Philosophy and Tragedy

Tragedy has always been an important topic in philosophy, ever since Aristotle first wrote about the subject in his *Poetics*. However, despite tragedy's consistent presence in post-Kantian thought, the relationship between tragedy and philosophy has never before been systematically addressed and investigated.

Philosophy and Tragedy is a unique and original collection of essays by some of today's leading philosophers on the encounter between philosophy and tragedy in the work of Hegel, Hölderlin, Nietzsche, Heidegger and Benjamin. The present volume asks the fundamental question why it is that after Hegel, philosophy seems to have been preoccupied with the 'tragic' and explores the dynamics of the relationship between tragic form and philosophical enquiry. The essays demonstrate how the model of tragedy affords the most extreme and thorough presentation of conflicts which are at the heart of continental philosophy, such as the topics of freedom, necessity, identity and historicity, and reveal why tragedy is so essential to modern philosophical thinking.

The contributors to this volume are: Miguel de Beistegui, Walter Brogan, Jean-François Courtine, Françoise Dastur, Günter Figal, Marc Froment-Meurice, Rodolphe Gasché, David Farrell Krell, Philippe Lacoue-Labarthe, Will McNeill, Simon Sparks.

Miguel de Beistegui is Lecturer in Philosophy at the University of Warwick. **Simon Sparks** is Leverhulme Trust Research Fellow at the Department of Philosophy, University of Strasbourg.

Warwick Studies in European Philosophy

Edited by Andrew Benjamin
Professor of Philosophy, University of Warwick

This series presents the best and most original work being done within the European philosophical tradition. The books included in the series seek not merely to reflect what is taking place within European philosophy, but also to contribute to the growth and development of that plural tradition. Work written in the English language as well as translations into English are to be included, engaging the tradition at all levels — whether by introductions that show the contemporary philosophical force of certain works, or by collections that explore an important thinker or topic, or by significant contributions that call for their own critical evaluation.

Titles already published in the series:

Walter Benjamin's Philosophy
Edited by Andrew Benjamin and Peter Osborne

Bataille: Writing the Sacred
Edited by Carolyn Bailey Gill

Emmanuel Levinas: The Genealogy of Ethics
John Llewelyn

Maurice Blanchot: The Demand of Writing
Edited by Carolyn Bailey Gill

Body- and Image-Space: Re-reading Walter Benjamin
Sigrid Weigel (*trans.* Georgina Paul)

Passion in Theory: Conceptions of Freud and Lacan
Robyn Ferrell

Hegel After Derrida
Edited by Stuart Barnett

Retreating the Political
Philippe Lacoue-Labarthe and Jean-Luc Nancy

On Jean-Luc Nancy: The Sense of Philosophy
Edited by Darren Sheppard, Simon Sparks and Colin Thomas

Deleuze and Philosophy: The Difference Engineer
Edited by Keith Ansell Pearson

Very Little ... Almost Nothing: Death, Philosophy, Literature
Simon Critchley

Blanchot: Extreme Contemporary
Leslie Hill

Textures of Light: Vision and Touch in Irigaray, Levinas and Merleau-Ponty
Cathryn Vasseleu

Essays on Otherness
Jean Laplanche

Philosophy and Tragedy

*Edited by Miguel de Beistegui
and Simon Sparks*

London and New York

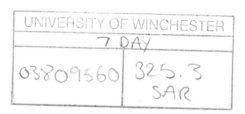
First published 2000
by Routledge
11 New Fetter Lane, London EC4P 4EE

Simultaneously published in the USA and Canada
by Routledge
29 West 35th Street, New York, NY 10001

Routledge is an imprint of the Taylor & Francis Group

Transferred to Digital Printing 2004

Typeset in Perpetua by
J&L Composition Ltd, Filey, North Yorkshire

British Library Cataloguing in Publication Data
A catalogue record for this book is available from the British Library

Library of Congress Cataloging in Publication Data
Philosophy and tragedy/[edited by] Simon Sparks and Miguel de Beistegui.
p. cm. – (Warwick studies in European philosophy)
Includes bibliographical references and index.
(pbk. : alk. paper)
1. Tragic, The–History–19th century. 2. Philosophy,
German–19th century. 3. Tragic, The–History–20th century.
4. Philosophy, German–20th century. I. Sparks, Simon, 1970–
II. Beistegui, Miguel de, 1966– . III. Series.
BH301.T7P45 1999
128–dc21 99–28329
CIP

ISBN 0–415–19141–6 (hbk)
ISBN 0–415–19142–4 (pbk)

Contents

List of contributors

Miguel de Beistegui is Lecturer in Philosophy at the University of Warwick. He has published essays on Heidegger in English and in French, and is author of *Heidegger and the Political: Dystopias*.

Walter Brogan is Professor of Philosophy at Villanova University. He is the author of several articles on Nietzsche and has published extensively in Ancient Greek Philosophy and Contemporary Continental Philosophy. He is the co-translator of *Heidegger's Metaphysics Θ 1–3: On the Essence and Actuality of Force*, and is currently working on a book for SUNY Press on Heidegger's interpretation of Aristotle.

Jean-François Courtine is Professor of Philosophy at the Université de Paris (X), and the Director of the Husserl Archives in Paris. Translator of Schelling's work into French, he has written extensively on German Idealism and phenomenology. His books include *Heidegger et la phénoménologie* and *Extase de la raison: Essais sur Schelling*.

Françoise Dastur is Professor of Philosophy at the Université de Nice. One of the leading interpreters of Hölderlin in France, she is the author of *Hölderlin, le retournement natal: Tragédie et modernité & nature et poésie*, as well as works on Heidegger, Husserl and the question of death. All her books are currently being translated into English.

Günter Figal is Professor of Philosophy at the University of Tübingen. One of Germany's foremost interpreters of recent German thought, he has published extensively on Nietzsche.

Marc Froment-Meurice is a Professor in the Department of Romance Languages, Vanderbilt University, Nashville, USA.

Rodolphe Gasché is Professor of Comparative Literature at the State University of New York, Buffalo. His books include *The Tain of the Mirror* and *Inventions of Difference*.

David Farrell Krell is Professor of Philosophy at DePaul University, Chicago. He is the author of, amongst other works, *Daimon Life: Heidegger and Life-Philosophy* and *Lunar Voices: Of Tragedy, Poetry, Fiction and Thought*.

Philippe Lacoue-Labarthe is Professor of Philosophy at the Université des Sciences Humaines de Strasbourg. Since the appearance of his first essays on and translations of Hölderlin in the 1970s, he has been one of the leading inter-preters of Hölderlin in France. Amongst his most recent works are *Musica ficta (figures de Wagner)* and *Metaphrasis*. In English his publications include *The Literary Absolute* and *Retreating the Political* (both co-authored with Jean-Luc Nancy), *Typography, Heidegger, Art and Politics* and *The Subject of Philosophy*.

Will McNeill is Associate Professor of Philosophy at DePaul University, Chicago. He has translated or co-translated several Heidegger volumes, and is author of *The Glance of the Eye: Heidegger, Aristotle, and the Ends of Theory*.

Simon Sparks is a Leverhulme Trust Research Scholar at the Université des Sciences Humaines de Strasbourg. He is the co-editor of *On Jean-Luc Nancy* and editor and co-translator of Philippe Lacoue-Labarthe and Jean-Luc Nancy's *Retreating the Political*.

Acknowledgements

The impetus for the essays collected in this volume was the conference 'On Tragedy' held at the University of Warwick on 24 May 1995. The contributions from Miguel de Beistegui, Françoise Dastur and Philippe Lacoue-Labarthe are more or less modified versions of the papers delivered there. The volume was also to have included Marc Froment-Meurice's 'Antigone: In (the) Place of Tragedy', included in his *C'est-à-dire* (Paris: Galilée, 1996) and now available in translation as *That Is to Say* (Stanford: Stanford University Press, 1999). Versions of the essays by Jean-François Courtine and Walter Brogan first appeared in *Extase de la raison: Essais sur Schelling* (Paris: Galilée, 1990) and *Research in Phenomenology*, volume xxiv (1994) respectively. We would like to thank Galilée and the editors of *Research in Phenomenology* for generously granting permission to reprint these essays.

Our thanks also to Oxford University Press for permission to quote from G.W.F. Hegel *Aesthetics: Lectures on the Fine Arts*, trans T.M. Knox (1975).

We would like to thank Andrew Benjamin, who commissioned this volume, and Tony Bruce, our editor at Routledge. Our thanks, equally, to Jonathan Derbyshire, Anne O'Byrne, Peter Poellner and John Protevi for their translation work, and for so readily approving our changes. Lastly, we owe debts of gratitude to Warwick University for their fine hospitality, and to the participants of Warwick conference for their invaluable contributions.

Introduction

Miguel de Beistegui and Simon Sparks

We take as our point of departure the following observation: apart from the texts of Greek philosophy which treat of tragedy, whether from the point of view of its political status (the *Republic*), or from that of its form and effects (the *Poetics*), there actually exists another tradition, indeed a group of traditions, anchored in the German thought of the end of the eighteenth century, which takes tragedy – and particularly Greek tragedy – as its theme. It is the philosophical import of such a tragic turning within philosophy that this collection aims to present.

The sole intention of this introduction is to raise the question of the origin of such a return to tragedy. If one can immediately, and perhaps entirely legitimately, offer purely external and contingent reasons for this apparently sudden infatuation with tragedy – an Antiquity made palatable by the work of Winckelmann or by a mimetic will to self-affirmation independent of the French cultural model – it remains none the less important to ask precisely what, at the very heart of philosophy, was able to render such a passage to tragedy decidedly possible. The hypothesis which we want to advance here is the following: if such a passage to tragedy was able to take place, then it was only because tragedy was itself envisaged as passage, as a bridge thrown over the abyss opened by the critical philosophy; it is because, in other words, tragedy was envisaged as a 'solution' to the problem inherited from Kant, and in the wake of a path opened by him: that of the (re)construction of the critical edifice by way of the mediating role of 'those judgements [*Beurteilungen*] which one calls aesthetic'.[1]

It is this question of the unity of philosophy, as critical philosophy, which is the outstanding object of the *Critique of Judgement*. The critical enterprise as such was an attempt to settle the disputes around the questions fundamental to the history of modern metaphysics by delimiting once and for all the field of philosophical speculation and the human faculties corresponding to it. The critical enterprise was thus to transform itself into what, in a letter to Marcus

Herz of 1766, Kant called 'a metaphysics of metaphysics', to elevate itself to the level of rigorous science. Yet, as is well known, by delimiting the field of philosophy, Kant also imposed severe limits on it, thereby rejecting its aspiration to elevate itself to the status of absolute knowing. With Kant, the sphere of knowledge is divided into the theoretical and the practical. And if it falls to the latter to grasp those metaphysical objects inherited from the history of modern philosophy (God, the soul, freedom), this knowledge remains partial insofar as it is not knowledge by means of concepts, but by mere Ideas to which, as postulates of pure practical reason, no sensible intuition may correspond. This amounts to saying that, with Kant, the balance of metaphysics tilts in favour of practical philosophy which recoups the speculative content of such metaphysics, but at the cost of a transformation: under the guise of freedom – as a mere idea of speculative reason, albeit one whose possibility we know *a priori* and whose synthetic demonstration is to be found in practical reason alone – it is now morality which forms the 'cornerstone' of the metaphysical edifice.

In the immediate aftermath of the critical enterprise, the Kantian heritage will thus have consisted in the affirmation of two absolutely heterogeneous – and apparently contradictory – orders. For if Kant rejects the particular use made by 'the modern philosophers' of the Wolffian distinction between the *mundus sensibilis* and the *mundus intelligibilis* as 'empty word-play' (A 257; B 312), he none the less admits of a distinction between the realm of sensible concepts and that of intelligible concepts: on the one hand, the realm of the sensible presided over by the mechanical causality of nature (in other words, the order of theoretical necessity), and, on the other hand, that of the intelligible, presided over by what he describes as a free causality (in other words, the order of practical freedom or morality). Thus if the critical philosopher is, in the words of the first *Critique*, a 'lawgiver of human reason', his legislative sphere, namely, philosophy itself, must itself be divided into two distinct systems comprising 'one single philosophical system': the philosophy of nature, which deals with '*whatever is*'; and the philosophy of morals, which concerns itself with '*whatever ought to be*' (A 840; B 868).

In the face of this bi-polar division of philosophy and of the respective faculties proper to it, it falls to the third *Critique* to take up the question of the possibility of a passage or transition (*Übergang*) from pure theoretical reason to pure practical reason, from the domain of nature to that of freedom. It becomes a matter of synthesis or of mediation, one in which the very unity of the critical philosophy will be played out. Thus, even if Kant will not cease to insist that investigation into the general principle of judgement which founds aesthetic judgement in particular is 'the most important part of a critique of this power' (Ak. V: 169), belonging to it 'essentially' (Ak. V: 193), it is to the mediating function of judgement, and to the often inextricable difficulties which accompany it, that the problematics of art and of the sublime remain subordinated. Put differently: the third *Critique* concerns itself with the beautiful and with the sublime only to the extent that aesthetic judgement itself carries the promise of such a passage. And, despite Kant's treating it as a mere 'appendix' to the analytic of aesthetic judgement in general (Ak. V: 276), it is the sublime which, far more than the beautiful, sets one on the path to this passage. For if Kant is to be believed, the beautiful and the feeling of pleasure which accompanies it proceed merely from the free play and from the harmonious union of the understanding and imagination, and concerns only the finite forms of phenomena; against this, the sublime stages the struggle between imagination and reason, which, as a faculty of the unconditioned, 'enlarges' the imagination, pushing it to the limit of its dysfunctioning and opening it to the infinity of the Ideas. What, in the beautiful, was a simple and harmonious 'play' between two faculties becomes, in the feeling of the sublime, 'effort' and extreme tension. For if the beautiful is nothing other than form in its pure agreement with self, its pure accord with the imagination, if it is, in sum, a matter of schematism as such, then with the sublime it is, quite the contrary, a matter of the *Unbegrenztheit* of presentation or of the figurative force (*Einbildungskraft*) of imagination itself in order that it open onto what Kant – somewhat unhappily – describes in terms of a 'negative' or 'indirect' presentation of that which does not present itself, or of that which presents itself only at the very limit of presentation. What presents itself in the sublime by way of a reflexive judgement is thus far more problematic than in the case of the beautiful. For how is this presentation staged? How does the imagination schematise the supra-sensible?

Such questions are surprising. Does not Kant explicitly state that, insofar as no sensible intuition can ever correspond to them, the Ideas cannot be schematised? 'Taken literally and considered logically,' he writes in the 'General Comment on the Exposition of Aesthetic Reflective Judgements', 'the Ideas cannot be presented [*nicht dargestellt werden*]' (Ak. V: 268). It is thus only through an entirely paradoxical logic of presentation that the sublime is able to constitute the site of the presentation of the unpresentable, or of the passage from the realm of the theoretical to that of the practical. And this logic, which reveals to the imagination its own limits precisely at the moment when it demands that it go beyond them, also and at the same time reveals the supra-sensible destination (*Bestimmung*) of man, unlimiting or infinitising it at the very moment when it inscribes it within its finitude:

> . . . the feeling of the sublime in nature is respect for our own destination [*Bestimmung*] but, by a certain subreption (the substitution of respect for the object for the Idea of humanity in our own subject)

3

this respect is attributed to an object of nature which renders intuitive [*anschaulich*] to us, as it were, the superiority of the rational determination of our cognitive faculties over the greatest faculty of sensibility.

(Ak. V: 257)

If to the Ideas of reason, and to the Idea of freedom above all, there can directly correspond no intuition or object of nature, no less certain is it that what is played out in the feeling of the sublime is precisely an involuntary opening onto the supra-sensible world, something like a transport of spirit to a higher destination than the single appearance by which we are confronted. How else are we to understand the fact that every so-called 'sublime' spectacle is not limited to the arousal in us of pain, dread or fear, but also arouses a certain pleasure which, as Kant says, immediately follows the initial repulsion? How is it, in other words, that we feel a certain attraction before the spectacle of a phenomenon hideous and terrifying in itself, and which seems to return us to the finitude of our sensible being? Ought not the sad joy which the sublime awakens in us be an index of a hidden – what Kant calls 'subjective' – purposiveness? Without this merest trace of purposiveness – even if this be a contrapurposive (*widerzweckig*) purposiveness – the phenomenon would no longer be sublime, but simply 'monstrous' (*ungeheuer*) (Ak. V: 253). Thus, the world of Ideas, in itself unformed and without figure, ought to open itself to another form, to something which would not be purely on the side of the unformed or of the monstrous (which could only provoke disgust and repulsion), but which would situate itself at the very limit of form, making it into the index of an order higher and more profound than the one which imagination most ordinarily constitutes for itself, for example in the beautiful. If, once again, the beautiful results in the harmonious free play of the understanding and the imagination in a figure susceptible of being contemplated, the sublime shakes imagination to its roots, stimulating or pushing it to the very limit of what it can bear, forcing it to teeter precariously on this limit in its attempt to unlimit it and open it onto what, in us, goes beyond every form, every figure, every image. It is thus always the imagination which bears the weight of this presentation, but now in the expression of its own failure or its own impotence:

That the mind be attuned to the feeling of the sublime it must have a receptivity for Ideas; for it is precisely the inadequacy of nature to these Ideas, and this presupposes both that the mind is receptive to Ideas and that the imagination strains to treat nature as a schema for them, that constitutes what both repels our sensibility and yet at the

4

same time attracts us: because it is a power that reason exercises over sensibility only merely in order to extend it in conformity with its own domain (the practical) and to let it look out to the infinite, which for sensibility is an abyss [Abgrund].

(Ak. V: 265)

Here, then, is the clear expression of this paradox: it is in the failure of the imagination before an absolutely great object of nature that the properly practical destination of man presents (or schematises) itself. It is in the shaking of the imagination in its effort to schematise the Ideas that the 'feeling of a destination which goes entirely beyond the domain of the imagination' is awakened in us.

Is this inadequacy enough to deduce an inadequacy of the imagination as a faculty of the presentation of nature in its relation to freedom, and of the sublime as the site of the passage from the theoretical to the practical? Without again calling into question either the necessity of such a passage or the sublime as its site, can one not ask whether there would be a way of envisaging other forms of the presentation of this co-existence? Even if he did so only in passing, Kant himself seems to have thought so at least twice, and this despite his having insisted on the fact that one cannot locate the sublime 'in products of art', but only in 'brute nature' (Ak. V: 252–3).[2] There is, first of all, the reference to poetry, which seems to harbour the power to evoke the suprasensible by means of the sensible and thus to schematise the world of the Ideas:

Amongst all the arts, *poetry* . . . holds the highest rank. . . . It fortifies the mind by letting it feel its ability [*Vermögen*], free, spontaneous, and independent of natural determination, to contemplate and judge nature, as appearance, according to aspects which it does not on its own offer in experience either to sense or to the understanding, and hence it lets the mind feel its ability to use nature on behalf of and, *as it were* [*gleichsam zum*], as a schema of the supra-sensible.

(Ak. V: 326, emphasis added)

Equally, and even more decisively, there is the following note from § 49 of the *Critique of Judgement*, where Kant does not hesitate to qualify a work – in truth, an inscription – as sublime:

Perhaps nothing more sublime has ever been said, or a thought ever been expressed more sublimely, than in the inscription over the temple of Isis (Mother Nature): 'I am all that is, that was, and that will be, and no mortal has lifted my veil.'

(Ak. V: 316n.)

Leaving to one side the reasons which led Kant to declare such a sentence sub-lime,[3] we can take from this, in what perhaps constitutes a prefiguration of the tragic turning, the *fact* that there *can* be sublime works – rather, works whose function might be analogous to that of the sublime in nature.

On the basis of this, therefore, and insofar as it infinitely approaches the world of Ideas, might not the work, and the poetic work in particular, function as a schema? This, at least, is what we want to suggest. Namely, that the work will have functioned as schema (and there, perhaps, would be its unthought), that it is in this problematic of presentation of what is in itself without form and without figure (the practical domain, and freedom in partic-ular) that the tragic problematic comes to be inscribed, at least to begin with. Prolonging the analyses of the sublime sketched out by Kant, and in particular the question concerning the possibility of a simultaneous presentation of the sensible being of man and his practical destination, tragedy allows for a certain German thought to breach the frontier separating the thematic of art from that of the sublime, and to displace the problematic of the imagination in the direc-tion of the – poetical – work.

Yet how could tragedy – Greek tragedy – provide a solution to the Kantian problem? How could tragic presentation succeed where, in its effort to schema-tise Ideas of reason, the imagination had failed? Answer: because the tragedy would be nothing other than the presentation, the exposition, precisely, of the conflict between immutable orders co-existing in man: the order of nature or of necessity, on the one hand, and the order of freedom, on the other, the order of sensible finitude, and the order of practical infinity. Pushing them to their ultimate expression, tragedy presents each of these orders in their own demand and according to their own logic. And it is precisely in the holding together of each moment in its most extreme exigency that the tragic takes place and, with it, tragic feeling (much akin to the sublime insofar as it con-stitutes a mixture of pleasure and pain, of attraction and repulsion): it is only at the moment when the hero sees himself constrained to act under the weight of a necessity (of a Law) which imposes itself upon him in all its force and vio-lence, provoking a sort of terror and fright in the spectator, that he affirms himself by going beyond this law and this order, revealing himself to be free, subject to *another* Law. In tragedy, moreover, it is freedom which reveals itself through necessity, just as in the sublime practical reason reveals itself through the absolute and terrifying grandeur of nature. But at precisely the point where the imagination, syncopated at the very moment of the presentation of the image, seems to undergo the test of its own limit, the tragic work of art seems to affirm itself in all its schematic power.

It is thus both in its content and its form – the two being inseparable, per-haps here more than ever – that tragedy constitutes a 'solution' (indeed, an

6

other solution, one perhaps already glimpsed by Kant) to the problem of the relation and the presentation of the relation between freedom and nature, the problem of the unity of the critical system as a whole. From the perspective of the content, insofar as what plays itself out in tragedy is precisely the conflictual relation between the two spheres identified by Kant (and not their harmonious union: it is perhaps in this that the tragedy would be more a sublime work than a simply beautiful one), a relation in which the spectator is led back to his own freedom as his ultimate end. Equally, from the formal perspective, precisely insofar as a schematic value is accorded to the tragedy which seems to distance the thematic of art and of the sublime from that of a faculty in order to bring it closer to that of the work. It is in this space that the entirety of modern aesthetic thought, from Schiller to Heidegger, will come to be played out. And if the thematic of art remained and remains so important in the eyes of modern philosophy, this is above all because of its capacity to present the unpresentable, to situate itself at the juncture of two disjoined orders, to effect the passage through which nothing, of itself, can pass.

*   *   *

In the end, then, the passage or the turn to tragedy will have been far more than a mere turning back to the tragedy of the Greeks. Such a return could only be the result of a failure, done out of pique. It could, above all, be only a reaction. The tragic turning within philosophy, then, will have been programmed by the horizon opened by the critical philosophy, and by which it will not cease to have been sustained. And if it is on the basis of this horizon that the Greeks can be seen to have thought more than we moderns – and that is to say, we Kantians – this will, paradoxically, be precisely because of Kant. It is the thought of Kant, and in particular his attempt to construct a passage from theoretical reason to practical reason, which will have been at the origin of this Greek reversal, and which will have contributed to reopening the space of the poetical – against which philosophy will not have ceased to measure itself.

Notes

1 Immanuel Kant, Preface, *Critique of Judgement* in *Kants Gesammelte Schriften*, ed. Preussiche Akademie der Wissenschaft (Berlin: Walter de Gruyter 1902–) V: 169. Excepting the *Critique of Pure Reason*, ed. Raymund Schmidt (Hamburg: Felix Meiner, 1956), where, following scholarly convention, we give the standard A and B pagination, all further references are to this edition, henceforth cited as Ak., volume and page number.
2 Of course, the sublime is not to be located *in* such nature, but only in the judge himself. Sublimity is, then, an effect of nature whereby the imagination is referred

7

to reason (and not, as in the case of the beautiful, to the understanding) in order *not* that there be a harmony between these faculties – and this even if Kant presents it as such on at least one occasion: Ak. V: 256 – but that the imagination find itself inadequate to reason's ideas. On the relation of imagination to reason in the effect of the sublime, see John Sallis, *Spacings – of Reason and Imagination in Texts of Kant, Fichte, Hegel* (Chicago: University of Chicago Press, 1987), 82–131.

3 The logic underpinning this declaration has been well documented elsewhere. See, for example, the texts gathered in *Du Sublime* (Paris: Belin, 1988), particularly those by Philippe Lacoue-Labarthe and Jacob Rogozinski.

Part I

Hegel

1

Hegel: or the tragedy
of thinking

Miguel de Beistegui

My aim here is to produce a genealogy of the tragic in Hegelian thought. Needless to say, I shall be forced to consider, if not all of Hegel's texts, then at least the corpus as a whole, from the early writings to the Berlin lecture courses, a choice which might thus reveal the evolution of a thinking. In the context of a simple study, such a genealogy can be only schematic. None the less, it should suffice to highlight a question which runs throughout the whole of Hegel's *oeuvre*, a question which, once unearthed, allows us to view that work in new light. As the guiding thread or key to the following remarks, the question of the tragic will allow us to return to the sources of Hegelian dialectics and to see how the *oeuvre* constituted as a system remains permeated by it.

If the tragic provides such a point of access, it is because, even when it is still only a matter of the rumblings of a thinking yet to come, it is indistinguishable from what will not cease to constitute the fundamental demand of that thought, namely 'reconciliation'. And if, as a question of *Versöhnung*, the last word will ultimately belong to philosophy, tragedy will until the very end be related intimately to this demand. This is, at least, what is suggested by the *Lectures on Aesthetics.*[1] Tragedy is analysed there in terms of contradictions whose solution is as necessary as the conflict itself. Certainly, and as Aristotle suggested, by presenting essential conflict, tragedy generates fear and pity on the part of the spectator but also, and beyond these passions, awakens in him a higher feeling -- higher because already philosophical -- namely, the feeling of reconciliation (*das Gefühl der Versöhnung*):

> Above mere fear and tragic sympathy there stands that sense of reconciliation which the tragedy affords by the glimpse of eternal justice. In its absolute way this justice overrides the relative justification of one-sided aims and passions because it cannot suffer the conflict and contradiction of ethical powers which according to their concept must be unified to be victorious and permanent in true actuality.[2]

11

To the cathartic Aristotelian framework, Hegel thus adds a third feeling, one which properly reveals the destination of tragedy. For him, tragedy serves to awaken in us the feeling of the necessity of the reconciliation of the powers of ethical life under their concept. By subordinating tragic action to the necessity of its reconciliation, Hegel turns dramatic representation into the figurative expression of the speculative, the prefiguration of the philosophical and of history as the 'site' or the 'stage' of the reconciliation of Spirit immersed in its negativity. Detaching himself from the timid mass of simple consciousness full of untroubled security, the tragic hero sees his destiny arising out of his actions as their very meaning, a meaning which he had thus far ignored.[3] Representing the refuge of the individual and collective soul from the very possibility of the awesome tragic conflicts, the chorus remains torn between an admiration for the audacity of the hero and horror at his destiny. In the shock of two individual *pathos*, the two ethical powers (rights or duties) are at odds and reveal themselves in their necessary mutual co-belonging. This revelation, the true stake of tragedy, is the proper mark of the Destiny which imposes itself as the absolutely rational in which Spirit is reconciled with itself.

*　　*　　*

In the early writings, however, the feeling of reconciliation linked to Destiny remains the privilege of Greek antiquity. In the absence of a dialectical–teleological philosophy of history, the modern age appears, in Hegel's eyes, as the stage of a theatre bereft of any Destiny, as the site of an errancy where, separated from the world, man lives under the illusion of a rich spiritual interiority and in a disincarnated ethical life. Torn between his private and public life, between his actions here and his life in the beyond, between his interiority and his relation to others, modern man lives separated from the State and from God, from other citizens and from other Christians. The modern age being that of division and separation, of timid individualism and alienation, man is not confronted by an authentic destiny through which he could realise himself and to whose tragic dimension he could thus elevate himself. The religion of the people, indeed the people itself, no longer exists, and, distraught and unfree, modern man traverses history, oblivious to the harmonious and beautiful age where once he lived united with others, the State and the gods.

Why should this be the case? And how can this state of separation be remedied? Is it possible to restore the antique *polis*, to revive the Greek gods, to measure oneself afresh against the tragic power of Destiny? These questions are at the heart of the Hegelian enterprise, and it is in trying to address them that, step by step, Hegel will set himself on the path of his own thinking. In the manner in which they are posed, these questions find answers within or in the context of a reflection that stages the tragic element as revealing – on a properly political level, as we shall see in the article on natural law dating from the Jena period, but also before that, in an apolitical religious reflection dating from the Frankfurt period – a destiny as reconciliative agent.

Indeed, it is in a text almost certainly written in 1798–9, namely *The Spirit of Christianity and its Destiny*[4] (to give it the title proposed by Herman Nohl), that Hegel attempts to find a religious solution to the characteristic alienation of modern man. Greece and, *de facto*, tragedy, insofar as the two are co-extensive, is thus not what is at stake in these religious-style considerations. As a destinal power, the tragic demand, although not at the forefront of things, none the less continues to orient the Hegelian enterprise, as if all historical reality could not but be measured by the yard-stick of Greek perfection:

> The great tragedy of the Jewish people is no Greek tragedy; it can rouse neither terror nor pity, for both of these arise only out of the fate which follows from the necessary slip of a beautiful being; it can arouse horror [*Abscheu*] alone.[5]

Thus the destiny of the Jewish people would itself also be tragic. But such a tragedy has nothing in common with that which marks the beauty and grandeur of Greek tragedy, namely the necessary and reparative confrontation of ethical powers opposed within the same sphere. Whereas the Greek Spirit truly incarnates Destiny as 'reconciliation of powers of action', Jewish destiny consists in never being able to elevate itself to the heights of Greek Destiny. In this sense, Jewish tragedy is bereft of any tragic dimension, consisting more in the structural impossibility of a union with the natural and political world, as well as with its own god. Jewish destiny is tragic only insofar as it incarnates the unhappiness of a consciousness forever severed.

Like Cadmus or Danaus, Abraham abandons his family and his nation. Yet unlike them, he does not carry with him the pain, symptomatic of a need for love, of lost freedom and broken bonds. Abraham leaves out of a concern for independence and freedom, but the act by which he decides to found the Jewish people is primarily an act of separation, a flight that allows him to avoid the encounter with the Other, with desire and love. He envisages his relations with nature and with others only as relations of need, and ends up estranged from everyone and everything. He wants to be alone and to dwell in his solitude; he refuses to attach himself to beings and to things. Eternally nomadic, he turns away even from the earth itself, which becomes hostile toward him. In this face-to-face bereft of any engagement, Abraham suffers the irreducible alterity of a nature that he does not even contemplate transforming, leaving to nature, to the Other, the job of reconciling man (envisaged as a simple animal) and nature (the satisfaction of animal needs). But insofar as it is the Other of man, nature cannot reconcile itself with man. Only a power other than nature would be in a position to reconcile man and nature. As Hegel will never cease to affirm throughout his writings, this power of transformation allowing man to relate to nature as to himself is, precisely, work. But Abraham refuses to work or to put others to work. Thus he calls upon a power foreign both to nature as well as to the rest of men. This is the Jewish God. Necessarily exterior to the world and to men, Abraham's God is created after Abraham's image and can sustain the image of the chosen people only for so long. The laws that he gives seem arbitrary and without love, and his commandments wholly abstract. It is not surprising, therefore, that the people of God try to escape these laws by rejecting their God, by throwing themselves into idolatry or by accepting servitude. The rare moments of happiness when they try to open themselves to the world and to love are, precisely, moments when they betray their God, who then immediately plunges them into the pits of despair. They find a solution to oppression, a return to independence, only in taking refuge in an enslavement to their God, a refuge more terrifying than any slavery insofar as it is devoid of the force of any actual relationship. Thus, the Jewish people are condemned to live the misfortune of a consciousness incapable of reconciling itself with the powers which face them – nature, other people, God. Nothing, therefore, is more foreign to the beauty of Greek destiny than the 'horrible' tragedy of Judaism.

Nevertheless, despite the unavoidable presence of the Greek tragic in *The Spirit of Christianity*, Hegel does not propose a return to the gods and to the *polis* of antiquity. The reconciliation of the sundered forces does not fall upon Greece, in what would amount simply to a retroactive illusion, but upon Christianity. With Christianity, a double relation to the tragic takes place: on the one hand, by envisaging the figure of Christ as this testament of love which allows for the historical reconciliation of the self-inflicted impasse of Judaism, Hegel sets himself on the path of what will become Hegelianism, namely the taking into account of historical becoming as the necessary unfolding of a rationality; on the other, the Christian reconciliation is still unable to raise itself to the heights of the *total* beauty of Greece. Put differently: if Greece is no longer the object of a nostalgia and seems to give way to a concern for a philosophical thematisation of historical becoming, its demand for unity none the less continues to govern Hegel's thought.

Jesus' merit lies in attempting to save the Jewish people from themselves and from their misfortune by introducing the law of love, the subjective purity of the heart as a replacement for the objective commandments.[6] What arises with love is the possibility of a new ethical community that suppresses the oppositions which, until now, could only be resolved by force. By reuniting the particularity of inclination and the universality of the law, love suppresses the opposition between subject and object, between identity and alterity. But this love is itself only a subjective reconciliation which, as such, turns away from the objectivity of the world by refusing to recognise it as its own realm. In violating the commandments in the name of a subjective morality, in measuring all forms of community by the yard-stick of this sole divine inclination, Jesus unveils his own destiny: to allow for the happiness of an ideal world without ever being able to reconcile himself with the actuality of this world. Thus, Jesus' own destiny was to see life turn against him and annihilate him; by opposing the totality of the Jewish world, Jesus was made to perish on the cross without ever having been able to overturn the world to which his message was none the less opposed.

Like the Jewish destiny, the Christian destiny will have fallen short of true Destiny, short of a true reconciliation of life with itself, for it is only in the acceptance of the tragic and of Destiny that reconciliation is produced. Both religions remained incapable of giving birth 'in beauty' (in this Hellenic beauty which is nourished by the tragic and overcomes it) to an authentic *Versöhnung*. But they none the less carry *their own* destiny within themselves, a destiny of being unable to lift themselves to the heights of tragic consciousness. In this regard, and in order to explain what it is that constitutes the essence of Destiny, Hegel has recourse to the analyses of crime and punishment.

If the criminal who has taken a life and negated nature sees in the law the only punishment equal to his fault, he will remain separated from life, without any possibility of reconciling himself with it. For him, death will be non-life, other than life. In the punishment inflicted by the law, the criminal continues to know himself as a criminal. His sentence only affirms what he already knew himself to be: a criminal. But this self-knowledge is unbearable for the criminal. So he turns to his master, Justice, in the hope that it will pardon him and thus efface his crime. By shutting his eyes to his fault, Justice would allow him to escape what he knows himself to be. In this logic of crime and punitive law, the impasse is total and the criminal is wholly unable to reconcile himself with the life he negated: if the sentence is carried out, the criminal suffers it like the rigour of a law in which he does not recognise himself; if the sentence is suspended, then the law is no longer the law and the criminal is discharged of a fault that none the less is his own.

The reconciliation ought thus to transcend this logic in the direction of another logic, that of Destiny: 'Punishment as destiny is of a wholly different nature.'[7] If, in other words, the criminal lives the punishment as that which, through his own death, reconciles life with itself beyond the fault, then, since his death will be the individuality *sacrificed* to universality, his sentence will be a destiny in the proper sense. Through this sacrifice, life is reconciled with itself. Contrary to punishment, destiny 'is situated within the sphere of life'

15

and constitutes its motor, its dynamic.[8] By killing another individual, the criminal 'thought he was confronting a life other than his own', without realising that, in truth, he had 'destroyed his own life; for life is not distinct from life, but is in the single divinity'.[9] By 'destiny', Hegel thus understands this capacity which an individual or a people has to live its separation or its sundering as its own, and that is to say as this tragedy which it has to assume as its own. For this people or this individual – tragic consciousness – life is what separates itself in itself: death is not the pure and simple negation of life, but life itself which separates itself from itself and sunders itself within itself, as Aeschylus' *Orestia* indicates:

> Destruction of life is not a non-being of life but its diremption, and the destruction consists in its transformation into an enemy. Life is immortal and, if slain, it appears as its terrifying ghost which vindicates every branch of life and lets loose its Furies.[10]

And a little further on, still commenting on the fortunate ending of the *Orestia*, Hegel adds the following:

> In the case of punishment as destiny, however, the law is later than life and beneath it. There the law is only the lack of life, defective life as a power; and life can heal its wounds again; the severed, hostile life can return once again into itself and annul the work [*Machwerk*] of a crime, the law and punishment.[11]

Reconciliation is thus inherent in life itself, which confronts the tragic of death and overcomes it. Only tragic consciousness is able to envisage life as destiny or as differentiated unity.[12] Jewish consciousness, in perceiving the law as punishment, and Christian consciousness, despite the love which it carries and which points toward a reconciliation of some sort, cannot quite reconcile themselves with life in its opposition to itself.

Given the failure of the attempt at reconciliation on the basis of religion, the question is now to know whether such a reconciliation can be effected in the ethico-political framework. Thus, at Jena Hegel turns toward ethical life, which he sees as the truly destinal power capable of elevating itself to the heights of the Greek tragic. It is in an article of 1802–3[13] that Hegel formulates the idea of a reconciliation elevated to the status of the absolute present in the ethical totality of a people. Such an idea might seem surprising. Has not Hegel already shown that such an ethical demand for the absolute had vanished with the collapse of the Greek *polis*? Although taking into account the irreducibility of modern ethicality as subjective freedom, Hegel will continue to measure it against the Greek model, namely that of the unity of the work of art and political life.[14] As in *The Spirit of Christianity*, only now on the level of the ethico-political, Greece continues to mark, in inverse relief as it were, the exigency of the absolute; it is no longer the Greek *polis* as such which is at stake, but the memory of a tragic beauty which now functions as the speculative aim or *telos*.

With the article on natural law, ethical life becomes the point at which the tragic is articulated in absolute terms. With ethicality, the question is the following: how can the modern State be the place of the reconciliation of two ethical powers which oppose and mutually exclude each other, namely the absolute ethical life, on the one hand, and, the relative ethical life, on the other? Whereas the first characterises the properly political moment, the organic nature of the State, that which includes the soldiers or the philosophers, and that is to say those for whom the universal is the whole, the second characterises the economico-juridical moment of the State, its inorganic nature, that which includes the sphere of needs and of right, in other words the family, the bourgeois state and the peasant state, for whom private interest is everything. Whereas the first state defines the State in all its purity, whether it be for the soldier sacrificing what is most his own, his life, to the survival of the universal, or for the philosopher-statesman, all of whose efforts are directed toward a thought and a government of the ethical totality, the second remains immersed in the sphere of particularity and, *de facto*, places the authentically political moment of the State in danger.

The ethical reconciliation of these two antithetical moments arises on the basis of a reading of Aeschylus' *Orestia* which, in its unfolding, reveals the very structure of the absolute. The tragedy of ethics (*die Tragödie im Sittlichen*) thus coincides with the emergence of the absolute, of life as such reconciled with itself. It renders explicit what remained only implicit in Frankfurt. From the start, one notes that the division of the State into free state, whether warrior or philosopher, and unfree state, whether peasant or artisan, to say nothing of the tragic solution of this division, undeniably evokes ancient Greece. None the less, it would be wrong to think that the stakes here are simply Greek. Rather, it is a question of thinking the modern State in its separation, taking into account the unavoidable presence of the bourgeois sphere and its economy, and of bringing a modern response to this state of sundering, without calling for a return to the Greek *polis*. Thus Greece can no longer function as a model, and if it continues to act as a reference then it is only from a perspective that is already largely dialectical and which accords to that demand for philosophical coherence proper to the notion of the absolute. Greece, the ethical life in particular, is subjected to a speculative reading which announces systematic thought.

17

What is this reading? How does Aeschylus' trilogy allow for the ethical life to be thought as absolute? By carrying out the orders of Apollo, god of the spiritual – properly political – ethical life, Orestes kills his mother, who has herself killed his father, and thus re-establishes the tarnished power of ethicality. But, at the same time, Orestes unleashes the fury of the Furies, goddesses of the natural ethical life and possessors of the powers of right violated by him. The conflict is brought before the judgement of the Athenian people, who, in the figure of Areopage, decide equally in favour of the two powers, thereby recognising their equal right of existence but thus also signalling their inability to rule on the conflict. The task of resolving this conflict will fall to Athena, goddess of the people itself. Restoring Orestes to the political or Apollonian life which he had himself chosen, on the one hand, and, on the other, incorporating the Furies within the City as benevolent divine powers – the Eumenides – Athena, and that is to say wisdom or the people as divine power, reconciles the people with itself whilst also laying down a mode of political organisation. Indeed, if a divine and unalienable existence is granted to the powers of private right, this remains subordinate to the absolute ethical life. But, in order to remain within its absolute ethical life, the State must recognise in turn the private sphere of right, of property and of enjoyment, all the while remaining free from the hold of this latter. In order to remain faithful to its spiritual or divine reality, the State must thus *sacrifice* a part of itself and refuse to be only absolute ethical life:

> This reconciliation lies precisely in the knowledge of necessity, and in the right which ethical life concedes to its inorganic nature, and to the subterranean powers by making over and sacrificing to them one part of itself. For the force of the sacrifice lies in facing and objectifying the involvement with the inorganic. This involvement is dissolved by being faced; the inorganic is separated and, recognized for what it is, is itself taken up into indifference while the living, by placing into the inorganic what it knows to be a part of itself and surrendering it to death, has all at once recognised the right of the inorganic and cleansed itself of it.[15]

This schema which emerges towards the end of the article on natural law defines the essence of the absolute as speculative reality. This is the very structure of the absolute or of 'life' now revealed as tragic. Thus, Hegel can write:

> This is nothing else but the performance, on the ethical plane, of the tragedy which the Absolute eternally enacts with itself, by eternally

18

giving birth to itself into objectivity, submitting in this objective form to Passion [*Leiden*] and death, and rising from its ashes into glory.[16]

Here, one clearly sees how the tragic defines the absolute in its very unfolding, and how, because of this, the tragic is wrested from the theory of tragedy and grasped in its content and its philosophical destination. It is precisely this inter-penetration of the two spheres which allows Hegel to weave together references to the New Testament (the Passion) and Greek mythology (the Phoenix being reborn from its own ashes). Tragedy thus resides in the fact that ethical nature 'separates itself and opposes to itself its inorganic nature as a destiny' (this is the difference with Judaism, which could never envisage separation as the unifying movement of life itself) and, in the struggle and sacrifice of this destiny, reconciles itself with the divine essence which is the unity of these two powers, the being-one of the universal and the particular, of the infinite and the finite. Which amounts to saying that ethical life is a universal which is not opposed to the particularity of the people as to its Other, but which contains this particular within itself as its own inorganic nature. Thus, it is the universal itself which particularises itself and which, in this movement of self-opposition, posits itself as destiny and reconciles itself with itself. The tragedy of ethics is nothing other than the ethical manifestation of the tragedy which the absolute itself is, and which fulfils itself only in the tragic completion of ethical totality. The being of the absolute is nothing other than the tragedy of its manifestation, and the originality of the Hegelian conception of the tragic is to conceive of it as the content of speculative philosophy. As Bourgeois rightly remarks,

> the exposition of the tragedy of ethics, which unfolds and absolutises the presentation of ethics as *self-sacrifice*, secures the decisive passage from a Schellingian approach that constructs the absolute on the basis of the *presupposition* of the *negative* within it, to the properly Hegelian approach which lets the absolute unfold as what posits itself in its self-negation, in identifying, for the first time, the transparent absolute with reason, with self-negation or infinite negativity.[17]

*　　*　　*

By posing the identity of the absolute and of sacrifice, the article on natural law thus effects a speculative translation of this identity, whilst forever integrating the logic of sacrifice and of tragedy into the unfolding of the absolute. It falls to the *Phenomenology of Spirit*[18] to draw all the consequences of this inter-penetration, by defining the absolute as negativity. In recognising the truly

19

ontological status of the negative, the *Phenomenology* is far from undoing the unity of sacrifice and the absolute, of the tragic and the true. Rather, it serves to emphasise it even further. The surging forth of the negative as the very force of the self-production of Spirit marks the speculative interiorisation of the tragic. At the same time, tragedy is granted a limited place and role within the *Phenomenology*, whether as the mere *form* of representation of Spirit, or as just one moment in the historical unfolding of Spirit. As the tragedy of ethicality, tragedy manifests itself as the primary form in which spirit surges forth in its concrete actuality. But in no way does it constitute the final word of the absolute in its in-itself. Nor can it constitute the final word of the absolute in its for-itself as a mode of artistic representation, precisely insofar as it remains bound to representation and has not yet managed to adopt the perspective of the concept. Starting with the *Phenomenology*, then, one must distinguish a threefold sense of the tragic, three ways in which the tragic may be envisaged:

1   As the sacrificial logic that underscores Hegel's conception of the negative, thus inscribing the absolute itself within this logic. In this first sense, it is the absolute itself which is tragic.
2   As the tragedy of ethics, or as Greek ethical life, in which the destinal power of the Greek moment is revealed. Thus, in this second sense, tragedy is seen as simply providing an access to ethical life. It is ethical life which is envisaged for itself, not tragedy. The tragedy is therefore that of ethics.
3   As a mode of spirit's self-consciousness or knowing of itself, in other words as poetic form. In this last sense, tragedy is envisaged from the perspective of aesthetics.

Leaving aside for the moment the question of the essentially tragic nature of the absolute – I shall come back to it at length in the third part of this essay – I now wish to concentrate of the last two senses in which tragedy is envisaged in the *Phenomenology*.

(1) It is towards the very beginning of the section on 'Spirit', when the substance has become subject or actual self-consciousness, that, in a passage entitled 'True Spirit. Ethical Life', the discussion of Greek ethical life and its tragic representation intervenes. In its actual or historical immediacy, Spirit is primarily 'ethical substance'. And it is Ancient Greece which here figures the absolute in its immediate actual self-consciousness. We should emphasise that, with respect to the article on natural law, what announces itself as the equivalent of the tragedy of ethics figures only a *moment*, albeit an initial one, of becom-

ing Spirit, and that this moment aims to make sense only of *Greek* ethicality. Consequently, it cannot be a question of reading these pages from the *Phenomenology* as the absolute's last word on the ethico-political, and thus of envisaging the tragic as the ultimate form in which it would present itself.

If Greek ethicality appears at this stage of the process it is because, according to Hegel, the characteristic feature of the Greek world was to attempt a direct and immediate conjunction, though the life of the people, between the singular and the universal, one in which each consciousness attained its own universality through an individual operation that integrates it to the laws, to the common customs, in other words to the ethical substance. One recognises here the fundamental theme developed in the article on natural law; but in contradistinction to this earlier work, Hegel is not concerned to outline the spiritual necessity by which the beautiful Greek ethical totality lived its own disappearance. And it is precisely this philosophical inflection which leads Hegel into a new interpretation of tragic conflict, the accent now bearing upon the irreducibility of the conflict rather than on its internal reconciliation. If, in its tragedy, Greek ethicality does indeed allow for a reconciliation of the ethical powers, this reconciliation is only immediate and abstract and, as such, destined to experience its own dissolution in what reveals itself to be a higher form of reconciliation.

This new interpretation of tragic conflict is no longer rooted in the Aeschylean trilogy, but in Sophocles' *Antigone*. Entirely assimilating the destiny of Greek ethicality to that exposed in Sophocles' tragedy, Hegel does not even bother to refer to it explicitly, thus giving the feeling of a total equation between the conflict inherent in the work and the becoming of historical consciousness. What does *Antigone* reveal? On the one hand, a political organisation; on the other, the limits of this organisation. Indeed, it is on the occasion of an apparently accidental conflict that the tragedy reveals the tragic destiny of the ethico-political organisation as a whole. The tragic conflict revealed by the work is organised on the basis of the opposition between the two dominant powers at the heart of ethicality, represented by Creon and Antigone respectively. In a 'normal', non-dramatic situation, these two principles live in peaceful union which reveals the beautiful ethical totality. But by putting each of these principles to the test, the tragedy will unsettle this too-perfect union and reveal its internal limits as well as its inevitable dissolution.

What, therefore, is the infra- or pre-tragic situation which will allow the drama to take shape and unfold? The equilibrium of ethical forces that are at work is that of two laws coinciding in a single place. On the one hand, Greek ethicality is constituted by the human law, which is also that of the *polis* and of masculinity. Hegel envisages this 'ethical community' from a double perspective: *in itself* it is 'actual substance', and that is to say it considers the individuals which constitute it as totality or 'people'; *for itself* it is Spirit that is reflected in the singular individuals and thus poses itself as 'actual consciousness' or 'citizen'. As universal, Spirit is public law and customs (*Sitten*); as singular, it is the individual certain of himself insofar as he belongs to this universal law: the citizen. The conjunction of these two perspectives results in government, which is 'certain of itself as simple and indivisible individuality'.[19] The realm of this first determination of Spirit is the open, the public, the 'light of day'. On the other hand, ethicality is the divine or feminine law, that of the family as 'natural ethical immediacy'. For if the family does indeed constitute an ethical entity in its own right, it is sheer 'being substance' (*seiende Substanz*); contrary to human law, which is a 'making' or an 'acting' (*Tun*), divine law simply *is*. Its immediate self-consciousness is neither mediated by political activity nor universalised through the recognition of the State. Its realm is that of Penates and obscure forces.

But this co-existence is clearly a relation, and the ethical life as such the truth of this relation. On the one hand, and insofar as it contains within itself the possibility of political community, the family is the *polis in potentia*: the individual is born into the family; in being born, it frees itself from the underworld with the aim of one day reaching the world above, namely that of the *polis*. The family, and that is in fact to say the woman or, more precisely, the mother, assures the passage from the first world to the second: she leads the adolescent to the threshold of adult life and delivers him over to the virile world of administrative, political and warrior duties. Although not participating directly in the properly virile life, she none the less knows that she belongs to an ethical order; but such a knowing is a mere *Gesinnung* – an unreflected *ethos* – an immediate ethical consciousness. On the other hand, as Hegel suggests here and as he had already developed further in the article on natural law, human or properly political law fully recognises the private and immediate moment whilst also affirming itself as that which frees itself from this initial moment. The political moment incorporates into itself the family and its economy but at the same time detaches itself from it and subsumes it under the universality of its own law.

Yet this relation is not entirely satisfactory. Even though there is the immediate perception of one power by the other and the resolute acceptance of the latter by the former, such an inorganic relation cannot account for the unity of Greek ethicality. There has to be a common ground, a place where both laws can coincide in their very being-separate. There has to be an ethical given through which each power is in a position to recognise the other power as *its* other thus allowing self-consciousness to realise itself as ethical consciousness. This mooring point, Hegel tells us, is death. Death is this ethical and natural given around which the two ethical principles commune. Why death? Why

22

does ethicality, as an organically constituted totality or as a living body, relate to death as to its constitutive horizon? The role of death, rather of the way in which it is taken up ethically in the funeraries, is double: from the standpoint of human law, the funeraries mark the recognition of the underworld, of the *genos*, of the naturality from which it itself is derived, from which it freed itself as virile law and to which it returns at the end of its stay in the world above; from the standpoint of divine law, the funeraries are the expression of a taking up of naturality in what constitutes its overcoming in the direction of ethics. In burying its own, the family honours the subterranean powers of naturality but, at the same time, elevates itself to the status of ethical community; for the family is primarily constituted not by its natural relation (husband–wife or parent–child), but by the spiritual relation which is incarnated in the brother–sister nucleus and which reveals itself most properly in funeraries. Whereas the relation between husband and wife or between parents and children, being too contaminated with naturality and with feelings which remain hostage to a sensible particularity, never reaches ethical plenitude, the 'uncontaminated' relation between brother and sister reaches a reconciliation between nature and freedom:

> They are the same blood which has, however, in them reached a state of rest and equilibrium. Therefore, they do not desire one another, nor have they given to, or received from, one another this independent being-for-self; on the contrary, they are free individualities in regard to each other. Consequently, the feminine, in the form of the sister, has the highest intuitive awareness of what is ethical.[20]

It is thus as sister, and only as such, that the woman truly reaches the level of ethics and participates in its sphere. Her brother is the sole link through which she can fully express this part of ethical spirituality which she incarnates. Now, funeraries are the actual place through which the sister can testify to her ethical relation with her brother. One sees why Hegel declares the absence of funeraries to be shameful and degrading (*entherende*), since it is an offence both to ethics and the gods. Were it not for this spiritual activity, the family would be irremediably repelled from the ethical world, forever attached to nature, riveted to being. It is only in being attached to this thread, the thread of death, that the family holds on to (spiritual) life. If the thread comes to be cut, or simply loosened, one can easily imagine the ensuing tragic consequences for the unity of ethicality. If, after some coincidence, the sister were to find herself unable to bury her brother, one can imagine how femininity (*das Weibliche*) would not hesitate to hurl itself against masculine law in what would amount to the conflict of ethics. Law against law, sex against sex, the ethical world would collapse into a fight to the death.

23

It is hardly surprising, then, that the tragic destiny of the *polis* is played out around the question of funeraries – the cornerstone of *Sittlichkeit*. Indeed, it is in a conflict around a cadaver that the internal organisation of the *polis* will reveal its insufficiency and live the drama of its own implosion. In Hegel's eyes, *Antigone* reveals a latent contradiction inherent in Greek ethical life, as the exposition of its destiny. Despite Creon's prohibition, Antigone insists on giving Polynices the honours and funeral rites to which, as a brother, he is entitled. Flouting Creon's authority, she faces death with resignation. The laws and will of men matter little to her; rather, it is the sacred rites of blood and the duties that go with them to which she submits. The law in whose name she acts is divine and immemorial and, consequently, stronger than the transient and human law of a man, albeit a king. From his own perspective, Creon justifies the prohibition of burial by claiming that Polynices, who had dethroned his brother, was an enemy of the *polis* and thus was to suffer the punishment meted out to those who turn against their own. Thus Creon speaks and acts in the name of the *polis* and its universal principles; his language is that of reason.

In the clash between these two laws and their principles, it cannot *for us* be a question of deciding in favour of one or the other. What is expressed by tragedy is the equal right to existence of both the conflicting powers, the essential contradiction of *Sittlichkeit*. Greek ethicality is lived as *destiny*: irremediably, it leads each power to the limit of its essence. It is only at the cost of a new distribution of its organisation that ethicality is victorious. In the play, each is culpable, and this culpability will be revealed as the *sense* – in the sense of both meaning *and* destination – of ethicality itself. In order to defend the ties of blood, Antigone has no other choice but to transgress the law of Thebes. Despite herself, she braves the authority of her king. And it is simply because she obeys the principle which she incarnates that she has to face death. As for Creon, he did not *want* to enter into conflict with the sacred powers of right that he was forced to flout. The logic of political governance alone lies at the origin of his misfortune. The two principles, perfectly legitimate so long as they respect the constitutive division of *Sittlichkeit*, reveal the deadly contradiction which silently animates it: 'a contradiction which is immediately deadly for the heroes who experience it without being able to dominate it, in the long run deadly for the *Sittlichkeit* itself possessed of and worked from within by the negative unity of destiny'.[21]

The tragedy thus reveals that an ethico-political organisation founded on the duality of a divine law and a human law, overlapped by a sexual partition of this *Sittlichkeit*, carries within it the latent conflict which can only lead to the total dissolution of the beautiful ethical totality. By proposing an *immediate* conjunction of nature and spirit within the sphere of the ethical life, the Greek *polis* condemned itself. From the standpoint of consciousness, this conjunction

24

reveals a disharmony and an opposition within consciousness itself between the 'unconscious tranquillity of nature' and the 'conscious tranquillity of ethics':

> The actuality of the ethical act simply reveals the contradiction and the germ of destruction inherent in the beautiful harmony and tranquil equilibrium of the ethical Spirit itself. For this immediacy has the contradictory meaning of being the unconscious tranquillity of Nature, and also the self-conscious restless tranquillity of Spirit. On account of this natural aspect, this ethical people is, in general, an individuality determined by Nature and therefore limited, and thus meets its *Aufhebung* at the hands of another.[22]

And it is only at the end of the advance of historical consciousness that a unity comparable to Greek unity, only more solid for being mediated by thought, will be regained. Through the formalism of Roman law, through Culture and Enlightenment and, finally, through the French Revolution and the revolution of thought initiated by Kant, a greater reconciliation will progressively have imposed itself. In this journey, consciousness will have experienced itself as the absolute power of thought immersed in phenomenality; it will have become absolute knowing.

(2) The *Phenomenology* broaches yet another discussion of tragedy, this time envisaged as a poetic genre, in the chapter devoted to the *Kunstreligion*. In both discussions it is a matter of the same life, the Greek ethical life, yet envisaged from two different perspectives, from the two sides of unified Spirit. Whereas the moment of ethicality considered Spirit from the perspective of its consciousness or its in-itself, art-religion, on the other hand, considers this same life from the perspective of its self-consciousness, or its for-itself. Such is the reason why the early passage on ethicality did not evoke tragedy so much as a genre, that is, as a figure of Spirit in the grasping of its own exterior content, as a specific tragedy, namely Sophocles' *Antigone*, which Hegel read as capturing the very content of this ethical life. In other words, *Antigone* functions as a way into the contradictions that belong essentially to the ethical life. Tragedy was not thought for itself, that is, as a genre, a mode of Spirit's self-presentation and self-apprehension, so much as it was used. And the legitimacy of such a use is revealed only now, that is, when the necessity of the link between ethicality and its representation is established. In tragedy, ethicality knows itself and presents itself to itself as this immediate, and therefore precarious and threatened, unity of the substantial (or the universal) and the singular. Yet if tragedy does indeed constitute a mode of ethicality's self-consciousness, it does not constitute its only nor, indeed, its ultimate mode. At least not apparently.

25

This becomes most clear in the section on 'Art-religion', where tragedy appears only as one genre amongst others, even if its function remains quite specific. Wherein lies this specificity?

Having thematised an initial form of art-religion (of Greek art), which, to the extent that it merely posits the god in its plasticity, independently of the spiritual activity by which it is born (as a form it is characterised by the sculpture–hymn–cult triad), Hegel qualifies as 'abstract', as well as a second form, in which man himself comes to incarnate and express the free movement of nature, and where his body is exposed like an animate and living work of art (such is the Dionysian frenzy), Hegel sketches the last and absolute form of the *Kunstreligion*: poetry. The medium that is specific to poetry in the most general sense or, if you prefer, to literature, is language – no longer the language of the oracle, the content of which is altogether singular and contingent, nor that of the hymn, which is nothing but a feeling in praise of a singular god, nor even, finally, that of the Dionysian frenzy, this stammering devoid of genuine signification, but this language which expresses a clear and universal content. Tragedy appears in this last moment, between the epic and comedy.

In the epic, the singer remains in a relation of exteriority with respect to the song. He narrates actions and events which are fictitious, and so is not himself integrated into them. The appearance of tragedy marks the passage to a mode of representation in which the narrator is also an actor, that is, one who takes part in the action which unfolds before the spectator. There is no longer the reserve and the distance which characterised the epic. The discourse is now the very discourse of the hero. And yet, the hero remains separated from the actor by a mask, by the last veil which separates man from his action. Furthermore, the chorus, which supposedly echoes the voice of the *polis* as a whole, remains powerless and passive in the face of the drama that unfolds, in the face, that is, of the destructive opposition of substances that takes place before its eyes. The chorus is witness only to the work of the negative: it is excluded from the action itself, and therefore can only *feel* – terror and compassion. Thus, there is at least a twofold exteriority or residual distance in tragedy, indicated by the presence of the mask and of the chorus. As a result of this exteriority, the chorus and the actors, but also, in what amounts to a mirroring effect, the audience as a whole, see the unfolding of the fate of the heroes as exterior and alien, instead of seeing it as the free activity of the absolute essence or of the necessary unfolding of the concept.

In order for this residual distance to be bridged, in order that the actor no longer be cut off from his action, and that the spectator be turned into an agent, thereby identifying himself with the truth of the action, it is necessary that the masks fall away and that the self-consciousness of the heroes become

26

one with the universal consciousness of the chorus. This is what takes place in comedy: in falling away, the masks reveal the true face of the actor to the spectator, the face of an ordinary man, which both the actor and the spectator recognise as their own. Consequently, the universal consciousness, thus far represented by the chorus, becomes the singular self-certain consciousness; it is no longer the consciousness that is *represented*, but the consciousness which apprehends itself immediately as its own content or as its unified substance.

*　　*　　*

The emergence in the *Phenomenology of Spirit* of a philosophy of intra-worldly becoming or, more exactly, of a temporality conceived as free unfolding of the rational, will thus have marked the *coup de grâce* inflicted upon the tragic grasped absolutely. Indeed, if the tragic is to a certain extent the bearer of the absolute, insofar as it expresses the essence of *Sittlichkeit* – if, in other words, it does indeed manifest a certain type of *Versöhnung* – it none the less does not coincide with the absolute grasped in the fullness of its unfolding. Indeed, as the mode of the self-presentation of the true it befalls philosophy or 'science' to articulate the unity of time and of the concept, of the finite and of the infinite, of the universal and of the particular, and to read history as the place where this reconciliation comes about. Does the discovery of this principle – which defines the internal coherence of the System – condemn the tragic to the dark corners of history and tragedy to taking on un-true and inactual modes of representation? Or, despite the 'official' place which is assigned to it within the System,[23] is it that the tragic continues to sustain certain aspects of Hegelian thought in what would amount to a philosophical *pathos*? If the tragic is incapable of making sense of what it presents, thus necessitating its own philosophical prolongation, does it not remain the locus *par excellence* of human existence, the locus at which the seriousness of history and of actions is presented, at which Spirit is revealed in its plasticity?

Without wanting to 'dramatise' Hegelian thought to the point of assimilating the true to the tragic, and at the cost of laughter and comedy,[24] one should recognise that the greatness of Spirit in history or of man in his action reveals itself primarily in sundering and in death, in sacrifice and in struggle, and that thought itself derives its depth only by taking the full measure of this tragic grandeur. Ultimately, then, the question of the relation between dialectics and the tragic ought to be raised. It is with a view to this that we must now turn to certain texts in which there can still be detected the continuity of tragic plasticity at the very heart of the System, despite the explicitly and supposedly secure place which the System attributes to the tragic within the *Aesthetics*.

In the reading of the article on natural law, we saw the relation which exists between the tragic and negativity. It is this latter which carries destiny and which reveals the absolute as the always re-inscribed place of its self-unfolding. Which amounts to saying that, in its very logical process, the speculative is tragic in the sense that it affirms its positivity only in and through a total engagement in its opposite (the negative) – an involvement which it lives as a struggle with that which has the force of necessity and in the unfolding of which it becomes itself. From this perspective, the preface to the *Phenomenology* constitutes a paradigmatic text. Everything, or nearly so, has already been said about this famous passage, which quite literally stages thinking as that which holds together the positive and the negative, life and death. None the less, from our perspective, namely that of an attempt to unearth an economy of the tragic, this text still warrants rereading:

> But that an accident as such, detached from what circumscribes it, what is bound and is actual only in its context with others, should attain an existence of its own and a separate freedom – this is the tremendous power of the negative [*die ungeheure Macht des Negativen*]; it is the energy of thought, of the pure 'I'. Death, if that is what we want to call this non-actuality, is of all things the most dreadful, and to hold fast to what is dead requires the greatest strength. Lacking strength, Beauty hates the Understanding for asking of her what it cannot do. But the life of Spirit is not the life that shrinks from death and keeps itself untouched by devastation, but the life that endures it and maintains itself in it. It is this power, not as something positive, which closes its eyes to the negative, as when we say of something that it is nothing or is false, and then, having done with it, turn away and pass on to something else; on the contrary, Spirit is this power only by looking the negative in the face, and tarrying with it. This tarrying [*dieses Verweilen*] is the magical power [*die Zauberkraft*] that converts it into being. This power is identical with what we earlier called the Subject . . .[25]

It would be exaggerated and, *stricto sensu*, erroneous to subordinate the truly speculative nature of this text to its plastic representation. Hegel's metaphorics remains subordinated to the expression of a logical or conceptual truth articulated in the *Logic*. None the less, it remains symptomatic of a tragic conception of truth.

Here, 'death' designates the original negativity, this 'prodigious power' by which Spirit relates itself to absolute otherness as to the most frightening (*das Furchtbarste*), by which Spirit loses itself in this otherness to the point of living its own sacrifice in this very exterioration before finding in it its own salvation and recognising in it the emergence of its own life. This power through which

Spirit relates to that away from which it wants to turn, so great is the fear that seizes it in the idea of its 'devastation' in opposition, is what demands the greatest 'force' – a 'magical' force, writes Hegel, for it is by staring the negative in the face, by tarrying in the absolute sundering, that life is able to 'overturn' the foreign and to relate to it as to its other. In the never-completed movement of this relation, substance is converted into subject and thought gains the realm of infinity. Thus, Spirit relates to its own death as to its own destiny. The inactual and frightening death against which life hurls itself and to which it agrees to *sacrifice* itself is the instrument of its own *reconciliation*. By elevating itself to the level of death, Spirit fixes the limits of its own drama and realises itself as tragic hero. As such, it can only arouse fear and pity. But above all, it becomes the theatre of a negativity portending reconciliation: in confronting death it experiences the negative as only one side of itself, as one determination of life thus far ignored, and experiences itself as that which can overturn the negative in being. Spirit is plastic or 'beautiful' only insofar as it is 'strong', and that is to say only insofar as it gathers and carries within itself the conflict of its essence. Whenever it turns away from this conflict, it is only 'beauty without force', that beauty which, devoid of life and of destiny, lulls itself through its own positivity, though an immediacy which give birth to no concreteness. As negativity, Spirit at once gathers within itself all the themes of the young Hegel: beauty, force, tragedy and destiny. It now bears the whole of history.

$$*\quad *\quad *$$

And in the same way that history is the stormy scene in which negativity is revealed, its actors are the heroes of this tragedy. Indeed, no one is closer to the tragic hero than the historical figure, this stylised and wholly dramatic figure of a personal destiny portending the universal. In history as in tragedy, only the hero counts, for through his actions he and he alone reveals reason to itself and to its intra-worldly inscription. Already, at Jena,[26] Hegel formulated the idea according to which the State owes its existence to great men and not to any social contract:

> All states were founded by the sublime power of great men, not by physical strength, since several men are physically stronger than one; but there is something about the features of the great man, such that the others want to name him their master; they obey him against their own will, and against their own will his will is their will – their immediate and pure will is his will – but their conscious will is something different. The great man has this pure will on his side, and they must obey, even where they do not want to. Such is the prerogative of the

29

great man: to know the absolute will, to express it; they all gather around his banner, he is their god.[27]

Much later, in the *Principles of the Philosophy of Right*,[28] Hegel writes in comparable terms:

> It is the absolute right of the Idea to make its appearance in legal determinations and objective institutions, beginning with marriage and agriculture . . ., whether the form in which it is actualised appears as divine legislation of a beneficial kind, or as violence and injustice. This right is the *right of heroes* to establish States.[29]

Certainly, from the perspective of immediately singular wills, namely the people, the power of these great men is often mere 'tyranny, pure and terrifying domination'.[30] Yet from the perspective of the result[31] – the obedience to the universal state on the part of these singularities wrested from their immediacy – this tyranny is both necessary and just insofar as it 'constitutes' and 'maintains' the State as the particular actuality which it is. It is precisely insofar as he is situated at the very forefront of historical action – in what constitutes a negation of objective reality and a transgression of those laws which, from the perspective of the Idea, have become outmoded – that the individual is a *hero*. In contradistinction to the ordinary man, the historical figure does not hesitate to oppose that which constitutes the basis of the existence of his people or his State. By opposing to the rights or duties of his people different rights or duties, rights or duties condemned by the people insofar as they contradict an already established ethics, the great man does not seek agreement from his fellow citizens or from his opponents. In this sense, he does not seek the Good, agreement or happiness. His medium is that of negativity, which, as such, produces more unhappiness and death than it does peaceful existence. Insofar as he incarnates a destiny, he cannot live peacefully while awaiting a death as sweet as it is certain. Like Alexander, his life is a struggle, a hard task which exhausts him and often leads him to a premature end. His fall is as spectacular as his rise: Caesar is assassinated, Napoleon dies in exile. Moreover, nothing is more tragic than the site of a hero at the moment of his fall.[32] Universal history is not the site of happiness: 'periods of happiness are blank pages in it',[33] for only private life is capable of happiness. By guaranteeing victory over his enemies, by dominating the provinces of the empire and by becoming the sole master of Rome, Caesar did not simply realise his personal ambitions. His personal gain was at the same time the realisation of the universal historical will and the completion of the demand of the age. The strength that the hero finds within himself as a hidden source is actually the sprit which wells up beneath the surface and which, 'impinging on the outer world as on a shell, bursts it in pieces, because it is another kernel than that which belonged to the shell in question'.[34] But only the very few can see this: the great man is usually judged as an individual who thirsts for glory, born by his passions and his destructive ambitions. If Alexander partially conquered Greece and Asia, was this not simply because he was overly ambitious and unscrupulous? And is not this irresistible tendency the sign of a bad nature which refuses to let others live in peace? This, at least, would be the opinion of the schoolmasters, these psychologising valets unable ever to reach the heights of tragic reason. In Hegel's critique of the moral standpoint and of smug individualism, one finds a hint of Nietzsche's critique: the slave will never be in a position to measure his own tranquil life against the universal destiny of the master; he will never grasp the necessity inherent in the destructive action of the historical figure who 'must trample many an innocent flower underfoot, and destroy much that lies in his path'.[35]

The destiny of the people themselves is also tragic, and history as such is the site of this tragedy. Like the great man, the people is a 'natural' individuality insofar as it has a 'life' of its own which is its destiny. The scale is different but, like any other individuality, the people undergoes a birth followed by a period of youth marked by a frenzied activity given over to realising its concept in the world to which it is opposed. During this period, the people overturns institutions and States, establishes its power at the heart of a new ethical life which everyone is willing to defend, and its negativity is the struggle that it must conduct against its opposition. This creative period is followed by that of its own success, the enjoyment of self-consciousness within a pacified world; but this peaceful life is that of habit, and 'just as man languishes through routine existence, so also does the national spirit through self-indulgence'.[36] Habit is mechanical life, life wound up like a clock, life which is no longer attracted by the chaotic movement of history. The medium of this existence is no longer internal struggle, and its negativity has ceased to be a struggle. Objectively, this period is often happy and devil-may-care. But this internal peace is an absence of destiny. Hence the happiness of a people already announces its own death: having completed its duty in the eyes of unfolding Spirit, all that is left to the people is to withdraw in the face of the emergence of other historical figures, all of which are destinies necessary to the realisation of History grasped according to its concept. Like the tragic hero, the people does not survive the completion of its destiny, a destiny which carries a reality the ultimate meaning of which escapes it and which it none the less serves to reveal. In this sense, history as the free unfolding of Spirit in time is indeed a tragedy: each of its moments lives its own existence as the destiny of a combat the ultimate meaning of which escapes it and which always ends with self-immolation in the purifying flame of the eternal sun of Spirit.

*　　*　　*

The typically tragic idea according to which Spirit lives only by elevating itself to the height of death reappears, now on a properly ethical (*sittlich*) level, in the *Elements of the Philosophy of Right*, §§ 321–9 of which, devoted to war, make this tragic moment perfectly clear. The sacrifice of the warrior which occupied so central a place in the organisation of the State in the article on natural law and the *System of Ethical Life*[37] is reinscribed towards the end of the *Philosophy of Right* when ethicality is posed as the State.

In its empirical existence, the State can be led to manifest itself under an exceptional form from the moment that its independence is threatened. This particular state is that of war against the outside. But – and, as far as we are concerned, this is what is essential – whilst being exceptional, this situation marks the most proper moment of the State, the moment which will reveal it in its truth:

> But this negative relation is the State's *own* highest moment – its actual infinity as the ideality of everything finite within it. It is that aspect whereby the substance, as the state's absolute power over everything individual and particular, over life, over property, and the latter's rights, and over the wider circles within it, gives the nullity of such things an existence and makes it present to consciousness.[38]

Again we find here a structure which resembles that of the Jena period, when Hegel saw war as the means by which the State affirms itself in its *pure* universality and returns to the spheres of the family, of right, and of the spiritual economy of its destiny.[39] Equally, war appears again as a necessary evil, as the necessity of a negativity which reveals the health of the State. For it is only in opposition and combat that unity comes about and independence is affirmed. In war, individuals learn that the preservation of the State is worth more than their personal interests and lives,[40] all of which would all disappear if the life of the State was genuinely threatened. But this much is clear: the State is not simply reducible to civil society, and its duties do not consist primarily in defending the interests of this latter. War is an 'ethical' moment in its own right, a moment, moreover, proper to the State – insofar as its true concern is freedom – and which thus has the necessity of a 'destiny' in the life of the State.[41]

It is only in its ability to die that the freedom of a people is evaluated.[42] Consequently, the State ought to be in a position to demand the sacrifice of each citizen, even if, for the most part, the sacrificial virtue belongs to a particular class, that of courage. Thus, the representatives of this class are the true

heroes of the State: in subordinating their life to that of the people in its universality, in renouncing the private sphere, the warriors incarnate the sacrifice
that the State demands of itself. They are the instrument of the preservation
of the political in its purity.

The courage of the warrior constitutes absolute value, virtue in itself, for he
confronts death as the sole horizon of his actions. But this confrontation with
death would not itself be an absolute virtue if – as is the case in the courage
of the bandit or the animal or even in the courage required by honour – it
were directed only to the particularity of this or that motive.[43] The warrior's
courage has as its goal the most universal and spiritual reality, namely the State
as such, the State as ethical substance. In agreeing to renounce what is most
his own and most dear to him – his life – in confronting death as that which
can allow the universal to live on, the warrior negates his own particularity
and elevates himself to the level of the universal. His action is what allows the
self-differentiated universal to maintain itself in the element of its spirituality.
Thus, sacrifice is the deed of a being whose freedom goes so far as to rid itself
of all sensible determination and raise itself to the level of a spirituality which
reveals the ethical horizon of the community. If it were not for this ability of
some to put their own death into play, ethicality as such would be exposed to
its own dissolution. In a sense, then, the warrior heroes reveal the State in its
purest form and incarnate the properly political moment, that against which its
destiny is silhouetted.

*　　*　　*

Thus, the tragic does not cease to sustain Hegelian thought: it accompanies the
genesis of the dialectic, it marks the seriousness of action and the essence of
history, in places it even comes to be confused with the absolute itself. In one
sense, tragedy is the site of this thinking. But for all that, can one categorise
Hegelian philosophy as tragic? Certainly, providing one conceives 'philosophy'
as the site of the articulation of the tragic, as the discourse in which the meaning of an intra-worldly negativity, which can be comprised only from out of
the tragic horizon of which it is the speculative outcome, elaborates and reveals
itself. As such, philosophy is indeed an onto-dramaturgy: wholly immersed in
the dramatic substance of the real, philosophy is the living presentation of that
substance, and constitutes the motivation of its theatricality. But this means
that, in the last analysis, the tragic, from the point of view of philosophy,
remains subject to the concept, which unveils its sense and reveals to it its own
destiny. In this sense, it would not be wrong to see the tragic as suppressed
in the concept, but as reinscribed, revisited, redeployed in its full meaning.
The tragic vision of the world remains subordinated to its speculative reconciliation, and the tragic is meaningful only insofar as it is understood on the

33

basis of its dialectic–teleological source. Hegelian philosophy has no choice but to be tragic since life itself is tragic, be it as subjective, objective or absolute spirit. But it is only insofar as life is the expression of negativity or of thought in the movement of infinity that it is the scene of an unending drama. In this sense, it is tragic only insofar as it elevates itself to the heights of thinking and, in the movement of this elevation, negates itself as tragedy so as to become philosophy.

Translated by Miguel de Beistegui and Simon Sparks

Notes

1 *Vorlesungen über die Ästhetik, Werke* (Frankfurt am Main: Suhrkamp, 1986) XIII–XV; translated by T. M. Knox as *Aesthetics: Lectures on Fine Art* (Oxford: Oxford University Press, 1975), 2 volumes. Henceforth *Ästhetik*, volume and page number. All translations have been prepared by the translators from the original sources. The text of this edition, established by Hotho on the death of his master, is based on one of Hegel's manuscripts from the Berlin period and students' notes taken on the occasion of Hegel's courses in Berlin in 1823, 1826 and 1828/9. The historico-critical edition being prepared under the direction of Annemarie Gethmann-Siefert poses serious editorial problems since the classes have to be reconstructed chronologically and, in the absence of all of Hegel's own written texts (these having been either destroyed or lost), the different sets of notes compared, in order to free the text from the occasionally authoritarian hold of Hotho's text. For more details concerning the Berlin course on aesthetics, one should consult Annemarie Gethmann-Siefert, 'Ästhetik oder Philosophie der Kunst – Die Nachschriften und Zeugnisse zu Hegels Berliner Vorlesungen', *Hegel-Studien* 26 (1991), 92–110. Once the Hegel-Archiv's meticulous and exacting work has been completed, we ought to be in a position to rely on a more definitive text, which, I mention in passing, might hold a few surprises on some points, without, however, calling into question the whole of the text such as we know it today. If I have continued to refer to the traditional text it is only because, thanks to Madame Gethmann-Siefert, to whom I am indebted, I have had at my disposal the lectures of 1823, which, moreover, as far as the passages which concern me here go, present no contradictions with Hotho's edition. None the less, these passages ought to be considered with due caution and reserve.

2 *Ästhetik* III: 526; II: 1198.

3 *Ästhetik* III: 523–4; II: 1196–7.

4 *Der Geist des Christentums und sein Schiksal in Hegels Theologische Jugendschriften*, edited by Herman Nohl (Tübingen, 1907); translated by T. M. Knox as 'The Spirit of Christianity and its History' in Hegel, *Early Theological Writings* (Philadelphia: University of Pennsylvania Press, 1971). Henceforth Nohl. With regard to its relation to the question of tragedy, this text has been analysed by P. Bertrand in 'Le sens du tragique et du destin dans la dialectique hégélienne', *Revue de Métaphysique et de morale* 47 (1940), 164–86; and by Otto Pöggeler in 'Hegel und die griechische Tragödie', *Hegel-Studien* 1 (1962), 285–305.

5 Nohl 260; 204–5.

6 Ibid., 261; 205.

7 Ibid., 279; 228.

8 One might say that the dialectic thus anticipates the final translation of this concept into speculative terms; but it is precisely in this translation that the systematic specificity of Hegelianism is played out.

9 Nohl 280; 229.

10 Ibid., 280; 229.

11 Ibid., 281; 230.

12 Thus, as Bertrand has explained, 'Macbeth seeks to establish a law of tragic equality between the deceptively strange life that he has offended, and his own lost life. Or rather, he sees the law born of his crime, thus illuminating the meaning and import of his actions' ('Le sens du tragique et du destin dans la dialectique hégélienne', 175).

13 Über die wissenschaftlichen Behandlungsarten des Naturrechts, seine Stelle in der praktischen Philosophie, und sein Verhältnis zu den positiven Rechtswissenschaften, SCHELLING–HEGEL, Kritisches Journal der Philosophie (1802–3), in Georg Wilhelm Friedrich Hegel, Werke II: 434–53; translated by T. M. Knox as Natural Law (Philadelphia: University of Pennsylvania Press, 1975). Henceforth Naturrecht.

14 On this question, and the Schillerian background which governs it, see Annemarie Gethmann-Siefert, 'Die Funktion der Kunst in der Geschichte', Hegel-Studien 25 (1984), 220–8.

15 Naturrecht, 494–5; 104.

16 Ibid., 495; 104.

17 Bernard Bourgeois, Le droit naturel de Hegel (Paris: Vrin, 1986), 448.

18 Phänomenologie des Geistes, Werke III; translated by A. V. Miller as The Phenomenology of Spirit (Oxford: Oxford University Press, 1979). Henceforth Phänomenologie.

19 Ibid., 329; 268.

20 Ibid., 336; 274.

21 Dominique Janicaud, Hegel et le destin de la Grèce (Paris: Vrin, 1975), 179.

22 Phänomenologie, 354; 289.

23 The task of expounding this place falls to the Aesthetics. As Otto Pöggeler emphasises ('Hegel und die griechische Tragödie', 296–7), and as our preliminary reading of the Kunstreligion has already indicated, tragedy and comedy figure as the last and highest forms of art, and, de facto, as the site of the passage from art to a higher form of absolute spirit, namely religion. In this sense, whilst preparing the way to religion, tragedy, insofar as it is a mode of expression of the beautiful, none the less remains an immediate and inferior form of absolute spirit. Furthermore, tragedy loses its Greek privilege in the Aesthetics – even if Greece still remains origin of the tragic type – in order that it can incorporate Romantic tragedy as well, thus proposing a larger definition of the tragic type, although one still faithful to the (Greek) model of 'ethical substances':

> The true content of the tragic action is provided, so far as concerns the aims adopted by the tragic characters, by the range of the substantive and independently justified powers that influence the human will: family love between husband and wife, parents and children, brothers and sisters; political life also, the patriotism of the citizens, the will of the ruler; then religious existence . . .
>
> (Äesthetik III: 521; II: 1194)

Although the themes proper to Greek tragedy (the public life, the religious life, the will of leaders) are easily recognisable here, one is forced also to recognise the place given to Romantic tragedy (subjective love).

24 It would be wrong to forget that life is also the place of levity and comedy and that its 'seriousness' in no way precludes laughter. Hegel himself, as, for example, certain aphorisms of the Jena period indicate, happily turned to irony and did not hesitate to be *witzig*. Also, as we have already begun to see, in Hegel's classification of the various poetic genres, tragedy gives way to comedy, which, despite the crudeness of its expression and the buffoonery of its situations, reveals a consciousness more developed than tragic consciousness. In a way, comedy is the completion of tragedy and the comic form continues that of the tragic: the masks fall away, plasticity gives way to irony and the objective equilibrium of the ethical substances cedes to subjectivity, which, through its laughter, masters everything:

> Whilst tragedy emphasises the eternally substantial in its victorious and reconciling mode, in that it strips away from the conflicting individuals their false one-sidedness and brings them together through what is positive in their respective will, it is, on the other hand, *subjectivity* which, in its infinite assurance, retains the upper hand in *comedy*.
>
> (*Ästhetik* III: 527; II: 1199)

Doubtless, the truly comic, characterised by 'infinite good humour and assurance' (III: 528; II: 1200), allows man to raise himself above the contradiction within which he is caught and to gain access to a certain felicity, instead of submitting to such contradiction and feeling gloomy. But this victory remains that of subjectivity, of that particular subjectivity which will would rather turn away from its destiny and close in upon itself than measure itself against ethico-political objectivity.

25 *Phänomenologie*, 36; 19.

26 *Jenaer Systementwürfe III, Gesammelte Werke* (Hamburg: Meiner, 1976) VIII. Henceforth *Systementwürfe III*.

27 *Systementwürfe III*, 258.

28 *Grundlinien der Philosophie des Rechts, Werke* VII; translated by H. B. Nisbet as *Elements of the Philosophy of Right* (Oxford: Oxford University Press, 1991). Henceforth *Recht*.

29 Ibid., § 350.

30 *Systementwürfe III*, 258.

31 And the result alone is what matters insofar as it alone is the true.

32 Thus, in a letter to Niethammer dated 29 April 1814, Hegel expresses himself as to Napoleon's destitution, in which he saw 'a fearsome and fantastic spectacle . . ., the most tragic thing there is'. See *Hegels Briefe*, edited by Johannes Hoffmeister and Friedhelm Nicolin (Hamburg: Meiner, 1981), letter 233; translated by Clark Butler and Christiane Seiler as *Hegel: The Letters* (Indiana: Bloomington, 1984), 307.

33 *Vorlesungen über die Philosophie der Geschichte, Werke* XII: 42; translated by James Sibree as *The Philosophy of History* (New York: Dover Press, 1956), 26.

34 Ibid., 46; 30.

35 *Die Vernunft in der Geschichte*, edited by Johannes Hoffmeister (Hamburg: Meiner, 1955), 105; translated by H. B. Nisbet as *Lectures on the Philosophy of World History: Introduction* (Cambridge: Cambridge University Press, 1975), 89.

36 Ibid., 72; 59.

37 Cf. *Naturrecht* 61–3; 92–4, and 'System der Sittlichkeit' in *Schriften zur Politik und Rechtsphilosophie*, edited by Georg Lasson (Leipzig: Meiner, 1922), 465–8; translated by H. S. Harris as *System of Ethical Life and First Philosophy of Spirit* (Albany: SUNY, 1979), 147–9.

38 Ibid., § 323.

39 Moreover, in § 324, Hegel himself cites the passage from the article on natural law according to which it is through war that 'the ethical health of people is preserved in their indifference toward the permanence of finite determinacies, just as the movement of the wind preserves the sea from that stagnation which a lasting calm would produce – a stagnation which a lasting and, *a fortiori* perpetual peace would also produce among nations' (*Naturrecht*, 61–2; 93).

40 *Recht*, § 324.

41 Ibid.

42 Cf. *Naturrecht* 59; 91: 'This negatively absolute, pure freedom, appears as death; and by his ability to die the subject proves himself free and entirely above coercion.'

43 *Recht*, § 327.

2

Self-dissolving seriousness: on the comic in the Hegelian concept of tragedy

Rodolphe Gasché

According to a commonly held view, Hegel's philosophy is a sort of panlogism in whose conceptual system the differences that compose existential experience lose all their singularity and definition. Hegel did, after all, assert the rationality of reality, and many would argue that he thereby proffered a philosophy that is inexcusably taken in by universal reason. But against this widely held view, some readers have emphasised the essential role of negativity in the positive achievements of speculative thought. Such readers would argue that, indeed, 'the tremendous power of the negative'[1] at work in both history and in the self-realisation of Spirit cannot be separated from the positive results of these realms. Jean Hyppolite, for one, suggests that the complicity of negativity and reason arguably establishes a relation between reason and the tragic; accordingly, he writes that the '"absolute concept" implies the permanence of the tragic in the most reasonable, rational and wise realisations of history'.[2] But the scope of Hyppolite's argument – like that of readers who have made similar claims – extends beyond merely acknowledging a permanent presence of a tragic vision in Hegel's thought, a vision whose presence would merely represent the 'reverse side of the positive', in order to construe this presence as 'the supreme condition of the historical dialectic'.[3] According to Hyppolite, a 'pantragism' remains 'always in the background of Hegelian thought'.[4] Indeed, as he asserts, in Hegel's *Phenomenology of Spirit*, the negativity of the tragic has become the driving subject itself. Hegel, he explains,

> introduces us to a history in which the tragic of negativity – the certainty of death which, as one can see from the *Phenomenology*, has become the subject itself – is linked in a strange fashion to the rational and reasonable work [*oeuvre*] into which the human *polis* shapes itself.[5]

Peter Szondi, in *Versuch über das Tragische*, makes the same point even more emphatically than does Hyppolite, when he argues that in Hegel (in contrast to Schelling) tragic and dialectic coincide. Tracing the evolution of Hegel's conception of tragedy from its first treatment in *Über die wissenschaftlichen Behandlungsarten des Naturrechts* to the *Lectures on Fine Art*, Szondi argues that 'this identity is not a late affirmation, but goes back to the origin of both ideas in Hegel.' Hegel's early theological writings of 1798–1800, in particular *Der Geist des Christentums und sein Schicksal*, advance an interpretation of the Christian ethical order (*Sittlichkeit*) according to which the law is not an objective rule to which the human being is subject (as in Jewish religion), but is itself the result of a self-division of absolute ethicity. Hegel terms this self-division 'fate' (*Schicksal*). This genesis of fate coincides, Szondi claims, with the genesis of dialectic, and he adds: 'Fate in the Christian realm means tragic fate, in the sense that it is shown to be the moment of self-division in the ethical nature according to the definition of tragedy in the text on natural law.'[6] According to Szondi, then,

> the *Phenomenology*, in distinction from the *Aesthetics* but in conformity with the text on natural law, puts the tragic, though without ever explicitly calling it by that name, into the centre of Hegelian philosophy and interprets it as the dialectic to which the ethical, or the spirit on its level as true spirit, is subjected.[7]

In other words, even when it exceeds its limited historico-theological determination associated with the spirit of Christianity and becomes the law of the world, dialectic remains another name for the tragic and for its overcoming.[8] Dialectic is structurally tragic, and tragedy correspondingly dialectic.[9]

It cannot be my ambition in this short essay to call into question this powerful and influential interpretation of Hegel's conception of tragedy and dialectic. The fact of the tragic protagonist's death at the hands of a power greater than himself seems unmistakably to raise tragedy to the essential and privileged mode in which the negative finds its expression. What, indeed, could be more negative than death? Subsequently, and in a move which is difficult to contest, the thinkers who hold that the tragic occupies a central place in Hegel's philosophy have also been led to accord tragedy an apparently incontestable ascent over comedy. Thus Hyppolite remarks regarding modern comedy – both the aesthetic genre and the comedy of the modern State – that even this prosaic state of the world 'cannot entirely eliminate a tragic perspective that, even when extended to all, is beyond the satisfactions of private and bourgeois life'. Hyppolite's point is that even in this new world, a world of modern comedy, the tragic has not disappeared.[10] In fact, he contends that quite the opposite is

39

the case: that the dialectic of comedy – in the modern sense, of course, but ultimately in the Attic sense as well – remains suspended from the tragic. Yet although I cannot hope simply to overturn this interpretation, I shall nevertheless express a hesitation about it; a hesitation that derives from Hegel's treatment of comedy both in the *Phenomenology* and in the *Aesthetics*. A careful scrutiny of Hegel's discussion of dramatic art as a whole may indeed force us to re-examine the evidence, and the self-evidence, of the proposed primacy of tragedy in the understanding of the Hegelian dialectic.

According to the *Aesthetics: Lectures on Fine Art*, poetry is clearly the art of all arts, since it is in poetry that the ideal reality of art is realised in exemplary fashion. Further, and for the same reason, dramatic art occupies a special position within poetry, and consequently within the entirety of art. As Hegel emphasises at the outset of the section dedicated to it, dramatic art is 'the highest stage of poetry and of art generally' (1158).[11] Indeed, as we shall see, in dramatic art, that is to say, an art whose centre is made up by actions, the spirit offers itself to real experience, and does so in its totality. Heinz Paetzhold explains:

> Insofar as drama has the action at its centre, it reveals the Spirit itself in its totality, that is to say, the Spirit which exteriorises itself in the process of the action, but also the contradiction (collision), and finally the dissolution of the conflict in the reconciling return to itself. The action is a paradigm for the Spirit's being with itself in the other, and hence it allows for the experience of the total structure of the movement of the Spirit. This constitutes the metaphysical status of drama. To put it bluntly, drama represents the art of all arts, not only thanks to its law of *artistic* construction, according to which it integrates the principles of the epic and the lyric and raises them to a new level, but because drama is that art which structurally depicts the Spirit, and makes it intuitably experiencable in its phases of being-with-itself, exteriorisation, division, and finally of its return to itself.[12]

But if drama enjoys the privilege in question amongst the arts in general, is it therefore obvious, as Paetzhold seems to hold, that this prime position is outstandingly occupied by one of its genres, namely tragedy? Speaking of drama, Paetzhold all but conflates drama and tragedy when he writes that 'the central thesis of Hegel's theory of drama is that drama – and, particularly, tragedy [a few sentences later, he writes: 'drama – and especially tragedy . . .'] – must be understood as an action that is meaningful in a form most appropriate to art'.[13] However, whilst both Hyppolite and Szondi have argued that the tragic is the centre of Hegel's philosophy, it is not, according to Szondi, the centre

40

of the *Aesthetics*. Szondi remarks that the *Aesthetics* is 'only the formal echo' of Hegel's philosophy,[14] and bases his conclusion on the 'obstinate refusal' of German Idealism in general 'to draw the dialectic into the centre of the examination of the tragic'.[15] Whatever may be the value of Szondi's comparison of the *Aesthetics* with the *Phenomenology*, I would contend that Hegel's explicit treatment of the tragic in the *Lectures on Fine Art* as one poetic genre -- one, moreover, in distinction from comedy -- significantly complicates any consideration of the tragic as a privileged art form. Moreover, the discussion of the tragic in the *Lectures on Fine Art* provides points of resistance to a conception whereby dialectic would be primarily linked to tragedy. This is not to imply in the least that Hegel simply valorises comedy over tragedy as an art form, even in the light of his confession that in modern drama, where fate depends more often than not on mere misfortune, 'for [his] part a happy denouement is to be preferred'. This preference is merely a result of the fact that modern dramas are rarely in a position to muster the 'higher outlook' that is required in order to stage conflicts and their resolution in a tragic manner. Nor is his astonishingly frank appreciation of Aristophanes' presentation of subjective gaiety proof of a preference on Hegel's part for comedy over tragedy. '*Ohne ihn gelesen zu haben, läßt sich kaum wissen, wie dem Menschen sauwohl sein kann,*' Hegel writes, which Knox demurely translates: 'If you have not read him, you can scarcely realise how men can take things so easily' (1221), but which literally reads: 'You can scarcely realise to what extent men can feel as good as hogs, be in hog's heaven, or in the pink.' I shall return to this statement, but let me hint that it will not be in order to suggest that it overturns Hegel's aesthetic appreciation of the art form of tragedy and contradicts what he says about the greatness of Attic tragedy. The point that I wish to make rather concerns a structural aspect of comedy (as understood by Hegel) that would suggest a principal priority of the comic over the tragic for the understanding of both tragedy and dialectics.

I return, then, to the section on dramatic poetry in the *Lectures on Fine Art*, but not before recalling the following point. Hegel emphasises right at the beginning of the section on dramatic art that drama is 'the highest stage of poetry and of art generally' (1158) – and I note that in the *Lectures* Hegel has modernity as well as Antiquity in mind – because it 'is the product of a completely developed and organised national life' (1159), and hence is Spirit in its actual totality. Indeed, the understanding of art as belonging to the realm of religion – in other words, to the realm of actual Spirit or *Sittlichkeit* as developed in the *Phenomenology* – is very much a part of Hegel's elaborations on art, and dramatic art, in the *Lectures*.[16] The ethical world order as 'the Divine made real in the world', and 'the substantive basis which in all its aspects, whether particular or essential, provides the motive [*Inhalt*] for truly human action', is acknowledged as 'the proper theme of the original type of tragedy' (1195); even further, it is the very object of aesthetic investigations in the *Lectures* insofar as it reflects on the modalities through which this content is made artistically effective and conscious.[17] Nevertheless, and more generally, the thrust of the *Lectures* consists in explaining 'the perfect totality of content and form' (1158) that distinguishes dramatic art on the basis of distinctions immanent to art itself, and this makes for its originality. To understand what such distinctions amount to, it is first necessary to bear in mind that the privileged position of poetry in the system of the arts is not merely owing to its designation as the last and final form of the successive art forms. Its special status derives from the fact that it is a synthetic form, one that comprises the previous forms of art in the shape of the poetic genres (epic, lyric, and drama). As Szondi remarks, the genres of the poetic art forms are thus 'the modes of presentations of the other arts on a higher level, beyond the sensible, namely in [inner] perception', that is to say, in representation (*Vorstellung*). Rather than being ideas, the genres of poetry – and of all the arts, poetry alone subdivides into different genres – are thus clearly of the order of modalities of presentation itself; and hence they are only understandable against the background of the system of the individual arts as it has been unfolded by Hegel.[18] As Hegel has noted in his reflections on these different poetic genres, poetry, because it is no longer 'confined by any one-sidedness in its material to one particular sort of execution . . . takes for its specific form the different modes of artistic production in general'. What follows from this is not only that poetry is the 'totality of art', and that the genres that compose it can, or rather 'must be derived from the *general* nature of artistic presentation [*Darstellung*]' (1037) itself, but also that the whole of poetic art emerges as an art within the medium made up by the different formal aspects of artistic presentation itself. Accordingly, dramatic art, which is the highest of the poetic genres, combines the two other poetic genres to the extent that they are modes of artistic production. Dramatic art 'unites the objectivity of an epic with the subjective character of lyric' (1158), Hegel writes. This generic approach to the question of dramatic art has significant implications for Hegel's understanding of both tragedy and comedy in the *Lectures*; these implications will need to be spelled out hereafter.

By uniting the epic with the lyric, the action that dramatic art places before our eyes 'originates in the minds of the characters who bring it about, but at the same time, its outcome is decided by the really substantive nature of the aims, individuals and collisions involved', Hegel holds. Now, 'the action itself in the entirety of its mental and physical actuality is susceptible of two opposed modes of treatment [*schlechthin entgegengesetzten Auffassung*], the tragic and the comic' (1158). At this point, I wish to look once more at the genre of dramatic

art itself, in order to define as clearly as possible what constitutes the difference between the tragic and the comic as two species (*Arten*) of this genre
(*Gattung*) (in view of what I seek to demonstrate, I can ignore drama as the
third species), to consider in what sense 'species' is to be understood here, and
also to speculate on the significance of the fact that the genre itself can and
must divide into species.[19] Since dramatic art, in its entirety, is a genre in
which 'the individual . . . character himself picks the fruit of his own deeds'
(1161), it is all the more important to be able to specify under what circumstances such a picking is either tragic or comic.

In the same way as does the epic, dramatic poetry stages an action. It is an
action in the dramatic sense, however, only if: (1) the material substance
(*Substantielle*), 'the eternal powers, i.e. what is essentially moral', proceeds
from subjects who are self-conscious and active individuals, and if these powers manifest themselves in the shape of passions; (2) this essential content separates 'into different and *opposed* ends' so that 'the action has to encounter
hindrances from other agents'; and (3) the 'decision on the course and outcome of the complications arising from the action . . . [displays] the vital working of a necessity which, itself reposing, resolves every conflict and
contradiction' (1162–3). In other words, dramatic action presupposes, on the
most general level, that the divine substance first become particularised and
one-sided (*einseitige Besonderheit*) in the shape of opposed passions, the collision
of which produces actions that steadily move forward 'to the final catastrophe'
(1168), and that 'finally their contradiction is annulled and the unity is
restored' (1166). As Hegel emphasises, the essential principle for discriminating between the kinds or species (*Arten*) of dramatic poetry 'can only be derived
from the relation of individuals to their aim and what it involves' (1193). The
distinction between the tragic and the comic (and their mediation in the species
of drama) concerns exclusively this relation. All distinctions derive from a preliminary difference in the relation of the individuals to the substantive aim of
the actions; for instance, the mutual hostility of the dramatis personæ in
tragedy, as opposed to their inward self-dissolution in comedy (1163). Before
further looking at how this difference in the relation of the characters to their
aims is to be thought, it is crucial to understand that the species to which this
difference lends itself are not just exterior modifications of the genre, distinguished for merely classificatory purposes. Instead, they are themselves the
means to achieving a total determination and completion of the poetic conception, and execution, of the dramatic action itself (or in totality); indeed,
they are the means without which such action could not proceed to 'visible
presentation'. Put differently, the function of the species of dramatic poetry
consists in rendering possible a phenomenalisation of dramatic action, its coming onto the stage. Tragedy and comedy are the very means that guarantee that

Rodolphe Gasché

dramatic action can become visible, apprehendable; in short, that it can *zur Erscheinung gelangen* in the first place. Hegel writes:

> if the action is thus to be made real objectively, it must itself be altogether determined and finished in itself in poetic conception and treatment. But this can only be done if . . . dramatic poetry is split into different *genres* which borrow their type, whether it involves opposition or their reconciliation, from the difference between the ways in which the characters and their aims, their conflict and the outcome of the whole action are brought onto the scene [*zur Erscheinung gelangt*].
> (1192–3)

The two 'modes of treatment' (*Auffassungsweisen*) for which the difference in question allows, the tragic and the comic, are of 'essential importance' because without them dramatic action could not 'be made real objectively'. Now, we must remind ourselves that poetic art (and religion, to which it belongs) achieves reality only through representation (*Vorstellung*). As the middle element, or 'the central element of imagination [*mittlere Element der Vorstellung*] . . . between what is directly visible or perceptible by the senses of the subjectivity of feeling and thinking' (1035),[20] representation defines the exact epistemic level on which Spirit experiences itself in this sphere of art. *Qua* representation, the mode of experience in question has already transcended the experience characteristic of sense-perception to which, however, it continues to relate by subjectively and reflexively processing it. Therefore representation, as the medium of poetic art, vouches for this art's 'spiritual *universality*' (1035), and hence for its proximity to thinking. But representation is not yet pure thinking. By continuing to refer to sense-perception, it remains tributary to something distinct from it, something it has not yet posited, that is to say, recognised as its own exteriorisation. Hegel defines representation's middle position in the following passage before elucidating several consequences of the phenomenal exteriorisation of action:

> . . . imagination [*Vorstellung*] is essentially distinguished from thinking by reason of the fact that, like sense-perception from which it takes its start, it allows particular ideas to subside alongside one another without being related, whereas thinking demands and produces dependence of things on one another, reciprocal relations, logical judgements, syllogisms, etc. Therefore, when the *poetic* way of looking at things makes necessary in its artistic productions an inner unity of everything particular, this unification may nevertheless remain hidden because of that lack of liaison which the medium of imagination cannot

44

renounce at all; and it is precisely this which enables poetry to present a subjective-manner in the *organically* living development of its singular aspects and parts, while giving to all these the appearance of independence.

(1035)

Representation, consequently, is the very way in which Spirit, by hiding its unifying operation and keeping it visible, makes it possible for a substantial content to come into actual appearance; more precisely, for it to come into an appearance that takes the shape of two seemingly unrelated and independent characters. But if dramatic poetry is thus enabled to represent 'the invisible aspect of mind and spirit in action at the same time, i.e. as an entirety of the circumstances and aims of various characters' (1168), the same representational principle also explains why dramatic art can, and must, split into seemingly opposed ways of relating to the substantial aim itself, and thus give way to the species of the genre. These species are the essential means by which the genre may accomplish its proper task, namely to be the representation of 'true action' (*wahrhafte Handlung*) (1193). Both species work at fulfilling this necessary condition for dramatic art, and they do this by determining the relation between character and aim in such ways that all the possibilities of this relation become realised. Subservient to the genre itself, the tragic and the comic foster between them a still-invisible totality. Whether it is tragedy or comedy which plays the decisive role in this fostering, or whether their share is truly equal, remains to be seen.

What, then, are the specific features that characterise the relation between individuals and their aims? Which features designate the particular manner of the unfolding of the dramatic conflict and its outcome; and hence also decide the kinds of artistic presentation that are possible within the genre concerned with 'true action'? I quote:

> In whatever form dramatic poetry brings the action on the stage, what is really effective in it is absolute truth, but the specific way in which this effectiveness comes on the scene takes a different, and indeed an opposed form according to whether what is kept dominant in the individuals and their actions and conflicts is their substantive basis or alternatively their subjective caprice, folly and perversity [*Verkehrtheit*].

> (1194)

The essential moments of true action consist of:

i. what is in *substance* good and great, the divine actualised in the world, as the foundation of everything genuine and absolutely eternal

45

in the make-up of an individual's character and aim; ii. the *subject*, the individual himself in his unfettered self-determination and freedom.

$$(1193–4)^{21}$$

Substance in its worldly reality, that is, as *Sittlichkeit*, is pervasive throughout the whole of dramatic poetry; but the way in which it takes on appearance and comes on to the scene (*zur Anschauung kommt*) can be shaped (*gestalten*) differently, more precisely, by way of figures opposed to one another. As I have already indicated, the true action with which dramatic art is concerned is that of subjects whose will and passions are determined by this spiritual substance. In these subjects, subjectivity and substantiality are thus unified. But within this unity itself a difference arises, depending on whether the substantial or the subjective aspect dominates. In all cases, dramatic art is based on the unity of substance and subject; but this unity itself can become biased, one-sided, if either one of the substance or the contingency and caprice of subjective life becomes the ruling principle. The fundamental unity of substance and subjectivity that characterises true action is one in which 'the gods . . . dominate the human heart' (*in der Menchenbrust waltenden Götter*) (1206); and only because it lets itself be dominated by one of the principles can there be kinds or species of dramatic art. We should note, moreover, that these two species, in that they are *schlechthin entgegengesetzt*, in absolute opposition, are susceptible of sublation: first by drama, but then by the prose of philosophy as well. By way of a first conclusion, we thus need to recognise that the tragic and the comic are theoretico-generic distinctions within the poetic presentation itself of what Hegel has called 'true action', that is, an action by subjects who have adopted aims of substantive bearing, and that they are distinctions for it alone, there being no other medium appropriate for it.

The question we face, therefore, is how Hegel's primarily generic approach to the differences in question in the *Lectures* – an approach which, obviously, rests upon a concern with the possibilities of artistic realisation, and not with simple (and exterior) classificatory concerns – affects the ways in which the tragic and the comic themselves must be understood.[22] Undoubtedly, the approach in question also pre-programmes all possible interpretations of the final catastrophe in both cases, and particularly of the resolution (*Auflösung*) of the catastrophe. In truth, the fact that tragedy and comedy are capable of resolution to begin with rests upon their being species of the same genre. Evoking the two discriminating principles of drama, Hegel writes:

> . . . granted the cleavage of dramatic poetry into different *genres*
> [*Arten*], it is only in these two fundamental features of action which

can confront one another as the basis of such *genres*. In tragedy, the individuals destroy themselves through the one-sidedness of their otherwise solid will and character, or they must resignedly accept what they had opposed even in a serious way. In comedy, there comes before our contemplation, in the laughter in which the characters dissolve everything, including themselves, the victory of their own subjective personality which nevertheless persists self-assured.

(1199)

As Hegel recalls, 'the original essence of tragedy' consists in the fact that within tragic conflict, 'each of the opposed sides, if taken by itself, has *justification*; while each can establish the true and positive content only by denying and infringing the equally justified power of the other' (1196). The ensuing opposition and collision sets up 'an unresolved contradiction', whose 'proper claim is satisfied only [*sein eigentliches Recht nur darin findet*] when it is annulled as a contradiction'. Hence, there follows from this the necessity 'of the tragic resolution of this conflict'. It is perhaps not unimportant to emphasise here that, at least as far as the *Lectures* are concerned, Hegel in no way implies that such resolution could only be brought about by the death of the hero. Indeed, it is also difficult to see, from Hegel's generic approach to the question of tragedy, why death would have to be the iron fate of any hero incarnating a particular aspect of ethical substance. In the *Lectures*, Hegel acknowledges that 'the tragic denouement need not every time require the downfall of the participating individuals in order to obliterate the one-sidedness of both sides in their equal need of honour' (1218). Indeed, he allows for tragic resolutions in which the protagonist does not meet his punishment (*Eumenides*), or he resigns (*Philoctetes*), or in which he even achieves reconciliation (*Oedipus at Colonus*) (1218–19).[23] Now, since the discriminating criterion of the 'tragic' species of true action is the predominance of substance in the union of substance and subject, the resolution of the conflict must manifest the conciliating power of substance. It could be said that with the resolution of the tragic conflict, one returns to only one of the moments necessary for true action – substance – even though it appears at this stage in its harmonising function. Indeed, Hegel notes that by means of the tragic resolution of a conflict, rooted in one-sided realisations of the ethical order,

eternal justice is exercised on individuals and their aims in the sense that it restores the substance and unity of ethical life with the downfall of the individual who has disturbed its peace . . . . The truly substantial thing which has to be actualised, however, is not the battle between particular aims or characters . . . but the reconciliation in

47

which the specific individuals and their aims work together harmoniously without opposition and without infringing on one another.

(1197)

In short, by the tragic resolution, eternal substance, which had suffered particularisation thanks to the 'nature of the real world' – the world of the acting subjects in which it took on reality and actuality – and had thus become 'perverted [*verkehren*] into *opposition* and collision' (1196), eventually 'emerges victorious in a reconciling way' (1199). But the perversion into opposition and collision, by way of which 'the blessed gods' are set in the real world, and which becomes annulled again in this reconciliation, remains nevertheless the point of view from which alone we can 'be really serious about those gods who dwell in their peaceful tranquillity and unity solely on Olympus and in the heaven of imagination and religious ideas' (1196). Is perversion of the divine substance into a dissolving one-sidedness truly to be qualified as serious? But is not perversion (*Verkehrtheit*) a characteristic of the comic? Hegel did indeed write that the specific form of the effectiveness of dramatic action varies 'according to whether what is kept dominant in the individuals and their actions and conflicts is their substantive basis or alternatively their subjective caprice, folly and perversity' (1194). Does the tragic resolution thus annul a comic aspect specific to the tragic, one without which no real seriousness in matters regarding divine substance could be attained? Or, more fundamentally, is tragedy in its very possibility a function of a trait that most properly belongs to what Hegel analyses under the rubric of the comic? I leave these questions in abeyance for the moment. Before I return to them, let me take up comedy.

> In tragedy the eternal substance of things emerges victorious in a reconciling way, because it strips away from the conflicting individuals only their false one-sidedness, while the positive elements in what they willed it displays as what is to be retained, without discord but affirmatively harmonised. In comedy, conversely, it is subjectivity, or personality, which in its infinite assurance retains the upper hand.
>
> (1199)

So whereas the outcome of tragedy restores the undivided substance and retrieves it as the reconciling power, the dominating principle of subjectivity in comedy means that the comic resolution brings about a victory of the 'infinite light-heartedness and confidence' (1200) of subjectivity over all the insubstantial actions that it pursues with 'great seriousness' (1201), while disregarding their contradictions. Compared to the tragic hero who is serious about a one-sided but substantial content, the comic character is '*serious in* identifying himself with . . . an inherently false aim and making it the one real thing in his life' (1200). Let me add right away that the seriousness that comic subjectivity brings to insubstantial aims is one that, in truth, only substantial aims deserve. Were it not for the subject's pathos, the comic protagonist would only inspire ridicule. The tragic and the comic heroes' worlds differ beyond the shadow of a doubt: the tragic hero's world is one in which the gods have become worldly (that is, serious) despite the fact – or precisely because of it – that they are split and opposed. By contrast,

> the general ground for comedy is . . . a world in which man as subject or person has made himself completely master of everything that counts to him otherwise as the essence of that he wills and accomplishes, a world whose aims are therefore self-destructive because they are insubstantial.
>
> (1199)

But on closer inspection, the tragic hero and the comic character differ only insofar as the first identifies with a one-sided truth, whereas the latter is dead serious or truthful only about petty and futile aims. Needless to say, this difference is not insignificant. But while there is certainly nothing tragic about the comic hero, is it entirely out of place to contend that there is something inherently comic about the tragic dramatis personæ? For the moment, let me only suggest a question concerning whether the tragic hero's stubborn fixation on a one-sided truth – notwithstanding that it is a truth – does not presuppose a structural trait that belongs primarily to the order of the comic.

The resolution of comedy requires a victory of subjectivity. Of the comic need for resolution, Hegel writes:

> The comical rests as such throughout on contradictory contrasts both between aims in themselves and also between their objects and the accidents of character and external circumstances, and therefore the comic action requires a solution [Auflösung] almost more stringently than does a tragic one. In comic action, the contradiction between what is absolutely true and its realisation in individuals is posed more profoundly.
>
> (1201)

If comedy is the kind of dramatic art that most urgently calls for a resolution, is it not because, within its world, all substantial aims are in dissolution? By adopting the most petty causes with great seriousness, the comic deepens the sense of limitation and finitude concerning the individual's ability to realise the absolute. If the comic poses this contradiction more profoundly than tragedy, it is because it reveals the individual's fixation on contents from which all substance has fled. It thus deepens (*stellt vertiefter heraus*) the contradiction between 'what is absolutely true and its realisation in individuals' by bringing to light the essential deficiency in any *individual* realisation of substantive aims. The comic thus also displays the truth of the tragic character who can only take a one-sided aspect of substance, rather than its entirety, upon himself. This is due to comedy's being precisely the seriousness with which an individual adopts ethical positions that always fall short of the ethical order in its entirety. Even though one would likely not find the tragic to be comic, tragic fate nevertheless hinges on the possibility that is specifically of the order of the comic.

The resolution of the comic collisions and final catastrophe consists in making 'the comic subjective personality . . . the overlord of whatever appears in the real world'.

> For even if what comes on the scene is only the show and imagination of what is substantive, or else mere downright perversity and pettiness, there still remains as a loftier principle the inherently firm personality which is raised in its freedom above the downfall of the whole finite sphere and is happy and assured in itself.
>
> (1202)

Hegel characterises victorious subjectivity repeatedly in terms of 'infinite light-heartedness' (*Wohlgemutheit*), 'bliss and ease' (*Seligkeit und Wohlkeit*), 'undisturbed cheerfulness' (*freie Heiterkeit*) (1200–1) or a 'naive fundamental "all is well within me"' (*unbefangenes Grundwohlsein*) (1222). But perhaps this is also the moment to recall his assessment of Aristophanes' comedies. Here, writes Hegel, the characters

> reveal themselves as having something higher in them because they are not seriously tied to the finite world with which they are engaged, but are raised above it and remain firm in themselves and secure in face of failure and loss. It is to this absolute freedom of spirit which is utterly consoled in advance of every human undertaking, to this world of private serenity, that Aristophanes conducts us. If you have not read him, you can scarcely realise how men can take things so easily [*wie dem Menschen sauwohl sein kann*].
>
> (1221)

By way of a caution, we might remark that for Hegel the only dramatis personæ who are truly comic are those who 'are comical [to] themselves' (*für sich selbst*) (1220), who can laugh about themselves (and who thus reveal a self-assuredness). In hog heaven, as it were, the comic subjects' ease, cheerfulness and 'pinkness' derive from their ability to put themselves in the pink, to laugh at themselves: more precisely, 'to dissolve everything, including themselves', in their laughter (1199). This victorious subjectivity, in which the final catastrophe in comedy finds its resolution, is, as Hegel puts it, 'the smiling blessedness of the Olympian gods, their unimpaired equanimity which comes in men and can put up with everything' (1222).

In that they are based on opposite ways of looking at human action with respect to its aims, the two kinds of dramatic poetry – tragedy and comedy – are 'firmly separated and strictly distinguished from one another' (1208). Yet in their organic development not only do they reach their respective summit of perfection one after the other – tragedy first, then comedy – but, furthermore, tragedy, at least in its early stages, displays features within itself that are clearly already of the order of the comic. As Hegel's discussion of *Oedipus at Colonus* demonstrates, Oedipus' final transfiguration and reconciliation already give rise to a *'subjective* satisfaction' and hence prepare 'the transition to the sphere of comedy, the opposite of tragedy' (1220). The subjective satisfaction in which comedy culminates is thus not entirely absent from tragedy; and if this can be so, it is only because the dissolving quality of subjectivity has an essential role to play in tragedy as well. Let us then have a further, and perhaps deeper, look at comedy.

> What is comical . . . is a personality or a subject who makes his own actions contradictory and so brings them to nothing [*auflöst*], while remaining tranquil and self-assured in the process. Therefore, comedy has for its basis and starting-point what tragedy may end with, namely an absolutely reconciled and cheerful heart. Even if its possessor destroys by the means he uses whatever he wills and so comes to grief [*an sich selber zuschanden wird*] because by his efforts he has accomplished the very opposite of what he aimed at, he still has not lost his peace of mind on that account.
>
> (1220)

Whether substance or subjectivity prevails, the subject destroys himself in dramatic action. I recall Hegel's criterion for upholding the excellency, among all tragedies, of *Antigone*: 'So there is immanent in both Antigone and Creon something that in their own way they attack, so that they are gripped and shattered by something intrinsic to their own being' (1217–18). What is great about the dramatis personæ, whether tragic or comic, is that *they themselves* dissolve themselves. Self-dissolution is comic in a strict sense, however, only if the subject

51

arises victorious from this destruction, and fully reconciled with himself. This possibility is explicitly present in tragedy as its potential end, but is only fully developed within the art form of comedy. But let us consider once again what such dissolution achieves. The comic characters, even if they belong, as they commonly do, to the lower class,

> reveal themselves as having something higher in them because they are not seriously tied to the finite world with which they are engaged, but are risen above it and remain firm in themselves and secure in the face of failure and loss.
>
> (1221)

The comic character's detachment from everything of the order of the finite world — that is, from an order from which all substance has fled, but also from all inevitably one-sided realisation of the divine order in the human world — makes his greatness. Yet this lack of seriousness as regards a worldly realisation of the ethical substance is the very condition under which one-sidedness can be overcome; and not only, in the first place, on the part of the comic character, but on the part of the tragic hero as well. The comic character exemplifies a dissolution of finitude and one-sidedness that is valid for the whole genre of dramatic art. At the beginning of the section on dramatic poetry, Hegel noted that:

> the drama is the dissolution of the one-sidedness of these powers which are making themselves independent in the dramatic characters, whether, as in tragedy, their attitude to one another is hostile, or whether, as in comedy, they are revealed directly as inwardly self-dissolving.
>
> (1163)

This concern with the self-dissolution of the subject is the ground for a certain excellency of comedy over tragedy. More urgently than does tragedy, comedy calls for a resolution and dissolution not only of its dramatis personæ, but also of itself as an art form, and even of art itself; at the end of the Lectures, Hegel states that on the peak where consciousness, satisfied with itself, no longer unites with anything objective and particularised, and 'brings the negative side of this dissolution into consciousness in the humour of comedy', 'comedy leads at the same time to the dissolution of art altogether' (1236).[24] What this is to say is that, within this concern with self-dissolution by one kind of dramatic art, in whose world everything has already dissolved, a principle reveals itself that is presupposed not only by tragedy but, ultimately, by dialectic itself.

Without self-dissolution, without the comic, without a comic self-dissolution, not only could the particularisation of substance which is necessary for true action of both variants not occur, nor the dissolution of these one-sided realisations of substance, but the comic hero could not even achieve the self-assurance of subjectivity that is his distinguishing feature. The comic, in the sense of a susceptibility or light-hearted readiness for self-dissolution, is the pervading trait of drama, the very condition of possibility without which there would be no such things as the art forms of the tragic and the comic, to name only them.

As Hegel reminds us, in his comedies Aristophanes loved to expose 'above all, [and] most mercilessly, the new direction that Euripides had taken in tragedy' (1221). Even though Euripides' tragic characters could be made into objects of ridicule only because he had already abandoned 'polished plasticity of character and action and [had gone] . . . over to subjective emotion' (1228), I would like, in conclusion, to ask whether it might be appropriate to suggest that tragedy is, as a whole, comical.

Hegel has made amply clear that dramatic poetry 'presupposes as past both the primitive poetic days of the epic proper and the independent subjectivism of lyrical outpourings' (1159). It thus comprises both genres. In the case of tragedy, the general background is even provided 'as it was in epic, by that world-situation which I have previously called the "heroic" age', Hegel remarks (1208). As in the epic, dramatic poetry brings before us a happening, a deed, an action; and even though these deeds are the actions of self-conscious individuals in dramatic art – of 'acting heroes [handelnde Heroen]', as Hegel calls them (1210) – still the 'fundamental essence [Substantielle] . . . asserted in individual agents acting independently and from their own resources . . . [is an] aspect of epic which is evidently effective and vital in the principle of dramatic poetry' (1160). However transformed the fundamental substance may have been by virtue of the hero's interiority and self-consciousness in dramatic art, 'the real thing at bottom, the actual pervasive cause is . . . indeed the eternal powers, i.e. what is essentially moral, the god of our actual life, in short what is divine and true' (1162). Finally, if the Divine is the innermost objective truth of the single hero's deeds, the outcome of his actions cannot lie in his own hands, 'but only in those of the Divine itself, as a totality in itself' (1163). The epic, then, is the pervading grid that, although it is internalised by the hero in dramatic art, still structures the relation between substance and object.

To highlight a particular aspect of this relation, I will turn briefly to Hegel's discussion of epic poetry in the chapter on 'The Spiritual Work of Art' in the *Phenomenology of Spirit*. As Hegel suggests here, the epic brings about a unity of the divine and the human by endowing both with self-consciousness and individuality. The gods of the epic world have human shape, and in the same way as do the humans, they also have 'the principle of action in them; what they effect appears, therefore, to proceed entirely from them and to be as free an action as that of men'. As a result, 'both gods and men have done one and the same thing', Hegel concludes. And in consequence, both appear ridiculous. In spite of their seriousness and superiority, the gods are ridiculous since they manifest themselves as mere mortals, whereas the latter appear ridiculous since all their efforts and labours are in vain, because it is the divine powers and not their mortal ones that are the true agents of the action. Hegel writes:

> The universal powers have the form of individuality and hence the principle of action in them; what they effect appears, therefore, to proceed entirely from them and to be as free an action as that of men. Consequently, both gods and men have done one and the same thing. The earnestness of those divine powers is a ridiculous superfluity, since they are in fact the power or strength of the individuality while the exertions and labour of the latter is an equally useless effort, since it is rather the gods who manage everything.[25]

But even this does not yet fully exhaust the ridiculousness of the epic relations between gods and human beings. Whereas the 'ephemeral mortals who are nothing' puff themselves up as the 'mighty *self*', the gods represented as individuals become involved in actions among each other that amount to nothing more than 'an arbitrary showing-off', given that their finite actions are directed against other gods, who, as gods, are invincible; thus, Hegel continues, 'their universality comes into conflict with their own specific character and its relationship to others'. And he notes that this conflict of the gods with one another demonstrates 'a comical self-forgetfulness of their eternal nature'.[26] In the *Lectures on Fine Art*, Hegel had warned against confusing ridiculousness pure and simple with the comic; but in no way does the comic exclude ridiculousness. Indeed, there is a specifically comic ridiculousness, and it is to this that Hegel refers when in the *Phenomenology* he ridicules the epic heroes and their gods. Comical ridiculousness of an individual requires that 'it is obvious that he is not so serious at all about the seriousness of his aim and will, so that this seriousness always carries with it, in the eye of the individual himself, his own destruction' (1220), he emphasises in the *Lectures*. Given that Hegel not only shows gods and men in the epic to be laughable, but even characterises them as comic, I can, in the present context, forgo the task of showing that the epic is intrinsically comic. But if the epic is comic, tragedy must be comic in a fundamental way as well; and perhaps most fundamentally, in that the relation between substance and subject that it takes over from the epic is in essence self-dissolving. Without the possibility of the dissolution of this relation, that is, without an element of the comic, tragedy would not be thinkable. The art form of comedy makes this explicit, and makes immediate self-dissolution its very theme. It thus also inaugurates the explicit passage from *Vorstellung* to thinking, which 'moves free in itself and in the spiritual world' (1236).

Notes

1 G. W. F. Hegel, *The Phenomenology of Spirit*, translated by A. V. Miller (Oxford: Oxford University Press, 1979), 19.

2 Jean Hyppolite, 'Le tragique et le rationel dans la philosophie de Hegel' in *Figures de la pensée philosophique* (Paris: PUF, 1971), 254.

3 Ibid., 258.

4 Ibid., 259.

5 Ibid., 258–9.

6 Peter Szondi, *Schriften*, edited by Jean Bollack (Frankfurt am Main: Suhrkamp, 1978) I: 167–8.

7 Ibid., 172.

8 Ibid., 173.

9 Following Otto Pöggeler's analysis of Hegel's references to Greek tragedy from the essay on *Naturrechts* to the *Phenomenology*, one can object to Szondi's claim of the centrality and continuity of the notion of the tragic in Hegel's conception of the dialectic throughout his philosophy (with the exception of the *Aesthetics*) that Hegel's understanding in Jena of the unity of the Absolute of the ethical world as a tragic reconciliation is a violent interpretation which is already abandoned in the *Phenomenology* where the Absolute of the ethical world is no longer conceptualised in the image of Greek tragedy. Moreover, as Pöggeler recalls, at the end of the Jena period, comedy becomes construed as the truth of Greek tragedy. Cf. Otto Pöggeler, 'Hegel und die griechiste Tragödie' in *Hegels Idee einer Phänomenologie des Geistes* (Freiburg: Karl Alber, 1973), 90–5.

10 Hyppolite, 'Le tragique et le rationel dans la philosophie de Hegel', 261.

11 G. W. F. Hegel, *Aesthetics: Lectures on Fine Art*, translated by T. M. Knox (Oxford: Oxford University Press, 1975), 1158. Unless otherwise specified, all page references in the text are to this work.

12 Heinz Paetzhold, *Ästhetik des deutschen Idealismus: Zur Idee der ästhetischen Rationalität bei Baumgarten, Kant, Schelling, Hegel und Schopenhauer* (Wiesbaden: Franz Steiner Verlag, 1983), 377.

13 Ibid., 387.

14 Szondi, *Schriften* I: 172.

15 Ibid., 208.

16 Hegel also recalls that

> truly *tragic* action necessarily presupposes either a live conception of *individual* freedom and independence or at least an individual's determination and willingness to accept freely and on his own account the responsibility for his own act and its consequences; and for the emergence of

comedy there must have asserted itself in a still higher degree the free right of the subjective personality and its self-assured dominion.

(1205)

17 The reference to dramatic art as a late product of national life provides another clear indication of the continuity between the *Phenomenology* and the *Lectures* on the matter of drama and ethical order.

18 Peter Szondi, 'Hegels Lehre von der Dichtung' in *Poetik und Geschichtsphilosophie* (Frankfurt am Main: Suhrkamp, 1974) I: 470, 475, 478. See also Paetzhold, *Ästhetik des deutschen Idealismus*, 361.

19 By translating *Arten* as 'genre', Knox blurs not only this question, but also the whole dialectic progression both within and beyond the genre.

20 Knox's translation of *Vorstellung* as 'imagination' is quite misleading, since imagination is only a modus of *Vorstellung*. Hegel distinguishes three modi of *Vorstellung*. They are *Erinnerung*, *Einbildungskraft* and *Gedächtnis*. See, in particular, G. W. F. Hegel, *Werke in zwanzig Bänden, Enzyklopädie der philosophischen Wissenschaft* (Frankfurt am Main: Suhrkamp, 1970) III: 257ff.

21 Hegel explains:

> the chief features implicit in the nature of dramatic action [consist in this: that] . . . in tragedy the whole treatment and execution presents what is *substantial* and fundamental in the characters and their aims and conflicts, while in comedy the central thing is the character's *inner* life and his *private* personality.
>
> (1205)

22 Ultimately, this question not only concerns Hegel's analysis of tragedy and comedy in the *Lectures*, but it also affects the *Phenomenology* as well, from which genre-related considerations regarding the tragic and the comic are not absent.

23 It is not uninteresting to note that these additional manners of tragic resolution, some of which are subjective in nature, are structurally not very different from the modes of the subject's self-dissolution which characterises the comic outcome.

24 Even though Hegel is uncompromisingly critical of Romantic irony, and of subjective humour *à la* Jean Paul, he does not despise humour in general. Indeed, quite the opposite is the case. As Wolfgang Preisendanz has shown, humour remains for Hegel 'the necessary head of a development immanent to the principle of the Romantic art form', even though 'he rejects it at first together with Schlegelian irony as the absolutisation of the one abstract moment of subjectivity'. Humour, in the shape of what Hegel terms 'objective humour', is not only instrumental in bringing about the passage from art to philosophical thinking; it is also, as Preisendanz demonstrates, the formal principle of art after art, of an art that, within its own medium, goes beyond itself as art. See Wolfgang Preisendanz, *Humor als dichterische Einbildungskraft: Studien zur Erzählkunt des poetischen Realismus* (Munich: Eidos Verlag, 1963), 121ff.

25 Hegel, *Phenomenology*, 441–2.

26 Ibid., 442.

Part II

Hölderlin

3

Of tragic metaphor

Jean-François Courtine

The question addressed in this study is already clearly delimited and, one could almost say, classic, well known in any case and generally accepted: it is, to put it briefly, the question of Hölderlin's relation to what is called 'German Idealism'. More precisely, the question of the 'historial' location of the poetological essays and *Aufsätze* of the Homburg period. Let us accept here, at least provisionally, this general problematic, even if it will mean adding later certain supplementary questions likely to complicate it. As is well known, it is principally Heidegger who has made us sensitive to the distance which separates Hölderlin from metaphysics in its absolute or completed form, even if his references to the poet's 'Philosophical Fragments' remain largely programmatic.[1] It is sufficient to recall here just one of these remarks, whose formulation remains, it is true, particularly abrupt and enigmatic. Heidegger, in a seminar devoted to Hegel and the *Differenzschrift*, having evoked the proximity – at the very least geographical (Frankfurt, Bad Homburg) – of Hegel and Hölderlin, goes on to say: 'This proximity is immediately questionable. For from this period on, despite the appearance of dialectic in his essays, the poet has already passed through and broken with speculative idealism, just as Hegel is in the process of constituting it.'[2]

What about this Hölderlinian passage through idealism? In what does this breaking free consist? What does an 'appearance' of dialectic mean? And what disguises itself under this appearance? These are all questions destined to remain on the horizon of the present study, and whose examination I want simply to initiate by way of the very specific issue of Hölderlin's meditation on tragedy, its essence and its historicity.

When seeking a precise vantage point from which to examine this *distance from* and *proximity to* the dialectical and speculative determinations of idealism, there are numerous compelling reasons for privileging, in the whole span of Hölderlin's poetological reflections, the question of tragedy. Indeed, from 1797 on, Hölderlin is writing the outline for a tragedy, and it is not an exaggeration to claim that the project of 'writ[ing] a true modern tragedy' will remain central up until 1804, that is to say, up to the publication of the translations of *Oedipus* and *Antigone*, as well as the accompanying 'Remarks'. It is not our aim here to follow the metamorphoses of this project and to elucidate the necessity which leads Hölderlin to engage in a decisive dialogue with Sophocles in order to delimit – destinally – the Greek and the Oriental, the modern and the Hesperian respectively, identifying in each case the 'proper' or the 'nationell [*das Nationelle*]'.[3] Let us concentrate instead on this singular insistence, for us all the more significant in that the tragic conflict or contradiction (*Widerspruch*) and its resolution orient, more or less explicitly, the meditations of German Idealism in the process of constituting itself as speculative or dialectical, and orient in any case the thought of the young Schelling, who, as early as the *Letters on Dogmatism and Criticism* of 1795–6, sees in tragedy, exemplified in *Oedipus Rex*, the heroic figure of an equilibrium between the power or 'superior strength' (*Übermacht*) of the objective world and the self-affirmation of the I in its absolute freedom (*Selbstmacht*).[4] In his lectures on the *Philosophy of Art* (Jena 1802–3, Würzburg 1804–5), Schelling will still regard tragedy as the highest manifestation of art (*Die höchste Erscheinung der Kunst*),[5] and will see in the 'hero of tragedy . . . the one who represents . . . the unconditioned and absolute itself in his person, . . . the symbol of the infinite, of that which transcends all suffering (*Leiden*)'. 'Only', Schelling goes on, 'within the maximum of suffering can that principle be revealed in which there is no suffering, just as everywhere things are revealed only in their opposites.'[6] It is thus that tragedy ('the essence of tragedy') can legitimately acquire a central function in the so-called 'Identity Philosophy', figuring concretely the ultimate absolutisation of freedom in its identity with necessity,[7] and so lay claim to the cathartic effect of 'reconciliation and harmony'.[8]

To this properly speculative interpretation of tragedy, which I have drawn only in its broadest outlines here,[9] I want to confront the Hölderlinian analysis, restricting myself to two essays in which the appearance of dialectic is most immediately striking: the fragment 'On the Difference of Poetic Modes' and the very brief sketch 'The Significance of Tragedies'. And since it is a matter of showing how Hölderlin, in a single gesture, 'collaborated . . . in the building of the edifice of speculative dialectic' and 'dismantles the speculative–tragic matrix',[10] of which tragedy was a privileged model, we will need to follow step by step the unfolding of the principal text in question.

*   *   *

In order to consider the first Hölderlinian interpretation of tragedy – the one which, it is worth repeating, is most explicitly articulated within the horizon of German Idealism – we should start with the provisional definition given at

60

the beginning of the study of the tragic poem in the Homburg essay 'On the Difference of Poetic Modes'.[11] Without taking into account the entirety of a text that is, in any case, unfinished and largely programmatic,[12] and without situating precisely the study of the tragic poem which occupies its central section (by far the most developed), let us recall briefly that Hölderlin considers the differences between the following three major genres or modes: lyric, epic and tragic, each genre subdividing in turn into sub-genres in respect of its basic tone. Hölderlin distinguishes in each genre or mode the appearance (*Schein*) or 'art-character', 'tendency' (*Richtung-Tendenz*), signification (*Bedeutung*), and the basic or fundamental tone (*Hauptton*), as well as the foundation (*Begründung*), stress or emphasis (*Nachdruck*), spirit, stance (*Haltung*) and dwelling (*Verweilen*). These different traits, which are, as it were, structural, themselves vary in respect of the three tones properly so-called: the naïve, the idealistic and the energetic or heroic (a classification borrowed in part from Schiller).[13]

The definition of the tragic poem given at the start of the essay runs as follows: 'The tragic, in appearance heroic, poem, is idealistic in its signification. It is the metaphor of an intellectual intuition.'[14] What are we to make of this? It is worth noting in the first place that the concept of 'metaphor' here figures in the preceding definitions of the two other genres (the 'lyric poem . . . is a continuous metaphor of feeling. The epic poem . . . is the metaphor of great aspirations'). The term does not appear to be reserved exclusively for the tragic poem (though we shall see that this is in fact the case), and indeed we can try to clarify Hölderlin's use of it with the aid of the first two definitions. It seems to be the case, then, that metaphor must be understood *à la lettre*, so to speak, as designating transport, transposition, transfer or translation (with all the deviation, substitution, impropriety, forcing and violence implied in the disclosure of an un-said integral to the 'source' language). However, the transfer here does not only affect a name, in conformity with the strictly Aristotelian problematic of *lexis*, but more generally an element, tonality or tone, a sphere, in order to displace it into what is always relatively 'improper' or 'foreign' to it. One thinks here of what Hölderlin will write later to Böhlendorff about Homer and the epic poem as a metaphor of great aspirations. In this famous letter, Hölderlin distinguishes, in everything 'worldly', the *Bildungstrieb*, the formative drive or genius, and the original ground, 'nature'. As far as the Homeric poem in particular is concerned, the great heroic aspirations which correspond to the 'nationell' or 'native' − sacred pathos, the fire from heaven, in a word, the Apollinian − are translated or transposed into the naïve tone (naïve here defining the art-character): Junonian sobriety, clarity of exposition and the foreign or alien element. What Hölderlin writes to Böhlendorff in 1801, in a meditation which, beyond all 'aesthetic' categories, turns on a rigorous delimitation of the Greek and the Hesperian, here finds its first poetological formulation:

The epic, in its outer appearance näive, poem, is in its basic tone the more pathetic, heroic, aorgic one; hence it strives in its art-character not for energy, movement and life, but for precision, calmness and pictorial quality. The opposition between its basic tone and its art-character, between its proper and its improper, metaphorical tone is resolved in the idealistic.[15]

In the case of the tragic poem, what is trans-posed and trans-lated in this way? In what space does the opposition between the proper and the improper unfold? In other words, in what does the tragic transport consist? The tragic poem is the 'metaphor of an intellectual intuition'; it allows passage or (sensible) egress, it presents, displays, exposes – properly speaking, stages [met-en-scène] – an intellectual intuition which is essentially an intuition of unity, of the originally one. The tragic poem is what 'gives rise' [donner lieu] to intellectual intuition; it allows it to take place [avoir lieu] insofar as it offers it the theatre of a possible 'propriation', even if, paradoxically, this unity – the unity of the 'primordially united' – only ever presents itself improperly by obscuring or annulling the very 'sign' properly (eigentlich) destined to manifest it. 'All works of this kind', Hölderlin continues, 'must be founded on an intellectual intuition which cannot be any other one than that unity with everything living.'[16]

The unity with everything living must be understood here as the unity (Einigkeit) of everything living, of everything which is, that is, as the dramatico-tragic version of the Hen panta, and not as a synonym of Einheit pure and simple – the unity of that which is one merely in its identity and particularity, the unity of that which is precisely vereinzelt – isolated, individuated, in itself a part. Unity (closer here to Innigkeit, inwardness and intensity[17]) is what reunites everything living in giving it unity, that which holds together and reconciles everything with everything else ('so that everything may encounter everything else'). Unity, as Einigkeit, reconciliation, mediation and mediacy, is properly speaking the work of spirit. Hölderlin says of the epic poem that what 'unites and mediates the basic tone and the art-character of a poem is the spirit of the poem'.[18] In the case of the tragic poem, however, the 'spirit of the poem' is nothing other than Geist itself, whose highest task is precisely Vermittlung or mediation. In the tragic poem, spirit is already fundamentally present in the tonality, in the ideal grounding (Begründung) of the poem; it is at work there all the way through.

This is why it is already possible to formulate the new Hölderlinian determination of the tragic effect (to tēs tragōdias ergon): one-whole! To display, to make sensible, to expose the unity of the whole. The tragico-dramatic poem – itself determined as 'what is highest in art' – can be properly defined as the total poem. It is in this sense that Hölderlin writes to Neuffer in July 1799:

[Tragedy] is the strictest of all poetic forms, which is entirely designed
to advance in harmonious alternation, without any ornament, almost
in grand tones of which each is a proper whole and which, in this
proud denial of anything accidental, depicts the ideal of a living whole
[*das Ideal eines lebendigen Ganzen*] as brief and, simultaneously, as completely full of content as possible, therefore more precise yet also
more serious than all other known poetic forms.[19]

Grounding the poem in intellectual intuition and the parts in the unity of the
whole implies, at the same time, making intellectual intuition sensible and
putting its unity to the test, to the extent of tearing the parts asunder.

Let us dwell for a moment on the function assigned here to intellectual intuition of maintaining the whole in its parts, in the unity of its partition. Granted,
infinite unity necessarily implies the infinite relation of belonging ('the more
infinite relation', *unendlicheres Verhältnis*[20]) in which whole and parts come
together. Intellectual intuition is always concerned with the originary totality,
though in order to recognise a state of the originally united in that which is
separated or partial; intellectual intuition maintains the whole in its parts, in
the unity of its partition. Certainly infinite unity necessarily implies the impossibility of the absolute separation or isolation of the parts. Everything which is
a part, separated into a subject and an object for example, must be *grasped* in
what is originally one. The task of intellectual intuition is the restoration of the
parts to this *arche*-unity, but it equally recognises what is 'separable' in each
part and in the unity of the whole 'the supremely separable', '*arche*-partition'
(*Urtheilung*).

Much more so than Fichte, who only employs the expression relatively late
on (in the second introduction to the *Wissenschaftslehre*), and then in order to
respond explicitly to Schelling's *Letters on Dogmatism and Criticism*, Hölderlin's
use of the term 'intellectual intuition' points us in the direction of the
Schellingian use of the term but also, and above all, beyond Schelling to the
short fragment entitled 'Urteil und Seyn' (judgement, original separation,
arche-partition and being) by its first editor, and written in all likelihood at
the beginning of 1795. Let me cite two brief passages of direct relevance to
our topic:

Being [*Seyn*] – expresses the connection between subject and object.
Where subject and object are united altogether and not only in part,
that is, united in such a manner that no partition can be performed
without violating the essence of what is to be separated, there and
nowhere else can Being pure and simple [*Seyn schlechthin*] be spoken
of, as is the case with intellectual intuition.[21]

Hölderlin opposes this absolute unity of being, this absolutely binding and properly unificatory unity, to the identity or self-identification of the I, Fichte's first principle and also Schelling's in *Vom Ich als Prinzip der Philosophie* (1795):

> Yet this Being must not be confused with identity. If I say: 'I am I', the subject ('I') and the object ('I') are not united in such way that no separation could be performed without violating the essence of what is to be separated; on the contrary, the I is only possible by means of this separation of the I from the I . . . . Hence identity is not a union of object and subject which simply occurred, hence identity is not = to absolute Being.[22]

Against Fichte and Schelling, Hölderlin is seeking here to distinguish being as such, insofar as it is expressed in intellectual intuition, from the putatively immediate identity revealed in the affirmation of the I by itself, in its absolute self-positing. For Fichte, the properly I is only that which can say of itself indifferently: *Ich = Ich, Ich bin Ich, Ich bin*. 'The I', he writes in 1794, 'posits its being originally. Which means, to use the terms I shall employ henceforth, that the I is necessarily unity of subject and object: subject-object. As such, it is without any mediation.'[23] Now this passage from selfhood to being, due to self-identity or self-positing, can, according to Hölderlin, only give access to a purely relative and thoroughly relational being, grounded less in a truly unifying relation than in the radical separation of the I from itself at the heart of self-consciousness. In order that unity be unity of being, mediation is always required. Granted, in the affirmation of self-identity, in the *judgement* I = I, one is justified in taking self-consciousness as the privileged figure of identity (properly speaking there is only identity of the I, of the subject of affirmation or self-representation). However, this identity is always mediate, one in which the I recognises itself in its opposition to itself. The identity of self-consciousness, far from being originary, always rests on an absolutely grounding mediacy, that of being as such once it is engaged in its originary partition, *Urtheil*:

> Judgement [*Ur-theil*], in the highest and strictest sense, is the original separation of object and subject which are most deeply united in intellectual intuition, that separation through which alone object and subject become possible, the *arche*-separation [*Urtheilung*]. In the concept of separation, there lies already the concept of the reciprocity of object and subject and the necessary presupposition of a whole of which object and subject form the parts. 'I am I' is the most fitting example for this concept of *arche*-separation as theoretical separation.[24]

It is being itself (now impossible to identify with the absolute I^{25}) which, in its unity, and in order precisely that there be infinite (more infinite) unity, splits off from itself, posits itself in its difference, differing absolutely and originally with itself. Pure being (*das reine Seyn*) is not identity in Fichte's sense, nor is it 'indifference' in Schelling's: it shows itself in its purity and originarity only insofar as differentiation is pursued 'adequately' (*hinlänglich*).^{26} To pursue differentiation as far as it will go is, for the young Hölderlin of 'Judgement and Being', a task and also an aporia to which the theory of tragedy gives a first (dialectical?) response – the aporia of the affirmation of *Seyn schlechthin*, which yields an intellectual intuition based on unity, and the radical *arche-partition* as fundamental to all opposition as to all identification.

Returning now to the essay 'On the Difference of Poetic Modes':

> . . . all works of this kind must be founded on an intellectual intuition
> which cannot be any other one than that unity with everything living
> which, to be sure, is not felt by the limited soul, only anticipated in
> its [the soul's] highest aspirations, yet which can be recognised by the
> spirit; it results from the impossibility of an absolute separation and
> individuation.^{27}

Unity with everything living, the unity of everything living, the unity of a single intellectual intuition which can be recognised by the spirit (inasmuch, once again, as it is really what reunites, mediates [*vermitteln*] and assures the communication [*Mitteilung*] of everything with everything else) 'results from the impossibility of an absolute separation and individuation'. It is when the parts are most thoroughly differentiated and dissociated, and are no longer anything but parts, that, paradoxically, unity is most determinate. Or again: unity, the 'primordially united', only appears at the extreme limit of partition, when the parts fully experience their splitting off, their breaking loose, their desolation, their dissidence, their isolation.

Hölderlin continues:

> [The unity of intellectual intuition in the tragic poem is explained]
> most easily if one says that the true separation, and with it everything
> truly material [and] perishable and thus, too, the union and with it all
> that is spiritually permanent, the objective as such and thus also the
> subjective as such, that they are only a state of the primordially united,
> a state wherein it exists because it had to transcend itself due to the
> stasis which could not occur in it.^{28}

It is not difficult to see here, in this necessity by which the self-knowledge or recognition of the primordially united or spirit consists in transcending itself [*sortir de soi-même*], one of the main motifs of German Idealism as a whole, one which Hölderlin himself was not slow in developing:

> . . . it is not at home, spirit, neither at the beginning nor at the source.
> It is enthral to the Fatherland.[29]

Indeed, in what is undoubtedly the most important essay of the Homburg period, 'On the Operations of the Poetic Spirit', the central question of the 'course and destination of man in general'[30] culminates in the determination of the way in which Spirit can know itself as such, and can be wholly present to itself. In order to reach this destination and accede to the 'true freedom of his essence', the spirit of man must 'transcend itself' and reflect on itself in differing from itself in the external sphere of the 'harmoniously opposed'. Such is the 'divine moment' in which the spirit is 'entirely present to itself in the infinite unity which is at once the point of separation for the unified as such, but then again also point of union for the unified as the opposed, finally is also both at once', in other words, the point at which 'the spirit is sensible in its infinity'.[31] But rather than Hegel or Schelling (even the Schelling of the Erlangen lectures, who is attentive to the ek-static dimension of the absolute as 'eternal freedom'[32]), one thinks here of Heraclitus, whose fundamental saying Hölderlin had already cited in *Hyperion*: *Hen diapheron eautō – das Eine in sich selber unterschiedne*.

Leaving aside the question of this proximity of Hölderlin and Heraclitus, let us hold on to the thesis that the primordially united remains as such only in mobility and in the antagonism of separation and differentiation. In order to be unity, the original or primordial unity must never be identical to itself; it must always be becoming other than itself, differing from itself: '[The] primordially united . . . had to transcend itself due to the stasis which could not occur in it because its mode of union could not always stay the same.'[33]

Stasis cannot find a place in the arche-unity, which is only unity by means of the *Vereinigung* within it, through the endlessly differing modality of unification and a specific mode of connection (*Verbindung*). The connection of the singular or unique must be an infinite connection which is not limited to referring different parts to each other in a simple relation (*Beziehung*), more or less strictly. Connection only becomes truly mediating in disconnecting or disarticulating merely unilateral relations. Only in this way can an authentic 'stance' (*Verhältnis*) arise, that of the binding tie (*entbindender Band*) which, releasing the parts, gives birth to the freest relation (*freiere Verhältnisse*) that Hölderlin also terms 'religious'.[34]

Arche-unity can only reveal itself in and through a modality of reunion and infinite connection unlike any other. As Hölderlin puts it in the essay

'Becoming in Dissolution', this unity only ever appears in a *world* or in the *decline*, the *instant* or the *becoming of the instant*, the metaphor of one world in another. As the most infinite connection, unity of intellectual intuition, it is 'the world of all worlds'.[35]

This modalisation of unity is demanded by the law of justice (*Gerechtigkeit*)[36] which wants each part to receive its due, and that is also to say its full measure; yet this share can always become an excess, receive overabundantly, beyond its share, and thus become over-measure (*Übermaß*).

Let me pick up the thread of Hölderlin's text once more:

> . . . stasis . . . could not occur in it because its mode of union could not always stay the same with regard to matter, because parts of the united must not always remain in the same closer and remoter relation, so that everything may encounter everything else and that all receive its full right and share of life, and that every part during its course equal the whole in its completeness; conversely, that the whole during its course become equal to the parts in determinacy, that the former gain in content [and] the latter in inwardness; that the former gain in life, the latter ones in liveliness; that the former feel itself more in its progress, and the latter ones fulfil themselves more in progress.[37]

That each part should equal the whole: Hölderlin is not yet evoking excess here. In effect, the part must find completeness and perfection (*Vollständigkeit*) and receive total fulfilment (*sich erfüllen*) at the height of its partition and individuation. Being equivalent to the whole, all the parts truly participate in the unity of the whole; they become *innig*, as intensively or inwardly united as the whole in its *arche*-unity (*alles ist innig*). The liveliness (*Lebhaftigkeit*) of the parts ensures the life of the whole, their fulfilment and completeness its determinacy. Thus 'everything may encounter everything else', the whole dividing itself in accordance with the highest justice. But this encounter or exchange takes place in a process in which the whole and the parts engage (uni-totality), at the risk, for the parts in their completeness and concentration, of becoming isolated and detached from the whole, of passing, in their excessive liveliness, from autonomy to dissidence (*Abseitigkeit*). The process is thus at once the condition of possibility of the completeness and perfection of the parts in their very partition, of their intensification (liveliness, *Innigkeit*), and also of the self-exposition of the whole in its determinate unity. The whole is only a living whole, determined and rich in content, on account of the liveliness of the parts, of their intensity. That is to say, on account of the always present possibility of an 'excess of this intensity' (*Übermaß der Innigkeit*), according to a formulation

of 'The Ground for Empedocles'. What, for the part, presents itself as a limit,
a threshold whose breaching must remain imminent, is for the whole necessary.
In their excessive liveliness the parts must know suffering in order that the
adjoining of the whole ('world of all worlds') appears in the conflict of one
against All, this adjoining only revealing itself completely in the absolute rift
of tragedy:

> . . . if it is an eternal law that the substantial whole does not feel itself
> in its unity with the determination and liveliness, not in that sensuous
> unity in which its parts – also being a whole, only more freely united
> – feel themselves; so that one may say: if the liveliness, determinacy
> [and] unity of the parts where their wholeness is felt, transcends the
> boundary of the parts and turns into suffering and, conceivably, into
> absolute determinacy and individuation, only then would the whole feel
> itself in these parts as lively and determinately as they feel themselves
> in a calmer yet also moved state, in their more restricted wholeness.[38]

Hölderlin tells us nothing about this eternal law (the law of justice) other
than what it decrees: that the whole cannot feel itself as the parts feel themselves in their integrality, their 'wholeness'. It can feel itself as the parts feel
themselves, to the same degree as them – when they feel themselves in a relatively tranquil, though still motive, state, such as that of lyric tonality – only
if these parts feel themselves excessively, sorrowfully, when this feeling of self,
in its liveliness, takes a step on the path leading to *Vereinzelung*, isolation and
solitude. The whole needs the part. It feels itself only at the price of the suffering of the parts; when the part has become *abseitig*, decidedly cut off, dis-
connected (*ungebunden*), in a state of secession with respect to the whole, when
its intensity has become an excess of intensity.

Splitting and partition (according to wholeness and liveliness) lead the parts
into the space of objectification, of self-feeling (*sich fühlen*). The feeling of self
is thus taken as far as it will go, in the face of the whole, against or in opposition to it, like Empedocles. The whole only feels itself in its parts and when
these become 'total'. Therefore separation does not undermine the whole or
dislocate it, since it is only thanks to this that the whole can return to itself,
and accede to the highest and most comprehensive uni-totality, giving rise to
a 'more infinite connection' (*unendlicher Zusammenhang*).[39] It falls to the part to
suffer on account of unity. The properly tragic pathos is that of *Vereinzelung*,
of a concentration on self leading to total dissidence.

The eternal law which is illustrated in the dramatico-tragic poem is that of
the justice or of the decision [*le partage*] which ensures partition *and* cohesion,
in other words the mediation of the whole and the parts; *the law of justice is*

mediacy. This is what Hölderlin will explain with the greatest possible force in the commentary accompanying his translation of fragment 7 of Pindar ('Das Höchste'):

> The immediate, strictly speaking, is impossible for mortals, as for immortals; the god has to differentiate several worlds. . . . Human beings, as cognisant ones, must also differentiate between several worlds, because cognition is possible only by contrast. That is why the immediate, strictly speaking, is impossible for mortals, as for immortals. But the strictly mediate is the law.[40]

Leaving aside the parenthesis which follows immediately the passage cited above and which has to do with the lyric mood and its 'individual world', let us return to the essay which has been serving as our guiding thread:

> The tangibility of the whole progresses precisely to the extent and in that proportion with which the separation itself proceeds within the parts and in their centre, wherein the parts and the whole are most tangible. The unity present in the intellectual intuition manifests itself as a sensuous one precisely to the extent that it transcends itself, that the separation of its parts occurs which, too, separate only because they feel too unified: either when, within the whole, they are closer to the centrepoint; or, when they are ancillaries, because they do not feel sufficiently unified as regards completeness, more removed from the centrepoint; or, as regards liveliness, if they are neither ancillaries nor essential parts in the above sense because they are not yet complete, but only divisible parts [*teilbare Theile*].[41]

The question subtending the entire essay, and which had already governed, as we saw, the fragment on 'Judgement and Being', is the possibility for the whole to be felt (*Fühlbarkeit des Ganzen*). How to think the necessary partition of being pure and simple in such a way that, in its absoluteness, it does not remain entirely unknown to itself, unknowable, unrepresentable and unpresentable? How to think the possibility of a *Darstellung* – of a presentation or *mise en scène* – of the non-objective? How can intellectual intuition become sensuous, make itself tangible to itself and thus become *aesthetic intuition*? The still abrupt response of 1795 declared: *Ur-theil*, *Ur-theilung*. Through his enduring meditation on Greek tragedy, Hölderlin will deepen this initial response and explain in concrete terms the meaning of this *arche*-partition. The primordial partition is part of a process, at the heart of a world which unfolds in its totality only *in passing*, in renewing itself at the price of a 'victim offered in sacrifice' (*Opfer*) 'to the destiny of time' (*Empedocles*): the process which marks the succession or substitution of worlds occurs temporally in and through the scission or separation of the parts. To the extent that the separate parts are only functions of a whole which is itself essentially and necessarily divisible into parts, the self-feeling of the parts (in the suffering and excess of isolation) ensures *Fühlbarkeit*, the sensuousness of the whole. It is thus that partition is already the becoming-whole of the whole. The whole achieves unity in its parts only thanks to their opposition and dereliction.

The separation of the parts (among them and in relation to their centre: uni-totality, the unity of the whole) can arise in different ways, corresponding to the sub-genres of tragedy: the parts can separate because they are too united, too close to the median point of unity (*Übermaß der Einigkeit*). Equally, they can dissociate when they no longer feel united enough, not related with suffi-cient intensity. Here again Hölderlin distinguishes two possibilities: (a) accord-ing to completeness, when it is a question of annexed or accessory parts, too distant from the centre; (b) according to liveliness, when it is a question of parts not yet entirely parts (de-parted), susceptible of a surplus of partition.

No doubt, in Hölderlin's eyes, there should correspond to this concrete analysis a rigorous determination of the different types of tragedy known to history, if not, within one and the same tragedy, of different 'scenes'. However, it is not our intention to undertake such a difficult enterprise of explanation or illustration. Let us simply remember, with Hölderlin, that the most general figure of splitting, which in fact constitutes the 'ideal beginning', is what he enigmatically names here *the necessary arbitrariness of Zeus*:

> And here, in the excess of spirit within unity, in its striving for mate-riality, in the striving of the divisible, more infinite aorgic which must contain all that is more organic – for all more determined and neces-sary existence requires a less determined and less necessary existence – in this striving for separation of the divisible infinite, which in the state of highest unity of everything organic imparts itself to all parts contained by this unity, in this necessary arbitrariness of Zeus there actually lies the ideal beginning of the real separation.[42]

The partition derives from the arbitrariness of Zeus – a Zeus characterised no less enigmatically as 'the highest separable': Zeus sets in motion (an *ideal* beginning or possibility of beginning in the sense of 'Becoming in Dissolution') a separation destined to reach out to all the parts. One thinks here of Oedipus, as elsewhere Hölderlin explicitly encourages us to, especially of the oracle's speech at Delphi, even if everything *actually* only begins with the *too infinite* interpretation which Oedipus gives of it. The ideal beginning (*das Mögliche*)

does not appear first of all: what shows itself to us immediately is the antagonism of the parts in their determinacy, the actuality of their separation.
Whatever the particular situation of the parts ('too united', 'not united
enough', 'not yet totally parts'), they must of necessity tend towards more particularity and concentration, since it is through this separation that they communicate and express unity. However, the necessity of the determinacy,
completeness and 'organic' character of the parts implies in turn, and no less
necessarily at that, the indeterminacy of what is partable, of an aorgic which one
can equally designate 'the excess of inwardness' (*das Übermaß der Innigkeit*),[43]
or else the excess of spirit in its unification, and which is named here by the
oxymoron 'the necessary arbitrariness of Zeus'.

I take up once again the path of Hölderlin's thought in its totality:

The whole – uni-totality – only feels itself in its parts; the whole only feels
itself to the extent that the parts feel themselves excessively, pathetically,
exposing themselves ultimately to *Vereinzelung*, desolation and absolute solitude.
The whole comes into view in the part. The (partable) whole comes on the
scene [*se met en scène*] thanks to the sublation of the part as this part, the part
taking the place of the whole (in the moment or instant, in passing). The necessary arbitrariness of Zeus is announced in this partition of parts and separation of the separable.

What is this strange figure of a god doing emerging at the end of the analysis of the tragic poem? How can we interpret this 'necessary arbitrariness' more
precisely? Before addressing this final question, let us consider for a moment
the eighth strophe of 'The Rhine':

> But their own immortality
> Suffices the gods, and if
> The Heavenly have need of one thing
> It is of heroes and human beings
> And other mortals. For since
> The most Blessed in themselves feel nothing
> Another, if to say such is
> Permitted, must, I suppose,
> Vicariously feel in the name of the gods,
> And him they need; but their rule is that
> He shall demolish his
> Own house and curse him like an enemy.
> Those dearest to him and under the rubble
> Shall bury his father and child,
> When one aspires to be like them, refusing
> To bear with inequality, the fantast.[44]

The gods feel nothing of themselves as long as their unity remains undiffer-
entiated and undivided; they become sensible to themselves only when mortals,

especially those who, tragically, pursue partition beyond their strict share, are allowed to feel 'vicariously' on their behalf.

Returning to the essay: how should we interpret this necessity which appears to weigh on Zeus himself? Is it a question of a new and ultimate principle governing partition and the separable, determining the whole of the process, transcendence and return to self? *Anankè* or *Nemesis*? And what, finally, of this arbitrariness (*Willkür*)? On this last point, fragment 37 provides a decisive hint when it explains human freedom as the 'supreme power [*Macht*] of lack or accomplishment'.[45] But can the one who passes for the first of the gods be said to be lacking and to be complete (*fehlen und vollbringen*)? Things start to become clearer if one hears in the obscure characterisation of Zeus as the 'highest separable' an anticipation of what Hölderlin will later call, in the 'Remarks on *Antigone*', 'the more real Zeus', Zeus as 'father of time': he who possesses [*depose*] time and dispenses with it only to remain, 'like ourselves, a son of time'.[46] Jupiter can establish his 'reign' or institute his 'laws' only by secretly receiving the inheritance from the 'ancient father' (Cronos–Chronos):

> For as from clouds your lightning, from him has come
> What you call yours. . .,[47]

namely the task of pursuing the work of time, in its failure as well as its completion.[48]

What thus comes to light in this recognition of the arbitrariness of Zeus is nothing less than the first stirring of the decisive meditation on the tearing or rending of time (*die reissende Zeit*) which will occupy the most important sections of the 'Remarks'. *Ur-theil*, we have noted, is concretely expressed in tragedy as a temporal process culminating in the *moment*; *arche*-partition itself is governed entirely by time in its spacing, better its agonal struggle [*son écartèlement*]. But the latter is only revealed as such in the passage, the transition from one world to another, from one figure to another, in the instant or sudden reversal: revolt, expulsion of the part, reunification, the renewed emergence of uni-totality.

Certainly one can say that, in a sense, Zeus, the father of time, is continually and eternally exposed, as 'world of all worlds' through them all. But far from offering himself in his eternity to some essentially atemporal intellectual intuition or other,[49] he only *properly* appears in the *moment*, the metaphor which is tragedy itself in its totality. It is thus (literally *and* metaphorically) that Zeus is able to grasp (feel) himself in his infinity, precisely in the impossibility of doing so in a stable or permanent state, since he only discovers himself *properly* through *Übergang*, in crossing, turning or passing over, in the 'catastrophe' of tragedy.

*   *   *

Rather than dwelling on this mirroring of time as the horizon of tragedy appre-
hended in its essence – which is in any case difficult to determine with any
degree of certainty – let us return to the central thesis of our main text:
tragedy is the metaphor of the absolute or of the primordially united, but in
this movement from unity to parts, through the dissolution of unity and the
resolution of the antagonism of all the parts (everything against everything
else), in the sudden unveiling of a 'more infinite' connection, of a 'religious'
relation of the whole provisionally (temporally) reunited, god reveals himself,
in the most immediate manner. Is it still possible to speak of a dialectic here?
Or should we not rather rethink, as Hölderlin urges, the category of the 'paradox' and its pertinence to the study of the essence of tragedy?

> The significance of tragedies can be understood most easily by way of
> paradox. Since all potential is divided justly and equally, all original
> matter appears not in original strength but, in fact, in its weakness,
> so that quite properly the light of life and the appearance attach to the
> weakness of every whole. Now in the tragic, the sign itself is insignif-
> icant, without effect, yet original matter is straightforward. Properly
> speaking, the original can only appear in its weakness; however, to the
> extent that the sign is posited as insignificant $= 0$, original matter, the
> hidden foundation of any nature, can also present itself. If nature
> properly presents itself in its weakest talent, then the sign is, nature
> presenting itself in its most powerful talent, $= 0$.[50]

And on 28 November 1798 Hölderlin writes to his brother: 'The divine, when
it emerges, cannot do so without a certain mourning [*Trauer*] and a certain
humility [*Demuth*]. Certainly, at the moment of decisive combat, it is no longer
the same!' The mourning here is precisely not that of tragedy (*Trauerspiel*);
rather, it is that which finds its ultimate manifestation in the agony of Golgotha.
With tragedy – in the tragic movement which is also the moment of decision,
the divine, the original, shows itself without equivocation; god shows himself
naked in his unbearable immediacy, and without sparing us by appearing in borrowed garb. 'The god of an apostle is more mediate', Hölderlin says in the
'Remarks on *Antigone*'. As a general rule, 'what is original appears not in
strength but, authentically [*eigentlich*], in weakness'. This is confirmed in the
doctrine of the *deus absconditus*, who only manifests himself clothed, hidden
under the humble form of a servant (Philippians 2: 7), in which, however, he
'properly' appears: 'Properly, the original can only appear in its weakness':

Always yet marvellously for the love of men
God clothes himself
And hides his face from all knowing. . . .[51]

But if, properly speaking, the original can only appear in weakness, what is really manifested in tragedy? Tragedy is precisely the site, the scene, of the decisive combat which is the encounter (the 'yoking together', as the 'Remarks' put it) of man and god in which the divine communicates so as to reveal itself, and in so doing ensures the communication of everything with everything else, allowing mediacy itself to appear in its absolute sovereignty. But this immediate presentation or irruption in time (and of time) both completes and interrupts partition: its sign (*pars pro toto*) is grievously shattered, becoming entirely insignificant ($= 0$). The divine, the original, the primordially united, manifests itself (authentically or inauthentically?) only in destroying the sign that is supposed to represent it 'in an authentic way' (*recht eigentlich*). The essentially tragic moment is the one in which god presents himself 'in person' – *deus ipse* – which he can only do, beyond all propriety and impropriety, by appropriating for himself a sign that has become insignificant, by destroying the very sign of presentation itself, remaining for ever in the tragic metaphor.

Thus tragedy is a metaphor in the very specific sense in which it properly presents the passage of god, that transport in which god shows himself, but as *nothing*. This transport is fundamentally 'empty' – nothing other than time, the tearing and wrenching of time.

Denn nirgends, bleibt er.	For nowhere it remains.
Es fesselt	No sign
Kein Zeichen.	Shackles it.
Nicht immer	Not always
Ein Gefäß ihn zu fassen.	A vessel to seize it.[52]

Translated by Jonathan Derbyshire

Notes

This text is the revised version of a paper presented at a colloquium on 'The Tragic and Tragedy in the Western Tradition' held in Montreal in 1979. An earlier version was published in *Revue philosophique de Louvain* 81 (February 1983). [*Translator's Note*. The text was subsequently included in a collection of Courtine's essays on Schelling, *Extase de la raison: Essais sur Schelling* (Paris: Galilée, 1990), 45–70. This translation is based on this latter version.]

1 This is still the case today, even after the publication of volume 39 of the Gesamtausgabe, *Hölderlins Hymnen 'Germanien' und 'Der Rhein'* (Frankfurt am Main: Klostermann, 1980). See also *Erläuterungen zu Hölderlins Dichtung* (Frankfurt am Main: Klostermann, 1971).

2 Martin Heidegger, *Vier Seminare: Le Thor 1966, 1968, 1969: Zähringen 1973* (Frankfurt am Main: Klostermann, 1973), 287. Cf. also Beda Allemann, *Hölderlin und Heidegger* (Zurich: Atlantis Verlag, 1954).

3 On this, see 'Hölderlin et Sophocles', Jean Beaufret's preface to the French translation of the *Remarks*, *Remarques sur Oedipe et sur Antigone* (Paris: 10–18, 1965).

4 See on this point Peter Szondi, 'The Notion of the Tragic in Schelling, Hölderlin and Hegel' in *On Textual Understanding and Other Essays*, translated by Harvey Mendelsohn (Minneapolis: Minnesota University Press, 1986), 43–55, and the chapter devoted to Schelling's poetics of genre in *Poetik und Geschichtsphilosophie* II (Frankfurt am Main: Suhrkamp, 1974).

5 Schelling, *Sämtliche Werke*, edited by K. F. A. Schelling (Stuttgart: Cotta, 1859) V: 690, henceforth *SW*, volume and page number; translated by Douglas W. Stott as *The Philosophy of Art* (Minneapolis: Minnesota University Press, 1989), 249. [*Translator's Note*. All quotations from German sources are my own translations.]

6 *SW* V: 467; *Philosophy of Art*, 89.

7 *SW* V: 690–1; *Philosophy of Art*, 249:

> Yet precisely in human nature too do the conditions of possibility obtain for necessity to be victorious without freedom succumbing, and in a reverse fashion for freedom to triumph without the course of necessity being interrupted. For the same person who succumbs to necessity can elevate himself above it through his disposition [*Gesinnung*] such that both – conquered and victorious at the same time – are manifested in their highest indifference.

8 *SW* V: 697; *Philosophy of Art*, 254.

9 Cf. again Szondi, who, in 'The Notion of the Tragic', emphasises the 'dialectical' traits not only of the Schellingian interpretation, but of the Hölderlinian one as well. See also, and especially, Philippe Lacoue-Labarthe, 'La césure du spéculatif' in *L'imitation des modernes: Typographies II* (Paris: Galilée, 1986), 39–69; translated by Robert Eisenhauer as 'The Caesura of the Speculative' in *Typographies: Mimesis, Philosophy, Politics*, edited by Christopher Fynsk (Cambridge, MA: Harvard University Press, 1989), 208–35.

10 Lacoue-Labarthe, 'Césure du spéculatif', 40–1, 43; 'The Caesura of the Speculative', 209, 211.

11 Cf. the letter to Chr. Gottfried Schütz (no. 203): 'As you know, the rigour with which our dear Ancients distinguished the different poetic genres has been totally misunderstood.'

12 See Friedrich Hölderlin, *Sämtliche Werke* (Große Stuttgarter Aufgabe), edited by Friedrich Beißner (Stuttgart: Kohlhammer, 1985) IV 1: 266–72, hereafter GSA, volume and page number; Friedrich Hölderlin, *Essays and Letters on Theory*, translated by Thomas Pfau (Albany: SUNY, 1988), 83–8, hereafter *ELT*.

13 On these poetological writings, see again the work of Szondi and especially Lawrence J. Ryan, *Hölderlins Lehre vom Weschel der Töne* (Stuttgart: Kohlhammer, 1960).

14 *ELT*, 83.

15 *ELT*, 83–4.

16 *ELT*, 84.

17 On this term, which in itself would require a detailed study, see Heidegger, *Hölderlins Hymnen 'Germanien' und 'Der Rhein'*, Gesamtausgabe 39), 249–50; cf. also the *Erläuterungen*, 36.

18 GSA O 0: 000; *ELT*, 84.

19 Letter no. 183, GSA IV 1: 339; *ELT*, 142.

20 'Über Religion', GSA IV 1: 277; 'On Religion', *ELT*, 92. See also Jaques Colette, 'L'Église esthétique' in *Cahier de l'Herne*, edited by Jean-François Courtine (Paris: L'Herne, 1989), 399–410.

21 GSA IV 1: 216; *ELT*, 37.

22 GSA IV 1: 216–17; *ELT*, 37–8.

23 J. G. Fichte, *Gesamtausgabe*, edited by R. Lauth and H. Jacob (Stuttgart and Bad Cannstatt: Friedrich Frommann, 1965), I 2: 261.

24 GSA IV 1: 216; *ELT*, 37.

25 See the letter to Hegel of 26 January 1795 (no. 94) and to his brother in 1801 (no. 231):

> What we were thinking together before, I am still thinking, simply with more application! Everything is infinite uni-ty, but in this whole there is something united in an eminent unifier which, in itself, is not an I; between you and me, this is God!

26 'Die Weisen aber . . .', GSA IV 1: 237; 'The Sages, however . . .', *ELT*, 49.

27 GSA IV 1: 267–8; *ELT*, 84.

28 GSA IV 1: 268; *ELT*, 84.

29 GSA IV 1: 261.

30 GSA IV 1: 263; *ELT*, 80.

31 GSA IV 1: 251; *ELT*, 71.

32 *SW* IX: 230.

33 GSA IV 1: 268; *ELT*, 84.

34 GSA IV 1: 277; *ELT*, 91.

35 'Das Werden in Vergehen', GSA IV 1: 282; 'Becoming in Dissolution', *ELT*, 96.

36 GSA IV 1: 274; *ELT*, 89: 'all potential is divided justly and equally'. See also the letter to Sinclair of 24 December 1798 (no. 171): 'It is good also, and this is even the first condition of life and of all organisation, that there is no monarchic force in heaven or on earth.'

37 GSA IV 1: 268; *ELT*, 84–5.

38 GSA IV 1: 268; *ELT*, 85.

39 GSA IV 1: 278; *ELT*, 92.

40 GSA V: 285; translated by Michael Hamburger as 'The Supreme' in *Hölderlin: Poems and Fragments* (London: Routledge, 1966), 639.

41 GSA IV 1: 269; *ELT*, 85.

42 GSA IV 1: 269; *ELT*, 85–6.

43 'Grund zum Empedokles', GSA IV 1: 157; 'The Ground for Empedocles', *ELT*, 56.

44 *Poems and Fragments*, 437.

45 GSA II 1: 325.

46 'Natur und Kunst oder Saturn und Jupiter', *Poems and Fragments*, 169.

47 Ibid., 167.

48 I am following here the interpretation suggested by W. Binder in his sadly unpublished dissertation *Dichtung und Zeit in Hölderlins Werke* (Tübingen, 1955). I am not convinced by the objections addressed to this work by Lawrence Ryan, *Hölderlins Lehre vom Weschel der Töne*, 25–6n., particularly since they end up making the high-

est separable not the father of time (Zeus), but the 'ground' from which 'time springs'. This strikes me as an example of combating an interpretation by replacing it with something absolutely identical.

49 I am thinking of Schelling in particular here; cf. *SW* I: 202, 206, 318.
50 GSA IV 1: 274; *ELT*, 89.
51 GSA II 1: 256.
52 Fragment 38.

4

Tragedy and speculation

Françoise Dastur

As is well known, tragedy was first interpreted by Aristotle in the *Poetics* in terms of its effects on the spectators and not in terms of what was represented in the drama itself. By defining tragedy as the imitation of an action which, by arousing fear and pity, operates the *katharsis*, the purgation of these passions,[1] Aristotle was the founder of a tradition which saw in tragedy a psychological or political medication. In *The Birth of Tragedy*, his provocative first book, Nietzsche demonstrated convincingly that considering tragedy from the perspective of the spectator and not from that of the tragic actor or chorus derives in fact from tragedy itself in its development and decline. For Nietzsche, it is with Euripides that the spectator climbs onto the stage, so that tragedy is no longer considered as the reflection of life and nature in its full strength,[2] but becomes only the mirror of the present social reality.[3] Because he no longer sees in tragedy a metaphysical phenomenon, Euripides is for the young Nietzsche the proclaimer of the death sentence of tragedy itself. It is true that Nietzsche will speak later on in his 1886 'essay of self-criticism' of his 'metaphysics of art'[4] in this early period still marked by the influence of Schopenhauer's idealism, but he will never reconsider the necessity that led him to give up the Aristotelian viewpoint of tragedy as *katharsis* for another viewpoint, the Dionysian, which allowed him to see in tragedy the very process of life and becoming in both its creative and destructive aspects.[5]

In fact, long before Nietzsche and *The Birth of Tragedy*, we find the development of a metaphysical theory of tragedy in Germany with Schelling and Hölderlin, and there we really can speak of a *speculative* theory in the strong sense of the word. But what does speculative – a word which will principally be used by Hegel, as we know, but which is already to be found in Kant – actually mean? This is the first point which needs to be clarified. The word *speculatio* comes, of course, from *specto*, to look at, to scrutinise, and was used by Boetius to translate the Greek *theoria* into Latin. But in Christian theology this meaning was forgotten, especially by Thomas Aquinas, who derives

78

speculatio from *speculum*, mirror, and relates the word to what Paul says in the first Epistle to the Corinthians (13. 12) concerning the vision of God whom we see now confusedly as 'in a mirror' but whom later, that is to say, after death, we will see 'face to face'. *Speculatio* means, therefore, partial and confused knowledge, as indirect and unclear as the image of oneself in the metal mirrors of these early times, and it is this meaning of the word that will be used by the German mystics. This explains Kant's tendency to give a pejorative turn to the word, which for him designates the mode of thinking of traditional metaphysics, whereas, for Hegel, the same word, now taken in a positive manner, will regain its original sense of *theoria* without, however, losing its mystical connotation. Thus speculation is connected with the *visio Dei*, the vision of the supersensible, or with what Kant calls 'intellectual intuition', an intuition which is refused to finite beings, which are only able to have 'sensible intuition', that is, an intuition of what is already given to them through their senses.

Kant insists on the finitude of human theoretical knowledge, which has to do only with the sensible *given* object, but he also recognises that a trespassing of the phenomenal limits takes place in the practical domain where the 'object' is not given but has to be realised by practical reason. This is why the post-Kantian philosophers, and Fichte in particular, immediately followed by Schelling, declared that such an intellectual intuition could be attributed to the human being in the practical domain. Thus they see Kant as a 'speculative thinker' in the practical domain, a view shared by Hölderlin, who, in a letter to his brother dated 1 January 1799, writes as follows: 'Kant is the Moses of our nation who leads it out of the Egyptian apathy into the free, solitary desert of his speculation and who brings the rigorous law from the sacred mountain.'[6] The comparison between Kant and Moses is clearly based on the importance given by both to the moral imperative, which requires the overcoming of the sensible desires and the limitedness of everyday life. The Egyptian apathy of the Pharaoh's Hebrew slaves is compared there to the 'rather conceited domesticity' of the Germans, who are too *glebae addicti*, too captive to their own soil and unable to accept anything 'that lies outside their anxious, narrow sphere'.[7] To lead them into the free and solitary desert of speculation is the task of the new philosophy, that is to say, Kantian philosophy, which, as Hölderlin underlines in the same letter, has the most beneficial influence on them by insisting 'to the extreme upon the universality of cognitive interest' and 'uncovering the infinite striving within man'. Speculation is therefore what is needed by the Germans, who have lost the ancient (that is, Greek) capacity of belonging to the surrounding world with sense and soul – in a word, the capacity of having a relationship with the All of nature and of gaining an insight into the totality of the universe.

But what does this insight into the totality, this 'intellectual intuition', have to do with this kind of art that is tragedy? We find in fact a very precise answer to this question in a short essay written by Hölderlin about the difference of poetic modes, in which he writes that 'the tragic is the metaphor of an intellectual intuition', as opposed to the lyric, which is the metaphor of a feeling, and to the epic, which is the metaphor of great aspirations.[8] Hölderlin takes here the word 'metaphor' in its literal sense, in Greek *metaphora*, meaning transposition, translation. The lyric poem, for example, is the transposition of the poet's feeling, whereas the tragic poem or tragedy is the transposition of the intellectual intuition or vision that the poet as an individual can achieve. Thus Hölderlin finds the possibility of intellectual intuition not, as did Fichte, in the practical realm, but in the realm of the aesthetic, as Schiller did in the *Letters on the Aesthetic Education of Man*. Hölderlin too wants to write philosophical letters, and he says in a letter to his friend Niethammer, dated 24 February 1796:

> In the philosophical letters, I want to discover the principle which explains to me the divisions in which we think and exist, yet which is also capable of dispelling the conflict between subject and object, between our self and the world, yes, also between reason and revelation, – theoretically, in intellectual intuition, without our practical reason having to come to our aid. For this we need an aesthetic sense and I will call my philosophical letters 'New Letters on the Aesthetic Education of Man'.[9]

However, Hölderlin is not actually the first to develop a speculative theory of tragedy. In spite of his Fichtean position, the young Schelling was led in the *Letters on Dogmatism and Criticism* to analyse Greek tragedy in order to understand how art is able to reconcile necessity and freedom, the opposed principles of dogmatism and criticism. For Schelling, in this respect, Oedipus is the tragic hero *par excellence*. As a mortal destined by fatality to become a criminal, Oedipus vainly struggles against the fate revealed to him by the oracle. He will be punished, therefore, for a crime which he did not in fact intend to perpetrate but which has none the less been accomplished through his hand. How could Greek reason bear such a contradiction? This is the question raised by Schelling in the last of the *Letters*. In his answer, Schelling tries to show that Greek tragedy was a homage paid to human freedom. It was a great idea, he says, to accept voluntarily to be punished for an inevitable crime because it was a way to testify to the reality of human freedom by the very loss of such freedom and to die by proclaiming the freedom of the will. The tragic hero is a being who refuses to see his actions as the effect of destiny alone. He chooses to be responsible for all that he has done, even for what he could in no way have done consciously, because this is the only way for him to have access to the level of an absolute freedom and to identify himself with the *fatum*. But he can do so only by dying in one way or another, so that he gains an absolute freedom and at the same time he loses it. Thus the tragic hero identifies himself with fate, with the All, and thus he achieves the intellectual intuition or *visio Dei* which allows the reconciliation of the object and the subject. In return, however, he must lose his life, sacrifice his own finitude. Schelling does not actually speak of 'intellectual intuition' in his analysis of the tragedy, but the idea that the aesthetic intuition is, as he will say later, 'the intellectual intuition which has become objective'[10] can already be seen in his work of 1795.

The same idea can be found in Hölderlin's short essay 'The Significance of Tragedies', in which he writes that this significance can most easily be understood by way of paradox. The word 'paradox' also occurs in a letter of 4 June 1799 to his brother, in which Hölderlin explains that the artistic and formative drive which constitutes human culture is an authentic service done by human beings to nature. Because, he says, all the streams of human activity have their source in nature and return to nature, and because the human being cannot create force in itself but can only develop productive forces, he should never regard himself as a lord and master of nature. In a previous letter to his friend Sinclair dated 24 December 1798, Hölderlin wrote:

> The first condition of all life and all organisation is that no force is monarchical neither in heaven nor on earth. Absolute monarchy suppresses itself everywhere because it is without object: in a strict sense there was never something like it.

And he goes on to say that absolute monarchy as well as pure *a priori* thinking is a nonsense because everything that exists is the result of subjective and objective elements so that it is not possible to completely set apart what is particular and what is whole. The main idea is here that the single totality – what Hölderlin, along with his school fellows Schelling and Hegel, called the *hen kai pan* – is always mixed with a particular point of view. That is the reason why in 'The Significance of Tragedies' Hölderlin says that 'all original element appears not in original strength but, in fact, in its weakness, so that quite properly the light of life and the appearance belong to the weakness of every whole'.[11] Every whole appears in a living point of view and everything that exists is internally divided. Nature cannot appear in its original strength but needs art as something weaker than itself in order to appear. But in art, nature does not appear originally but through the mediation of a sign, that is, the hero. As such a sign, the hero is insignificant and without effect (*unbedeutend und wirkungslos*) because he can do nothing against fate and nature and because he will finally be destroyed by them. But when he declines, when, as Hölderlin says, the sign is equal to zero, 'the original element, the hidden foundation of any nature can also present itself', nature can properly present itself as the winner 'in its most powerful gift'. For Hölderlin, tragedy is a sacrifice through which the human being helps nature to appear as such, to come out of its original dissimulation, of its original *krupthestai*.[12] But in order to do such a service to nature, the sign has to become equal to zero, which means that the hero has to die. The conflict of nature and culture is therefore what is represented in all tragedies, but it becomes the subject itself, the theme of the tragedy in *The Death of Empedocles*, the tragedy that Hölderlin wants to write, but leaves unfinished in 1799.

During this period, Hölderlin sees Empedocles as the figure *par excellence* of the speculative thinker. Empedocles becomes for him a tragic hero because he possesses, as Hölderlin says in 'The Ground for Empedocles', *diese ungewöhnliche Tendanz zur Allgemeinheit*, 'that uncommon tendency toward universality',[13] that tendency which could have made a poet of him insofar as it is this tendency which, in the poet, becomes the ability to view a totality, the capacity of intellectual intuition. There is, then, a similarity between his hero and Hölderlin himself. Upon leaving the Seminary in 1793, Hölderlin wrote to his brother that he wanted to be active in a universal sense (*Ich möchte ins Allgemein wirken*), and that he also felt in himself *das ungeheure Streben, Alles zu sein*, 'the immense aspiration to be everything' of which he speaks in *Hyperion*.[14] Like Empedocles, he can find no satisfaction with anything that is particular, and again, as he wrote in the 'Thalia-fragment', *Hyperion*'s first version, what is not everything is nothing for him.[15] He often spoke of his 'ambition' to be a poet and had constantly to fight his mother's desire to see him become a priest and be satisfied with the peaceful and limited life of a rural minister. But his 'ambition' was not of this world, it was an 'ontological' aspiration, the same aspiration of gaining a view over totality which leads Empedocles to his suicide, *das idealische Tat*, the ideal act which for Hölderlin constitutes the fulfilment of the purpose of all human life, namely, as he makes clear in the Preface to *Hyperion*, reunion with nature: 'To be united with nature, with a unique infinite totality, is the goal of all our aspirations.'[16] We find the same idea in the *Frankfurt Plan for Empedocles*, the first draft of the play: Empedocles hates culture, has only contempt for all particular occupation, is an open enemy of all one-sided existence; he suffers from all particular conditions simply because they are particular, and from not being a God, that is, not being an omnipresent heart and intimate with everything – he is in pain because he is tied to the law of succession, to time, and, in this respect, he is the very incarnation of the spirit of impatience, the speculative spirit that cannot stand any limitation or positivity.

Now, we find the first mention of Empedocles in the second part of *Hyperion*. He is presented there in the same way as in the *Frankfurt Plan*, as the great Sicilian who was *des Stundenzählens satt*, tired of counting the hours and who, because he was close to the world's soul, threw himself in the fire of the volcano; not because he liked death in itself but, on the contrary, *in seiner kühnen Lebenslust*, in his bold desire to live. In the *Frankfurt Plan*, Hölderlin writes that Empedocles considers his death as a necessity which follows from his innermost being. But the plan in itself is very dry and abstract, without any real dramatic action, in spite of the fact that Hölderlin's intention at that time is to write, in a very classical manner, a tragedy in five acts. One wonders, in fact, why such a desire to be reunited with the All should take so long to be fulfilled. For a drama, contradictions and conflicts are needed, and that is why, as soon as Hölderlin begins to elaborate his tragedy, he will have to find another motivation for the death of the hero than the natural fulfilment of his being. I cannot enter here into the details of the first, second and third versions of the drama, but I want only to mention a marginal note to the first version which is quite clear in this respect. It says that Empedocles' decision to die must appear 'more forced than voluntary'. Hölderlin's problem here is to find a motivation for Empedocles' death which could be an external factor and therefore could allow the representation of a scenic action. But this poetological problem has also a philosophical basis: how is it possible to develop a dramatic action on the basis of the philosophical idea of the desire for totality? The philosophical question of the conception of totality is not, in fact, a purely Hölderlinian problem. It is a question shared by all his contemporaries, by Novalis, the philosopher who was the first to say that suicide is the ideal act, by Schlegel, Schelling and Hegel. How is it possible to conceive totality and to gain access to it in order to make it appear as totality? This question is the question of the age, the question raised by the new philosophy which had brought the Germans to the desert of speculation. But for Hölderlin alone this philosophical and speculative question is *at the same time* a poetological one.

Hölderlin tries to solve this question in his essay on 'The Ground for Empedocles'. In the first part of the essay, Hölderlin develops the idea of the opposition and reconciliation of nature and art, of the unlimited and unformed with the formed and limited. The idea of an exchange of the two opposites is, as it was already the case in *Hyperion*, strongly emphasised, but such an exchange has a temporal character and, as Hölderlin underlines, the reconciliation is only an appearance (*ein Schein*), and even a mirage (*Trugbild*), the uniting moment being essentially unstable and doomed to dissolution. Appearance and temporality, or better temporarity, are here the same, and the tragedy of appearance is nothing but the tragedy of time itself, which does not allow a final rest, but goes on endlessly in an infinite series of always new dissolutions

83

and structurations. This is why Hölderlin underlines the fact that Empedocles is 'a son of his heaven and time', 'a result of his time', which means that his fate is also a 'momentary union' (*eine augenblickliche Vereinigung*) doomed to dissolution. But in the same passage, Hölderlin adds: 'He seems indeed born to be a poet.'[17] Hölderlin imagined Agrigent at the time of Empedocles in analogy with his own time. In other times Empedocles could have been a poet, a Sophocles for example, but 'his time demanded a sacrifice', and because his time is individualised in the figure of Empedocles, Empedocles was destined to become a victim of his time. One imagines that this passage of the essay was read carefully by Heidegger in the thirties, and we can see some trace of it in 'The Origin of the Work of Art'.[18] Hölderlin says here that some times demand a poet and allow the formative drive to work in a peculiar sphere; but Empedocles' time, which was the time of the tremendous opposition of art and culture, could only allow a sacrifice, not an act which could help and be efficient in a peculiar way, but the ideal act of sacrifice which requires that the individual perishes. So the need of the time, *das Bedürfnis der Zeit*, as Hegel says, was the sacrifice of the individual, because the danger of this time is positivity, crystallisation, freezing of life in dead structures, which is precisely what Empedocles, who dies out of *Lebenslust*, of desire to live, fears above all. In his impatience, Empedocles – who, as the figure of speculative desire, wanted to be a god, was unable to understand that God is nothing other than time itself, as the 'Remarks on Sophocles' makes perfectly clear – represents the premature union (*die vorzeitige Vereinigung*) which is only an apparent solution to destiny. We could perhaps say that Empedocles is still too Greek or that he reacts as a Greek in an age which is already marked by modernity. His sacrifice is a solution, insofar as the premature union of God and man requires the death of the mediator, who is similar to Christ, because, as Hölderlin says, 'the universal would otherwise be lost in the individual and, which is even worse than all great movements of destiny and by itself impossible, the life of a world would expire in some particular instance'.[19] If the reconciliator does not die, then the divine dimension will be lost, the totality will become particularity, the intensity of life will crystallise in a particular being and thus there will be no world, no sphere simultaneously human and divine, but a total flatness of a 'human, too human' life. In fact, this is never possible, yet it remains the danger itself that menaces, this danger being not the death of the individual, of the mediator, but the death of light itself, of the divine horizon of human existence.

There is obviously a strong similarity between Empedocles and Christ. At the same time, in 1799, Hegel writes *The Spirit of Christianity and its Destiny* and, in a similar way, speaks of Jesus' death and of the coming of the Holy Spirit in the souls of the disciples after the disappearance of Christ. The

84

disciples no longer need an external authority but are able, after Jesus' death, to carry out the Christian message by themselves. But Hegel does not see the necessity of death as clearly as Hölderlin; he does not emphasise the necessity of dissolution for life and becoming in the same way as Hölderlin does in the essay he wrote just after 'The Ground for Empedocles', the title of which, although not given by Hölderlin himself, describes exactly his main idea: 'Das Werden in Vergehen', 'Becoming in Dissolution'.

Hölderlin sees the objective law of life with utter clarity, the formal condition which allows for the life of the totality, its staying alive: the death of the individual. But, as it will become clear in the 'Remarks on Antigone', there are two different kinds of death, the Greek and the Hesperian, a death which is a farewell to the world and a death which is a living death, the endurance of separation. The possibility of this other kind of death begins to appear in the third version of the tragedy with the figure of a new protagonist, the adversary, who is also mentioned in the last part of 'The Ground for Empedocles'. The adversary also gives a solution to the problems of the time, not by achieving a 'positive' union or reconciliation like Empedocles, but by maintaining the tension between art and nature and keeping both within their respective limits. The figure of the adversary is the incarnation of patience, of perseverance, of steadiness, whereas Empedocles incarnates impatience and *hybris*. He is not inclined to unite the extremes but tries to 'tame them and tie their reciprocity to something permanent and stable',[20] which can only be a political structure or a work of art. Compared to Empedocles, the adversary is 'a daring open soul', a more passive kind of person who is able to endure the opposition and to remain caught within their difference.

This becomes clear in the third version of the tragedy when the figure of the adversary seems to take two different forms: on the one hand, the royal brother who maintains the opposition, and, on the other, the priest sent by God, Manes, 'the one who remains',[21] who questions Empedocles' right to reconcile the extremes. On both hands, on the side of the human *polis*, as well as on that of the heavenly domain, Empedocles' speculative drive of reconciliation is contested, and both the king and the priest warn him and try to show him that the human being is committed to finding his dwelling in the *Zwischen*, in the in-between of earth and heaven.

From here we can perhaps understand why Hölderlin gave up writing his tragedy. If the theme of *The Death of Empedocles* is the justification of 'speculative suicide' and if, in working out the drama, the necessity of enduring separation which was already Hyperion's final discovery was once more revealed to him as constituting the only solution to the problem of modernity in the sense that, after having crossed the desert of speculation, modern man has to go back to his natural sobriety, it becomes clear that the kind of death

85

Empedocles wanted cannot be compatible with what Modernity requires. Whereas Empedocles' desire to escape all determination, to leave behind the law of succession, is the speculative drive itself, the desire to escape finitude into death, in the 'Remarks on Antigone' Hölderlin stresses, on the contrary, that 'the striving from one world to the other' has to be reversed into 'a striving from another world to this one'.[22] He could not confer an authentically modern meaning upon Empedocles' death because, as he says in the first letter to Böhlendorff, 'this is the tragic for us: that, packed up in any container, we very quietly move away from the realm of the living and not that, consumed into flames, we expiate the flames that we could not tame'.[23] The modern *Schicksal*, the lot of the modern, is not as impressive as the Greek one, but is, as Hölderlin stresses, 'more profound', because it requires that the limits between humanity and divinity should be maintained and acknowledged.

Seen from this point of view, Hölderlin's failure to write a modern tragedy might appear as 'positive' in the sense that it could perhaps give us to understand that lyric poetry is better fitted than tragedy to exposing the patriotic reversal of the Hesperian, a patriotic reversal which leads from the assumption of the speculative drive to the maintaining of limits, from Empedocles' sacrifice to Oedipus' living death. The necessity of this reversal from one kind of death into another one will lead Hölderlin to the *translation* of Sophocles' tragedies and not to the completion of his own modern tragedy. For the poetical form of tragedy, which is the most rigorous form of poetry, cannot resist when it tries to expose *das Schicksallose*, 'the lack of destiny'[24] of modern beings, of which Oedipus' living death is only the presentiment. Only lyric poetry can be fitted for the exposition of the *dysmoron*, the lack of *Moira* or share (the word is Sophocles' own in *Ajax*) of modern beings, as Hölderlin's great poetry from the turn of the century shows.

Notes

1 *Poetics, Peri Poietikes* 1449 b 25ff.
2 *The Birth of Tragedy*, § 8.
3 Ibid., § 11.
4 'Attempt at a Self-Criticism', ibid.
5 *Ecce Homo*, 'The Birth of Tragedy', § 3.
6 Friedrich Hölderlin, *Essays and Letters on Theory*, edited by Thomas Pfau (Albany: SUNY, 1988), 137.
7 Ibid., 136–7.
8 Ibid., 83.
9 Ibid., 131.
10 F. W. J. Schelling, *System des tranzendentalen Idealismus* in *Sämtliche Werke*, edited by Manfred Schröter (Munich, 1927–59) III: 625.
11 Hölderlin, *Essays and Letters on Theory*, 89 (translation modified).

12 Nowhere does Hölderlin quote Heraclitus' fragment saying that 'nature likes to dissimulate itself', but his understanding of nature is as near as it can be in modern times to the Pre-Socratics' approach to *physis*.

13 Hölderlin, *Essays and Letters on Theory*, 56.

14 Hölderlin, *Werke und Briefe* (Frankfurt am Main: Insel Verlag, 1969) I: 306.

15 Ibid., 440.

16 Ibid., 168.

17 Hölderlin, *Essays and Letters on Theory*, 55.

18 Cf. Heidegger, *Holzwege* (Frankfurt am Main: Klostermann, 1963), 50, where, amongst the ways in which truth can find its own foundation, Heidegger names 'the essential sacrifice'.

19 Hölderlin, *Essays and Letters on Theory*, 56.

20 Ibid., 61.

21 The name 'Manes' can be related to the Latin verb *manere* (to stay), but it can also relate to the Greek noun *mantis* (diviner). Cf. W. Binder, 'Hölderlins Namenssymbolik' in *Hölderlin-Jahrbuch* (Tübingen: Mohr) no. 12 (1961), 201ff.

22 Hölderlin, *Essays and Letters on Theory*, 112.

23 Ibid., 150.

24 Ibid., 114.

5

A small number of houses in a universe of tragedy: notes on Aristotle's περὶ ποιητικῆς and Hölderlin's 'Anmerkungen'

David Farrell Krell

Tragedy is no small matter. It is big. It has size and grandeur. Its elevated status derives from its plot and characters, its action and diction. Tragedy is serious. It gives serious pleasure, provoking fears and evoking compassion, then blowing them all away. No form of embodied presentation is as important for serious individuals and for a serious city as tragedy is.

And yet the stories enacted in the tragedies have their source in a very small number of houses – very special houses. Tragedy therefore ought to be a minuscule matter, involving as it does only a handful of families, which have very particular and very peculiar stories to tell. Yet Plato was concerned enough to construct his entire polity – not merely in one of its particulars but from top to bottom – in opposition to tragedy. Aristotle in turn was concerned enough to rescue the art of tragedy for philosophy, as though everything in his ethics and politics could be best viewed through its bizarre prism, and as though perhaps even physics and the philosophy beyond physics (μετὰ τὰ φυσικά) were somehow bound up with that art.

Centuries later, Hölderlin heard his own voice resonating with the timbre of tragedy. His novel *Hyperion* and mourning play *The Death of Empedocles* became steps toward Sophoclean tragedy, not departures from or progressions beyond it. It was as though, for Hölderin, all the world – and every mortal and every god in it – depended on that small number of plays that told of an even smaller number of households.

If I am mistaken about the consequences of this awe that was felt by both Aristotle and Hölderlin in the face of tragedy, an awe that arose from their belief that a small number of very quirky houses were home to the matters that were most important to them, then let it be a big mistake, one equal to a Nietzsche or a Heidegger, a Lessing or a Racine, a Goethe or a Shakespeare. It is already much too much to want to write about both Aristotle and

Hölderlin, however, and so I will advance from the megalomania of these opening remarks to the micromania of a reading – in this case, reading a few lines of Aristotle's *Poetics* and Hölderlin's 'Notes' to his translations of Sophocles' *Oedipus the King* and *Antigone*.[1]

In chapters 13 and 14 of περὶ ποιητικῆς, Aristotle identifies the types of events that excellent tragedies portray. These events have to do with domestic economy and household management – in a broad sense. How the tragic poet manages the events themselves, husbanding their portrayal in the orchestra, will decide whether or not the pleasure that is peculiar to tragedy will eventuate in the spectators. The οἶκος governs everything here: in two pages of text Aristotle will use cognates of this word five times.

Tragic events involve the change of fortune in an ἐπιεικής, that is, a 'decent' or just and equable human being, one who is perhaps not entirely noble, serious and elevated, but certainly superior to us – a human being whose grave error in judgement and action drives him or her from happiness to misery. The 'proper pleasure' of tragedy requires such a reversal. 'Proper' here means the pleasure that accompanies tragedy, the pleasure that is 'at home' in tragedy, as it were (1453b 11: ἡδονὴν ἀπὸ τραγῳδίας . . . τὴν οἰκείαν). Were the change of fortune to go from misery to happiness, we would find ourselves moving out of the household of tragedy into that of comedy (1453a 36: τῆς κωμῳδίας οἰκεία). Euripides, the 'most tragic of the poets', never made this mistake. Even if he often did not 'manage well' in other respects (1453a 29: μὴ εὖ οἰκονομεῖ), he always remained within the house of tragedy. He did so by selecting only those houses for his dramas in which the events and reversals of fortune were inherently tragic. For tragedy is a matter of special families or family lines (γένη, perhaps what Heidegger, following Trakl, calls *Geschlechter* and Gabriel García Márquez *estirpes*) and special houses or households (οἰκεῖαι), the family of Oedipus, the House of Atreus, and those like them.

Those like them are few. Rare though they may be, however, these tragic families are essential to the art – presumably inasmuch as they reveal something catastrophic in the city, and possibly in nature and in all being. For if these special families and rare households were mere exceptions to the rule, if they were merely quirky or kinky, no one would pay them any mind, and their stories would be pointless eccentricities. Kinky families may found burlesque and perhaps even comedy, but not tragedy. No, such tragic families and houses are memorable, and they are remembered as having suffered serious setbacks. Why and how do poets remember them?

'At first the poets told the stories they picked up wherever by great good luck they found them,' says Aristotle. In Aristotle's own day, however, the 'finest tragedies' were 'constructed around a few households' (1453a 18–19:

David Farrell Krell

νῦν δὲ περὶ ὀλίγας οἰκίας). Chance, τύχη, originally played a role in the gathering of these myths and sagas, although by Aristotle's time poetic τέχνη made the selection of those households on the basis of insight. True, the oligarchy of households in the present instance is a disastrous one. For these are families and houses 'which happen to have had dreadful things done to them, or to have done them themselves' (21–2). Here we encounter a second moment of τύχη – actually, the first moment, the moment when the deeds themselves were done. Here, in line 21, the troubling word συμβέβηκεν, troubling especially for physics and metaphysics, refers to those horrifying and uncanny things (δεινά) that were either suffered or committed (22: ἢ παθεῖν δεινὰ ἢ ποιῆσαι) in those rare and special houses where, by chance, the poets first found their stories.

Aristotle repeats the same set of claims at the end of chapter 14. There he is describing the most suitable kinds of incidents for a tragic plot, finding them precisely in the family home – where loving relationships ought to prevail. When enemies fight or strangers quarrel, no one is surprised; neither dread nor compassion is aroused in such cases. 'But when suffering happens within loving relationships [1453b 19: ἐν ταῖς φιλίαις ἐγγένηται τὰ πάθη], such as brother against brother, son against father, mother against son or son against mother . . . this is what we are looking for.'

This is what we are looking for?! If so, then what we are looking for is what the treatise on friendship in the Nicomachean Ethics decries as the most horrid of crimes – a child raising its hand against the father (1160a 5). One might have thought that raising one's hand against a mother, who is the very excess of loving, especially where her own children are concerned, is still more horrifying (1159a 27, 1161b 27, 1166a 9, 1168a 25); in either case, however, the crimes in question are a matter of house and home, where φιλία ought to have held sway. Tragic art, the highest and most serious of poetic arts, superior to epic, dithyramb, comedy and all the rest, searches out those households in which φιλία has gone missing. Why? The short answer is that the pleasure that is at home in tragedy requires such households for the arousal, refinement, distillation and purgation of pity, fear and all such emotions. The longer answer is that the pleasure evoked in embodied presentations of the sufferings of the rarest households produces the sublime art, the art that is replete with the pleasures of music and μίμησις, the art that is vivid, concentrated and serious – the art that presumably teaches us most about the world. It is precisely in the rarest of households that we learn something serious about the universe of being, insofar as that universe enjoins or permits suffering:

It is for this reason, as was said a moment ago, that the tragedies are not about a great number of families [1454a 9–10: οὐ περὶ πολλὰ γένη]. The poets went in search [10: ζητοῦντες] of these families in order to render such situations in their plots; they found them, not by means of their art, but by good fortune [10–11: οὐκ ἀπὸ τέχνης ἀλλ᾽ ἀπὸ τύχης εὖρον]. They saw themselves constrained to return always and again to those same households, the ones that happened to suffer these same passions [12–13: ἀναγκάζονται οὖν ἐπὶ ταύτας τὰς οἰκίας ἀπαντᾶν ὅσαις τὰ τοιαῦτα συμβέβηκε πάθη].

So many things in the universe of being lend themselves to embodied enactment or μίμησις: the music of flute, lyre and voice, and in voice language, harmony and rhythm; all the forms of mime and dance, the rhythms of their gestures bodying forth characters, passions and actions; literature, whether dithyramb, epic or comedy. Further, embodied enactment is the natural secret of all learning – and all human beings, as we know, desire to know and to learn. Yet if all these things offer themselves to μίμησις, whence in all the world the need for that small number of houses?

Let us go back to basic definitions. 'Tragedy, then, is the embodied presentation of an action that is serious' (1449b 24–5: μίμησις πράξεως σπουδαίας). Serious; not playful, but elevated in character; noble. Serious and complete, 'as having magnitude' (μέγεθος). It is otiose to argue whether magnitude is meant mathematically or dynamically, as extension or grandeur. For tragedy became grand when it surrendered its little plots, its improvised sketches and satires (1449a 19). The language of tragedy is 'embellished' or 'refined', as each of its parts requires, and the events of tragedy are acted out, not narrated. Finally, tragedy moves us to pity and fear, 'purifying us of all such emotions' (1449b 27–8: τὴν τῶν τοιούτων παθημάτων κάθαρσιν). Tragedy embodies and bodies forth as the deeds of serious characters (1448a 2: σπουδαίους), elevated personages of excellence and virtue (3: ἀρετή); or, at least, tragedy depicts its characters in such a way that they appear to be better than we are (4: βελτίονας, 12: βελτίους). The persons who are born into the small number of special households that lend tragedy its incidents are 'better' than the norm, and they prove it by killing their fathers and sleeping with their mothers, or by serving up their brother's children to him, or by sacrificing their children in order to assure the success of a military adventure, so that they in turn are killed by their wives, who for their part will be killed by . . ., and so on.

Why and how to take pleasure in such embodied enactments? Aristotle hints at the answer when he tells us that the pleasures of μίμησις, by which the human animal learns whatever it does learn, are extreme pleasures – or, rather, pleasures taken in extremes. They are 'best felt in the perfect embodiment of the forms of the most repugnant animals or of cadavers' (1448a 11–12: οἷον θηρίων τε μορφὰς τῶν ἀτιμοτάτων καὶ νεκρῶν). Mimetic pleasure, remarkable for the extreme repugnance of the objects of its embodiments, is the secret joy of learning, the very ἔρως of νοῦς. The repugnance of the deeds of our betters, and the catastrophic reversal of fortune our betters undergo, may be precisely what make poetry more philosophical and more serious than scholarly inquiries such as the one in which we are now engaged (1451b 5–6: φιλοσοφώτερον καὶ σπουδαιότερον). Whereas ἱστορίαι merely recount a succession of past events (τὸ γενόμενα), tragic dramas enact in an embodied way what may happen (τὸν δὲ οἷα ἂν γένοιτο, or, as a recent French translation puts it, ce à quoi l'on peut s'attendre [117]). Tragic dramas thus speak to the universal or general (7: τὰ καθόλου) with regard to verisimilitude and necessity (9: τὸ εἰκὸς ἢ τὸ ἀναγκαῖον), even though the deeds depicted in them are attributed to particular characters. A small number of particular characters in a small number of very special households apparently reveal – if only in uncanny and unhomelike hints – what the universal condition may be. Which would suggest how desperately all philosophy and all logic need tragedy.

Is such a reading tenable? Can one really take the battered and tattered text περὶ ποιητικῆς as one's prism and examine Aristotle's entire philosophical position through it? To see science through the optics of art, but art through the optics of life: such was Nietzsche's project. Would it be legitimate to make one further cut, add one more facet to the prism, and attribute that prism not only to Nietzsche but also to Aristotle? To see science through the optics of art, art through the optics of life – and life through the optics of tragedy?

No doubt, certain sites in the Aristotelian corpus would be more accommodating to such a reading than others. Kevin Thomas Miles argues that the need for what is translated as equity in Nicomachean Ethics (5: 10) exposes the tragedy of justice.[2] For the law must declare in universals, but universals never speak to the particulars that justice must respect – unless they do so in and as tragedy, which, we recall, speaks to the universal. 'Equity', ἐπιείκεια (we have already seen the word in Aristotle's description of the 'decent' or equable human being who must serve as the tragic hero), is that 'fittingness' or 'suitability' of what is 'meet and just' that must supplement the law if there is to be justice. Aristotle writes:

> What creates the problem is that it is the equitable that is just – not the legally just, but a correction of legal justice. The reason is that all law is universal, but about some things it is not possible to make a universal statement that will be correct. In those cases, then, in which it is necessary to speak universally, but not possible to do so correctly, the law takes the usual case, though it is not ignorant of the possibility of error. And it is none the less correct; for the error is not in

the law nor in the legislator but in the nature of the thing, since the matter of practical affairs is of this kind from the start.

(*Nic. Eth.* 5: 10; 1137b 10–20)

The logic of the supplement is never more relentless in its essentially tragic character than it is in the supplementation of legal justice by equity. None other than Friedrich Hölderlin describes the difficulty, with reference to Sophocles' *Antigone* and to the 'more intrinsic nexus of life', not first of all in his 'Notes to *Antigone*', but in a text (dated *circa* February 1796) entitled 'Fragment of Philosophical Letters':

> If there are higher laws that determine the more infinite nexus of life [*jenen unendlichern Zusammenhang des Lebens*], if there are unwritten divine laws, the ones of which Antigone speaks when in spite of the strict public prohibition she buries her brother – and there must be such laws if that higher nexus is not a mere phantasm – I say, if there are such laws, then they are in any case insufficient [*unzulänglich*], inso-far as they are represented as being *merely* for themselves and not as caught up in life [*im Leben begriffen*]. They are insufficient in the first place because, precisely to the degree that the nexus of life is more infinite, so too the activity and its element, the manner in which the activity proceeds, and the sphere within which all this is observed, encompassing the law and the particular world [*besondere Welt*] in which the law is being exercised – all this too is bound up more infinitely with the law. Thus, even if it were a universal law for all civilised peoples, the law could never be thought at all in abstraction from a particular case. It could never be thought if one were unwilling to take into account its very own peculiarity [*Eigentümlichkeit*], namely its intimate imbrication [*innige Verbundenheit*] with the sphere in which it is exercised.[3]

So much in the *Nicomachean Ethics* may strike us as essentially tragic: the insufficiency of virtue for happiness; the residual need for prosperity and great good luck in the virtuous life; the inevitable acknowledgement of death in Solon's affirmation, 'He was happy'; the incapacity of φρόνησις to offer any-thing like assurance of right or fitting action; the imprecision of ethical delib-eration and moral theory; the dispersion of 'the good'; the identification of 'the better' as always 'the more difficult'; the wish of friends that they spend their days and lives together – as a *wish*; and, to end the list, the very fact that the good is what we aim at rather than possess.

By contrast, it is doubtless difficult if not impossible to regard Aristotelian circular motion, whether in the heavens or in the mind, as essentially tragic.[4] Yet precisely how such eternal circuits are to be thought as proper to embodied human existence on this earth is a grand aporia. If ideas or forms, thought as the being of things, cannot be separated from the things, then Aristotle's own anti-Platonism militates against the putative separability of the thinking soul – which is in a way all things – from the body. And that would bring us closer to a tragic conception of being, perhaps closer than Aristotle himself may have desired. Yet in this we would be constrained, as it were, by the things themselves (*Met.* 1: 9). Thus the question raised of old, raised now and always, 'is always the subject of doubt'; the question of being (τί τὸ ὄν;) invariably broaches the tragic. For 'if nothing is by accident perishable' (*Met.* 10: 10), then perishing belongs to the essence. To the essence of *perishable things alone*, one might reply. Yet the aura of those perishable things – the aura of deleterious time, chance and accident – radiates outward to the perfect circles of the universe of being, perhaps contaminating even them with tragedy. While eternal being, utterly unmoved, moves perishable beings as the object of their desire as well as their thought (*Met.* 12: 7), it must surely hope that nothing comes to break into the narcissistic circle of its autonoesis and autoerotics. Yet that very hope shows that Aristotle's god, his unmoved mover, never felt the delight of loving – in Aristotle's own view, the superior delight. For loving, not being loved, is the dream of the finest friend and the most energetic mother. Indeed, the *hope* for autonomy is evidence of rupture itself – Io's interruption of Prometheus' wretched solitude, Aphrodite's of Zeus' absolute sway – and it presides over the very birth of tragedy.

Arguably, there are an infinite number of places in the Aristotelian corpus where the optics of tragedy enable us to see Aristotle's problems and achievements in a new light. While it may not be the usual way to read and teach Aristotle, the prism of tragedy reveals possibilities for *thinking through* in an unfamiliar way a number of classic problems of philosophy. Allow me, then, the following preliminary, cursory, hastily compiled list of sites – a dozen of them, seven from the *Organon*, five from the *Physics* – simply as a beginning.

1. In the *Organon*, the problematic relation of οὐσία to 'individuals' in a 'primary' or 'secondary' sense, the apparently inevitable slippage between any given *this* and the genus to which it belongs, creates a situation in which we form impressions that are 'not strictly true' (*Cat.* 5).
2. The 'awkward results' of the reign of necessity, which operates in the 'fullness of time', also point to a tragic situation. For necessity does not seem to admit of any alternatives in human destinies, alternatives that could be introduced by 'deliberation and action' (*De int.* 9).

3. The indemonstrability of 'basic premises' and 'basic truths' about which 'it is hard to be sure' (*Post. Anal.* 1: 3, 9).
4. The possible untruth of valid argumentation (ibid. 1: 19).
5. The unavailability of being (τὸ ὄν) to genus-species differentiation, and the inexhaustibility of being – 'one can always ask why' (ibid. 2: 7).
6. The risky induction of primary principles: 'It is like a rout in battle stopped first by one man making a stand . . .' (ibid. 2: 19).
7. The impossibility of a radically reflexive or perfectly autonomous knowledge: 'Demonstration cannot be the originative source of demonstration' (ibid. 2: 19).
8. In the *Physics*, the fact that matter ('a mother, as it were') *desires* the form, 'as the female desires the male and the ugly the beautiful – only the ugly or the female not *per se* but *per accidens*' (1: 9), a disconcerting reduction of matter to desire and desire to accident – precisely with a view to form.
9. The supposition that 'art imitates nature', or that art 'partly completes what nature cannot bring to a finish, and partly imitates her', inasmuch as in both art and nature 'mistakes are possible', shows us that even self-doctoring doctors suffer not only from illness and demise but also from professional incompetence and malpractice (2: 2, 8).
10. If τέχνη is mimetic of φύσις, one must wonder whether the most imitative of arts, poetic art, and in poetic art the elevated art of tragic drama, imitates nothing less than φύσει ὄντα, the entire universe of nature, which is therefore in some sense itself tragic (ibid.).
11. Nature is the scene not only of causality, which is the object of philosophy as such, but also of chance (τύχη), which is 'inscrutable to human beings': '. . . it is with reason that good fortune is regarded as unstable; for chance is unstable, as none of the things which result from it can be invariable or normal', except for the fact that chance normally and even invariably plays a role in both ethical and natural life (ibid.).
12. The identification of time as 'the cause of decay, since it is the number of change, and change removes what is' (4: 12). Whereas time may seem to be as much the cause of coming to be as of passing away, it is more properly described as the cause of oblivion and senescence, decrepitude, destruction and demise (4: 13). Sometimes it seems that sheer succession – time tearing ahead and tearing us away with it – suffices for tragedy.

Such a list, although a mere beginning, truncated and presented without sufficient reflection and patience, may nevertheless encourage us to take Aristotle's *Poetics* as more central to the Aristotelian corpus than it is usually considered to be. If such a list fails to overcome our scepticism, however, what now follows

David Farrell Krell

will seem even more fantastic. For even if we succeed in reading Aristotle as
a tragic philosopher, can we make of Hölderlin an Aristotelian?

There are only two references to Aristotle in Hölderlin's works, as far as I
am aware, one explicit, the other a mere allusion having more to do with
Sophocles than Aristotle. The direct reference apparently has nothing to do
with tragedy, although it does seem to arise from an experience of having read
the *Poetics*. We will take up the allusion to Aristotle later, in the context of
the 'Anmerkungen' to Sophocles' *Antigone*, where it appears. For the moment,
let us examine the sole explicit Hölderlinian reference to Aristotle. It appears
in a poem sketched in 1789 but left incomplete: an ode to the *Sacra via* of
poetry, the sacred way of poetry as a way of life, 'Die heilige Bahn' (1: 67–8):

Ist also diß die heilige Bahn?
   Herrlicher Blik — o trüge mich nicht!
      Diese geh' ich?? schwebend auf des Liedes
         Hoher fliegender Morgenwolke?

Und welch' ist jene? künstlich gebaut
   Eben hinaus mit Marmor beschränkt
      Prächtig gerad, gleich den Sonnenstralen —
         An der Pforte ein hoher Richtstuhl?

Ha! wie den Richtstuhl Purpur umfließt
   Und der Smaragd wie blendend er glänzt
      Und auf dem Stuhl, mit dem großen Scepter
         Aristoteles hinwärts blikend

Mit hellem scharfem Aug' auf des Lieds
   Feurigen Lauf — und jenes Gebirg'
      Eilt sie hinweg — muthig in die Thäler
         Stürzt sie, ungestüm, und ihr Boden

Ist wie des Nordens Flammengewölk
   Wallend vom Tritt des rennenden Gangs —
      Waffengeräusch rauschen seine Tritte
         Über alternde Wolkenfelsen.

Ha! sie ist heiß die heilige Bahn —
   Ach wie geübt der Große dort rennt
      Um ihn herum — wie da Staunen wimmelt
         Freunde — Vaterland — fernes Ausland.

Und ich um ihn mit Mükengesums
   Niedrig — im Staub — Nein Großer, das nicht.
      Muthig hinan! — ! — Wanns nun da is, voll ist

96

Is this then the sacred way?
  Splendid prospect – oh, do not betray me!
    This is the way I shall go?? hovering on the
      High-flying clouds of the hymn?

And what is that way? artfully built
  Smoothly paved, curbed in marble,
    Splendidly straight, like the beams of the sun –
      At the gate a lofty seat of judgement?

Ha! how the royal purple flows over the seat of judgement
  And the emerald – how blindingly it gleams,
    And on the seat, wielding the great sceptre,
      Aristotle gazing ahead

With his bright keen eye on the hymn's
  Fiery course – and the sacred way
    Flies across those mountains – bravely into the valleys
      It plunges, untamed, and its roadbed

Is of the flaming clouds of the north,
  Surging in the wake of the race that is run –
    Clangour of weapons, its footsteps
      Sweeping over the ageing cliffs of cloud.

Ha! the sacred way is hot –
  Oh, the great one runs its circular course
    As though accustomed – how astonished
      Are his friends – fatherland – foreign shores.

And I go that way plagued by a swarm of flies,
  Cringing – in the dust – No, great one, not that.
    Bravely onward! – ! – When it is there, when it is full

If Aristotle holds the sceptre (but where? on the sacred way? or on that artful, artificial avenue? is there but one path here, or two?), it seems strange that Hölderlin's mourning play *The Death of Empedocles*, and his translations of Sophocles' tragedies, along with the 'Notes' that accompany his translations, should ignore Aristotle. It seems stranger still that Hölderlin's theoretical essays on tragedy should report nothing of Aristotle's views. It is therefore perhaps perverse to argue for a certain proximity in their views – perverse, even though no one can doubt the overwhelming force of Aristotle's *Poetics* for all criticism that came after it, including that of Hölderlin.

Allow me to present another list, it too quite hastily gathered, of places in

Hölderlin's 'Notes' where a kind of Aristotelianism seems to prevail. I will not be able to discuss all these places in what follows, so that the list is meant as an invitation to commentators who are more competent and comprehensive than I can ever be. Five brief points, again by way of a beginning:

1. It seems to me that Hölderlin's 'lawful calculus' (*gesetzliches Kalkül*) of tragedy is quite close to Aristotle's ubiquitous yet poorly defined διάνοια. Especially in chapter 19 of περὶ ποιητικῆς, Aristotle comes close to what Hölderlin defines as *das Idealische*, namely the fact that tragedy has to do with *ideas*, with thinking and language. The plot and incidents of tragedy are also matters of 'the idea', and are therefore essentially dianoetic. Would not Hölderlin affirm that intense focus on the *idea* is what the school of poetry needs in our own time – that even though no calculus can ever calculate the content of a play, the *idea* must dictate the sequence and the speed of its embodied presentations?

2. As obvious as it may seem, one must ponder the fact that Hölderlin's famous *caesura* or counterrhythmic interruption may be read also in terms of τὸ δέσις and τὸ λύσις, the tying and loosening of the knots, the complication and resolution of the plot. For even though the term *caesura* is borrowed from versification, Hölderlin applies it to the faculties of human knowing and to the events and actions of the tragic plot. Would not Hölderlin affirm that the *caesura* is a protracted instant or elongated point within which we can see how and why matters are tearing ahead so relentlessly?

3. Similarly, Hölderlin's notions of *Metapher* (as transport) and *Umkehr* (both as categorial reversal and the reversion to one's place of birth) need to be thought not only in terms of Aristotelian diction (and of metaphor in particular) but also in terms of the μεταβολή and περιπατεία that guide the selection, order and velocity of incidents in the plot.

4. Likewise, Hölderlin's notion of an ecstatic removal to the eccentric sphere of the dead (*Entrükung in die exezentrische Sphäre der Todten*) needs to be discussed in terms of the peculiar pleasure (ἡδονή) that Aristotle espies in tragedy, the universally discussed yet ever mysterious κάθαρσις of emotions. Nothing seems farther removed from Hölderlin's understanding of tragedy than pleasure. Yet it may be that Aristotle's insistence on the word ἡδονή will prove particularly instructive for Hölderlin's calculus, especially when it comes to the father of time and the earth, to wit, Zeus. Zeus and pleasure? Let us see.

5. Finally, in order now to truncate the list, what Hölderlin calls 'the deadly factical word' (*das tödtlich faktisches Wort*) may provide a bridge for our discussions of peripety to issues of diction (λέξις), considered in chapters

19–22 of the *Poetics*. The factical word, as both deadly and mortifying, Greek and Hesperian, may be the key to understanding why and how we are to experience the choruses and dialogues of the plays as the bodily organs of a suffering godhead.

Yet none of these five points speaks directly to our paradox – that the smallest number of houses prevail in a universe of tragedy. We may take it that Hölderlin is at home in the tragic universe, that even his gods are destined to experience tragedy. This we know not only from the late hymns but also from the early novel *Hyperion*, and also especially from the three versions of *The Death of Empedocles*, inasmuch as Empedocles, the author of books on both nature and κάθαρσις, is the tragic thinker *par excellence*. However, how do Hölderlin's thoughts on Greek and Hesperian tragedy, on the tragedy of space, time and history, relate to those few exceptional houses that Hölderlin too was seeking all his life?

Perhaps the most telling of the ties between Hölderlin and Aristotle is the fact that for both of them Sophocles' *Oedipus the King* is the exemplary Greek tragedy. Hölderlin's fascination with *Oedipus* and *Antigone* surely has to do with that *family*, that *household*, in which 'raging curiosity' and 'mournful calm' alternate. For the moment, here in my own remarks, that most telling of ties will be the only one discussed at any length. I will begin with the 'Anmerkungen zum Oedipus', and then proceed directly to the 'Anmerkungen zur Antigonä'.[5]

If Hölderlin admires 'the μηχανή of the ancients', desiring to enhance the craft of poetry in the German lands by attending to the skill or *Geschik* of the Greeks, it may not be too far-fetched to think of his 'lawful calculus' as a meditation on Aristotelian διάνοια – since 'reasoning' has to do equally with the contrivances of plot, the mechanics of poetic diction and the intricate flying machines of metaphor. Hölderlin is quick to admit that the 'particular content' of any given tragedy cannot be reduced to a calculus. Neither the content nor 'the living meaning' of any given play can be calculated in advance. The lawful calculus of tragedy is further complicated by the fact that it involves an entire 'system of sensibility', that is to say, 'the whole human being' viewed under the influence of 'the element' (presumably, the element of tragedy) in all its essential respects. Tragedy presents us with a succession – but also and especially an *equilibrium* – of presentations, sensations and reasonings (*Räsonnement*, perhaps to be understood in terms of διάνοια). The lawful calculus has essentially to do with 'tragic *transport*', which is 'properly empty and utterly unbound'. Empty of what? Perhaps, once again, of any particular content. Utterly unbound? Perhaps, one again, more infinite and undetermined, thinking the infinite in an Anaximandrian way, as Hölderlin so often does, as ἄπειρον. In any case, tragic transport is what Hölderlin means by *metaphor*.

He thinks of metaphor as a mode of transport(ation), the μεταφορά, as others of his texts suggest (2: 80, 102; 3: 398). The tragic has its significance in its 'ideal character', and is the bearer – or metaphor – of an 'intellectual intuition'. The editors of the Hanser edition of Hölderlin's collected works offer a useful summary statement concerning 'intellectual intuition', which may suffice for an initial orientation:

> Intellectuale [or intellectuelle] Anschauung: a spiritual–intellectual envisaging, the supreme form of knowing in the Neoplatonic doctrine of spirit (νοῦς); excluded from theory of knowledge by Kant as impossible for the human understanding, treated by Reinhold in the context of a general theory of the faculty of representation, appropriated by Fichte as the supreme act of the (absolute) ego for the grounding of the 'doctrine of science' ['Wissenschaftslehre'], and finally taken up by Schelling as the constitutive act of the ego. For Hölderlin it is an intuition – the intuition that 'all is one' – that exceeds theoretical and practical consciousness alike.[6]

Thus Ancient Greek tragedy responds to the modern philosophical quandary of the subject–object split. It does so by proffering the unity of a world in which subject and object are either not yet or no longer separated. In the same poetological sketch (from late autumn or early winter 1799) in which the concept of metaphor is extensively deployed, 'Das lyrische dem Schein nach idealische Gedicht . . .', Hölderlin defines the unity of subject and object in terms of 'the unity with everything that lives'. Such unity is therefore not theoretical and cannot be broached by epistemology. While it may be closer to practical philosophy, at least in Fichte's and Schelling's conceptions of it, it properly pertains to aesthetics in the broadest sense – a sense that would embrace major parts of Kant's third Critique, along with the Transcendental Aesthetic of his first Critique. For the unity we are seeking has to do with life. Viewed negatively, intellectual intuition arises from 'the impossibility of an absolute separation and individualisation' (2: 104). Viewed positively, the unity established in intellectual intuition achieves its 'rights' only when it partakes of 'its entire measure of life' (2: 105). Yet precisely in this most positive moment the negative reasserts its prerogative. Once again the element of excess, of the too much, arises. Subject and object are, in intellectual intuition, 'too unified' (zu einig), precisely in the way that Empedocles proved to be 'too intense, too singular' (zu innig, zu einzig) for his historical age.[7] Something akin to Empedoclean 'Strife' (Νεῖκος) disrupts the sphere of intellectual intuition. Aesthetics does not succeed where theory and practice had failed: Hölderlin's preferred analogies for the attainment and the disruption of intellectual intuition are the quadrature of the circle and the infinite approximation of the asymptote. Aesthetics gets us as close as one can get – and then drives us away. Hölderlin attributes 'the ideal beginning of the actual separation' of subject and object to 'the necessary *arbitrariness of Zeus*', or, more neutrally, inasmuch as *Willkür* means both, the necessary *will* of Zeus. In either case, it almost seems that what the ancient author of *Prometheus Bound* asserts of Zeus is true, namely that Zeus himself is a member of one of those rare and factious households of ancient Greece that open their door to tragedy. Intellectual intuition, for Hölderlin, *is* tragic thinking.

Finally, in this early text Hölderlin distinguishes Sophocles' *Antigone* from *Oedipus the King* in terms of the type of intellectual intuition presented in each. If the intellectual intuition is 'more subjective', and if the separation of subject and object arises from the 'concentrating parts' of the play, as it does in *Antigone*, with its highly compacted final scenes, the style of the tragedy is lyrical. If the separation of subject and object is more objective, that is, if it proceeds from the supreme possibility of separation, which is Zeus himself, as in the case of *Oedipus*, then the tragedy is eminently tragic. In *Oedipus the King* the sweeping succession of incidents separates all the characters radically from the divine. Thebes is besieged by plague not only because the temples of Apollo at Delphi and Abae are sick but also because some dread illness has spread to the father of time himself. Zeus' pleasure exacts of him its price. But let us return to the 'Notes to *Oedipus*'.

Oedipus – the most famous scion of that very rare Theban household that embraces Cadmus, Pentheus and Dionysos himself – struggles to achieve consciousness through an intellectual intuition. Yet what he achieves is disruption. The rhythmic sequence of embodied presentations in which he struggles for unification and consciousness of self will itself be subjected to a counterrhythmic interruption, the dramatic equivalent of *caesura*, which will prevent the play from tearing ahead too quickly, in ec-centric rapidity, to its violent conclusion. Slowing down the process of dissolution will not stop it, however. In *Antigone*, by contrast, the final scenes are compressed by the initial ones, so that the equilibrium of the piece inclines toward the end, with the consequence that the end must be 'protected from' the beginning. Here too, however, protection of the end will not stop or fundamentally alter it.

In both cases, as we know, the appearance of Tiresias marks the moment of *caesura* or counterrhythmic interruption, if only because Tiresias is the mediator between the immortals under the reign of Zeus and the mortals under the reign of nature's more aorgic power, represented by Cronos the Titan, a power that will eventually transport them into the underworld. Yet Tiresias has as much to do with Cronos as with Zeus, who, after all, are father and son. Of Tiresias Hölderlin writes:

> He intervenes in the course of destiny, as overseer over the power of
> nature, which tragically snatches the human being from its life-sphere,
> from the midpoint of its inner life, and transports it to another world,
> tearing it away into the eccentric sphere of the dead.
>
> (2: 310–11)

The midpoint must be understood both formally (in terms of the problem of
the ec-centric or decentred equilibrium of the sequence of scenes in the plays)
and materially (in terms of the unified life of the hero or heroine in an essential yet tenuous equilibrium with its world). Even if the transport (*Entrükung*)
or tearing (*Reißen*) of the hero out of the midpoint of life into the sphere of
death *seems* to have nothing to do with Aristotelian notions of pleasure or purification, (ἡδονή κάθαρσις), it remains true that the upsurgence of the more
aorgic and elemental nature does serve as something of a corrective to the
hyperorganized human order of the city. For if what *Hyperion* calls 'the School
of Destiny' has deprived Hyperion of all the pleasures that nature has to offer,
will not 'the School of Nature' compensate all the more violently, all the more
aorgically?

Something about that 'special house' of Oedipus comes to the fore in
Hölderlin's detailed analysis of the play in section 2 of the 'Anmerkungen' (2:
311–15). Ironically, it is Oedipus' 'marvelous, furious curiosity', which interprets the quite general pronouncement of the Delphic oracle all too particularly, that is his undoing. Oedipus' ὀργή, his fury, is a family story: as he
begins to break through the barriers of his unknowing with regard to his origins, he is 'as though intoxicated in his regal harmonic form', at least 'at first',
until he can 'no longer bear what he knows'. His suspicion of Creon betrays
how insecure Oedipus is under the burden of his 'unbounded thought, freighted
with mournful secrets'. Angry excess, or 'unmeasure', soon follows upon
Oedipus' splendid harmony, an excess that is 'gleefully destructive' and that
blindly obeys the imperious time that rushes ahead to doom.

Something else about that 'special house' of Oedipus becomes clear at the
formal midpoint of the play. Jocasta almost succeeds in soothing her son-and-
spouse's *second* nightmare, which is the nightmare about her. Her worlds instil
in Oedipus a 'mournful calm' (*traurige Ruhe*), a 'stupor' or an *embarras*. We
hear the powerful man deceive himself about his parentage for the last time.
Indeed, one might think of Jocasta's intervention as a second *caesura*, a kind of
shadowy *caesura*, interrupting the stormy sweep of disaster with a mother's
tranquil, lucid and utterly remarkable words to her little boy – who is about
to be cut away. Hölderlin does not cite them in his 'Anmerkungen', but how
magnificently he has translated them! He finds a language that gives us contemporary readers the entire Oedipus Complex in so sovereign and tranquil a
form that it seems to pre-empt all psychoanalysis (2: 287):

Jokasta

Was fürchtet der Mensch, der mit dem Glük
Es hält? Von nichts giebts eine Ahnung deutlich.
Dahin zu leben, so wie einer kann,
Das ist das Beste. Fürchte du die Hochzeit
Mit deiner Mutter nicht! denn öfters hat
Ein Sterblicher der eignen Mutter schon
Im Traume beigewohnt: doch wem [8] *wie nichts*
Diβ gilt, er trägt am leichtesten das Leben.

Jocasta

For what does a human being have to fear if his luck
Holds? There is no clear presentiment of anything at all.
To live straight ahead, as well as you can,
That is best. Do not fear marriage
With your mother! For oftentimes
In dreams a mortal has slept with
His own mother: yet whoever takes this as counting for
Nothing at all can most readily bear life.

Hölderlin has already used the phrase *Im Traume* fourteen lines earlier. If in Jocasta's mouth the phrase translates ὀνείρασιν, in the mouth of Oedipus it translates Polybus' longing (πόθῳ) for his lost adopted son:

Oedipus

. . . wenn er anders
Im Traume nicht umkam, von mir. So mag er
Gestorben seyn, von mir . . .

Oedipus

. . . unless
He died in dreams of me. In this way
He may have died of me . . .

No doubt dreams of longing play a large role for both father and son, and perhaps even for mother-and-wife and son-and-husband, in the special economies of tragedy and psychoanalysis. Indeed, there are moments when one is convinced that Freud *read* the play, perhaps in Hölderlin's more aorgic translation, and that he merely extrapolated from this very special household in the direction of the universal – as others before him had done.

   If Oedipus 'desperately wrestles in order to come to himself', he is at this

103

point in the play – the eccentric midpoint, the shifting fulcrum, at which in Pier Paolo Pasolini's film version of *Oedipus Rex* Oedipus and Jocasta join hands as young lovers – 'tempted back into life once again'.[9] Indeed, there are grounds on Hölderlin's own terms to see this shadow *caesura* as a more striking interruption of the rapid rhythm of the scenes of the play than the earlier confrontation with Tiresias was. Even so, the rush continues. Life is soon in the dust, or hanging from the roofbeam, as Oedipus strives 'almost shamelessly' to get control over himself. Hölderlin calls this Oedipus' 'foolishly savage search [*das närrischwilde Nachsuchen*] for a consciousness'; soon he will call it an 'insane questioning after a consciousness' (*das geisteskranke Fragen*). If it is intellectual intuition that Oedipus is after, the vision that will make him one with his world, only the blind Tiresias can show him the way. From the instant of his birth, or at least from the moment his heels are pierced and his toes sewn together, Oedipus is caught up in violent relationships, trapped in 'the more violence nexus' (*in gewaltsamerem Zusammenhang*). Jocasta herself will be tangled in the knots of her hair, 'hanging together', as it were, with her son-and-spouse in their very special house. Yet let us push on the paradox a little harder, as Hölderlin does.

In the third section of his 'Notes', Hölderlin reflects on the monstrous union of god and human being, of external nature and inmost humanity, in *wrath* – where boundless unity purifies itself by means of boundless scission. Perhaps this monstrous unification or coupling (*sich paaren*) of god and human in wrath (*Zorn*), followed directly by boundless separation (*gränzenloses Scheiden*), is what Hölderlin takes κάθαρσις to be. At all events, without apparent rhyme or reason, Hölderlin now makes an allusion to Aristotle. He cites the tenth-century Byzantine lexicon, the *Suda*, on Aristotle, implying perhaps that Sophocles is the true Aristotle, or that Aristotle is truly tragic. Hölderlin cites the phrase from the *Suda* without translating it, and without diacritical marks, as follows: Της φυσεως γραμματευς ην τον καλαμον αποβρεχων ευνουν. 'He [Aristotle, according to the *Suda*, but here apparently Sophocles] is the grammatologist of nature, writing with his pen dipped in pure mind.' Perhaps more than the union of Aristotle and Sophocles, or more than the replacement of the former by the latter, is at stake here, however: perhaps it is here a matter of a boundless pairing – and an equally boundless separation – of the more aorgic realm of nature (τῆς φύσεως) and of the human being, whether philosopher or tragedian, who tries to comprehend through the agency of the written word (γραμματεύς εὐνοῦν). Such boundless couplings and separations – one thinks of the intermittent couplings of Apollo and Dionysos cited by Nietzsche at the very outset of *The Birth of Tragedy* – take place in those much maligned and admittedly maddening yet undeniably very special houses in a universe of upsurgent, self-concealing being.

In the famous concluding lines of section 3 of the 'Anmerkungen zum
Oedipus', it is the betrayal of the gods – and betrayal *by* the gods – that
Hölderlin exhorts us to remember. Such betrayal occurs in a time of vanity
and futility (*in müßiger Zeit*), a time of pestilence and confusion of meaning, a
time out of work, a time that reminds Hölderlin as much of his own age as of
the tragic age of the Greeks. In order that the course of the world show no
gaps (see also 2: 73–4, 'Das untergehende Vaterland . . .'), and in order '*that
memory of the celestial ones not be extinguished altogether*', such memory '*communicates itself in the all-oblivious form of infidelity*, inasmuch as divine infidelity is the
most readily retained' (2: 315–16). It is not easy to say what such mutual
betrayal between god and mortality may be, their monstrous and furious union
now ruined by boundless separation, their covenant now revoked simultaneously by both sides, their sole prophet now an agent of death. We will continue to encounter such betrayal in *Antigone*, even if the 'Anmerkungen zur
Antigonä' no longer mention *göttliche Untreue*. These moments of oblivion and
betrayal are instants of reversal (*Umkehr*). In the 'Notes to *Antigone*', Hölderlin
will think this reversal in national-political terms, or, better, *natal*-political
terms, as the fatherland in tumult. At the present moment, in the context of
Oedipus the King, he thinks it in terms of the abandoned temples and barren
altars of plague-ridden Thebes. 'What should I sing?' asks the leader of the chorus in desperation, who then announces that he will no longer go to the erst-
while sacred places (2: 284):

> *Unglüklich aber gehet das Göttliche.*

> For divinity wanders in misfortune.

Divinity suffers the same misfortune as the wrathful and violent Oedipus,
who now, after the eccentric midpoint of mournful calm has passed, dreams
that his mother is Lady Luck, τύχη, the maid of the moon, otherwise known
as Chance and Hazard (2: 292):

> *Was soll, das breche . . .*
> *Ich aber will, als Sohn des Glüks mich haltend,*
> *Des wohlbegabten, nicht verunehrt werden.*
> *Denn diß ist meine Mutter. Und klein und groß*
> *Umfiengen mich die mitgebornen Monde.*
> *Und so erzeugt, will ich nicht ausgehn, so,*
> *So daß ich nicht, ganz, weß ich bin, ausforschte.*

> Whatever is to be, let it break upon me . . .
> Yet will I account myself a son of Fortune,
> Fortune replete with gifts, and not to be dishonoured.

For this is my mother. And small and tall
My sibling moons surrounded me.
And, thus engendered, I will not be extinguished, no,
Not thus; not until I have searched out whose son I am.

In this universe of lunar voices, of chance encounters with the dark side
and the new, what happens in a very particular family touches on solar space
and initiates solar time. 'For in the extremity of suffering nothing subsists
other than the conditions of time or space' (2: 316). The human being,
caught up in the moment, forgets himself and herself; the god, who is nothing other than time, forgets itself. All are unfaithful. All forget the unity with
the world that intellectual intuition, through the mediation of the poetic
word, promised. All suffer the sudden disruption or ecstatic displacement of
a turning, a 'categorial reversal', in which all our ends will not rhyme with
their beginnings; as the god shivers and founders in oblivion, the human being
is swept along in the sequence of events that break the bounds of space and
time. Hölderlin adds: 'Thus stands Haemon in the *Antigone*. Thus Oedipus
himself in the middle of the tragedy of *Oedipus*.' Haemon? He wanted to
found a special house of his own with the daughter–sister of Oedipus.
Oedipus in the middle? That is the point at which Jocasta tells him to keep
on dreaming, dreaming is best.

Oneiric, naïve language *is* the language of Sophocles, Hölderlin tells us in
the 'Notes to *Antigone*', to which we must now turn. Sophocles speaks and
writes the language of human understanding 'wandering among unthinkable
things'. The 'Anmerkungen zur *Antigonä*', after outlining a more technical
account of the calculable law of the *caesura*, pick up where the 'Anmerkungen
zum *Oedipus*' left off, with the categorial turning of time. If the *caesura* comes
quite late in *Antigone*, again with the appearance of Tiresias, the highest flight
or supreme moment of the play comes much earlier, immediately after the
midpoint (occupied by Haemon), in the fourth choral song. The song juxta-
poses Eros and Hades, the spirit of love-and-peace and 'the all-silencing god of
death'. Antigone's subsequent dialogue with the chorus invokes the fate of
Niobe (at line 852: '*Ich habe gehört* . . .'). Both here and in the fifth choral
song, superlatives of juxtaposition are achieved – superlatives of beauty and
horror, sacrilege and divine visitation. With regard to these superlatives,
Hölderlin writes:

When the soul labours secretly, it is of enormous help to it that at
the point of supreme consciousness it eludes the grasp of consciousness. And before the present god can actually seize the soul, the soul
goes to encounter the god with bold words, often the very words of

blasphemy. And in this way it preserves the sacred, the living possibility of spirit.

(2: 371)

As we shall see, Sophocles brings Niobe, Danaë, Lycurgus and Pentheus together in this moment of human genius and virtuosity, a moment that hovers between the sacred and the profane, between blasphemy and openness to the god. That moment is entirely 'orgic' and thus ready to be swept into the more aorgic realm of nature. These special women and men defy the gods and bring disaster on themselves and their children, but they also introduce the gods to their own divine disaster – to the lunar and solar disaster that they themselves are. Danaë for example, reveals to Zeus, the father of time, who he *is*. She does not serve merely as the receptacle for Zeus' golden shower, but retains her kinship with Ἀνάγκη by showing him what time is, and what time it is. She shows him what Aristotle called the superior delight, the delight in loving; she also shows him what such loving entails. Hölderlin deliberately 'mistranslates' Sophocles' lines, in order to enable us to better understand what is happening, he says, but in so mistranslating he gives an extraordinary twist to Zeus' arbitrary nature (2: 353).

Sie zählete dem Vater der Zeit
Die Stundenschläge, die goldnen.

She counted for the father of time
The strokes of the hour, the golden

Danaë did something *for* the god? She counted *for* him? Well, he was *there*, with her, and for reasons that were *not* arbitrary.

Instead of being the unwilling recipient of the father's golden shower, Danaë becomes a figure of λόγος. She is the one who *counts*. She counts the sequence of events, metes out destinies according to the lawful calculus of time, proclaims the counterrhythmic interruption that can only forestall (so that Zeus and we may see it better) but not quash calamity. Hölderlin's mistranslation is in fact uncannily close to the Greek: καὶ Ζηνὸς ταμιεύεσκει . . . Ταμιεύω means to serve as treasurer, not in the sense of collecting and hoarding gold within a thesaurus, but in the sense of dealing out and dispensing. *She* dispenses, *to* and *for* the father.[10] Danaë teaches the father what his very own golden flow, γονὰς χρυσορύτος, means. Hölderlin notes that when the names of the gods are spoken *seriously* (*Im Ernste*), σπουδαῖος, Zeus must mean the father of time, or father of the earth. Yet the genitive is more subjective than objective, inasmuch as Zeus belongs to time and to the earth. Hölderlin

107

David Farrell Krell

explains: 'For it is his [Zeus'] character to be in contrast to the eternal tendency, that is, to reverse the *striving from this world into another world* in such
a way that it becomes *a striving from another world into this one*' (2: 372, emphasis added). A god striving *to enter into* this world? Well, he was *there*, with her,
and for reasons that were *not* arbitrary. Perhaps an unheard-of fidelity under-
lies all of Zeus' flamboyant betrayals; perhaps a faith undergirds all his infi-
delities; perhaps a truth that is a troth will accompany him to the death? Ever
since *Hyperion*, this striving of the absolute to enter into the world of mortals
had fascinated Hölderlin. In an early draft of the novel, a sage tells the hero:

> Allow me to speak in a human way. When our originally infinite
> essence first came to suffer something, and when the free and full
> force encountered its first barriers, when Poverty mated with
> Superfluity, Love came to be. Do you ask when it was? Platos says it
> was on the day Aphrodite was born. At the moment therefore when
> the world of beauty commenced for us, when we became conscious,
> we became finite. Now we profoundly feel the confinement of our
> essence, and inhibited force strains impatiently against its fetters. Yet
> there is something in us that gladly preserves the fetters – for if the
> divine in us were bound to no resistance, we would know nothing
> outside ourselves and therefore nothing about ourselves either. And to
> know nothing of oneself, not to feel that we are in being, and to be
> annihilated – these are one and the same.
>
> (1: 513)

The categorial reversal of time discussed above, along with this reversal of
the eternal tendency to an earthbound, temporal tendency, may best be understood through a reading of the myth of Plato's *Statesman* (269d 5–274e 3). I mean
the myth of the eras of C(h)ronos and Zeus, the myth that accompanied
Hölderlin throughout the gestation-period of *Hyperion*. Cronos' categorial
reversal of time returns to the earth and to the Chaos of mortal bodies – especially the bodies of mortal women – who dwell in the gap. For the human
body initiates the time of what 'Der Rhein' calls *uralte Verwirrung*, 'primal confusion' – in *Statesman*, τῆς παλαιᾶς ἀναρμοστίας, 'the ancient dishar-
monies' (273d 1). If 'golden' means the beams of the sun, the sun of the
Golden Age, and if the light of the sun pertains to the great sky gods, Ouranos,
Cronos and Zeus, those beams must be refracted by a lunar reckoning.

> That happens always and only when time is counted in suffering [*wenn
> die Zeit im Leiden gezählt wird*], because then our heart of hearts follows
> with much greater compassion the course of time, and thus compre-

108

hends the simple passing of the hours – but this is nothing like an intellectual deduction of the future on the basis of the present.

(2: 372)

These remarkable lines, which are lines in search of a more appropriate relation to time for both mortals and the father of time, suggest that the infidelity of the gods and mortals alike induces suffering. Danaë gives Zeus the time of day, and in so doing gives him the time of night. Zeus comes to suffer for it. Presumably, he could have quit the dungeon – that most narrow of narrow houses – at any time. But he was *there*, with her, and for reasons that were *not* arbitrary. We may be assured that it was his choice, his *will*, his *liberum arbitrium*, to be there, to stay for a time; but it was a time *she* would count, she in her very special house. If he proved fickle, if he persisted in moving house, it was always only in order – like Old Faithful itself – to learn, through suffering, about time and fidelity. Myth has it that all of Zeus' mortal women were children of Niobe, and that he was seeking from them a son who would protect him and his fellow gods from the fate that Prometheus had predicted for them all.

From here, of course, one would have to proceed to the (impossible) third section of the 'Notes to *Antigone*'. One would have to make sense of so many (impossible) things: of the god who becomes present in the figure of death, of the 'deadly factical' nature of the word in Greek tragedy, as opposed to the 'mortifyingly factical' word of our own presumably 'more humane' era, in which a 'more genuine Zeus' reigns; of the course of nature, so inimical to human beings, a course now '*compelled more decisively back to the earth*' (emphasis added); of the Hesperian fatherland and its need to grasp, understand and depict clearly, along with its peculiarly dismal form of suffering – from its lack of destiny; and finally of *Antigone* as a republican play, in the sense of a celebration of the French Republic, caught up in tumult and listing awkwardly to port (*aus linkischem Gesichtspunkt*). All this is too demanding. Besides, Hegel said it all showed signs of derangement, as he urged Hölderlin's editors to omit *The Mourning Plays of Sophocles* from Hölderlin's collected works.

Let me therefore try to come to a conclusion. In the fifth choral song, immediately prior to the *caesura* (Tiresias/Creon), Hölderlin sees the conflict between Antigone and Creon presented in the purest possible fashion, in which these two characters differ 'solely with regard to time'. Their conflict and suffering arise from the unalterable turning of time (*wie . . . sich die Zeit wendet*), a turning we first see when Haemon rushes off the scene, heading for his botched patricide but successful suicide, and which we later see when Creon survives Antigone – differing from her by grace of time alone (*nur der Zeit nach verschieden*), she the loser simply because she presides over the beginning, he the winner – in the sense of *Winner Take Nothing* – simply because he succeeds upon her time, as upon his own son's time. Sometimes it seems that sheer succession suffices for tragedy. Meanwhile, the fifth choral song places Creon in the family-line of Lycurgus, Pentheus and Oedipus. It places Antigone in the family-line of Niobe, Danaë, Semele, Io and Persephone. Whereas in *Oedipus the King* the words of both chorus and dialogue are only *mediately* factical, inasmuch as the word, in proper Greek fashion, first becomes deadly when it seizes 'the more sensuous body', *Antigone* points toward a later, more Western or Hesperian age, when the word becomes *immediate*, attacking 'the more spiritual body'. 'The Greek tragic word is factically deadly, because the human body that it seizes is actually killed.' In our own Hesperian time, by contrast, 'because we stand under the more genuine Zeus', who does not merely dwell between earth and the savage world of the dead but compels the course of nature (which is always inimical to humankind) more decisively back to the earth, the materials and modes of tragedy shift. If the principal tendency of Greek tragedy endeavours to get hold of itself (*sich fassen zu können*), so that it may not perish utterly in the flames of passion (what the earlier letter to Böhlendorff called 'the fire of heaven' [2: 912]), the Hesperian tragedy struggles for aptness of depiction and skill of representation, inasmuch as its weakness is its lack of destiny, *das Schiksaallose*, δύσμορον, to wit, the misfortune of having somehow passed by its destiny. Admittedly, Hölderlin's use of *Schiksaal* seems especially here to cross with *Geschik*, skill of representation. The factically deadly word, the word that seizes the body in rage, 'actual murder through words', is eminently Greek. By contrast, in modernity, in the land of evening, the word seems rather to mortify, to kill the spirit by poisonous draughts. *Oedipus at Colonus*, which induces awe by means of its words uttered from an inspired mouth, seems more suited to the Hesperian age than to the athletically Greek age, the tragic age, whereas *Oedipus the King* seizes the body. It hangs or enucleates its nexus of characters.[11]

At this point in the long third and final section of the 'Notes', Hölderlin turns from the suffering of heroes to the suffering of gods, and especially of the father, who betrays one mortal woman after another, but who never escapes from the house of Niobe. Zeus' suffering – his captivation and captivity – enables him to plight his troth and then to hear the hours, *his* hours, the golden, being counted. One must concede that divine infidelity has as such dropped out of Hölderlin's discussion – surprisingly, inasmuch as Antigone seems to be a victim of divine manipulation as much as her brother and father were. The god in question is not Zeus, however, but Zeus' brother Hades. The fourth and fifth choral songs identify Antigone as a girl torn in two by the gods of love and death. She is the sister–daughter who finds her brother-and-lover in death. One must wonder whether divine betrayal is not even more readily remembered here than in *Oedipus the King*. But now to the sufferings of gods.

In *Antigone* the gods' names are systematically translated by Hölderlin in a 'livelier' fashion, that is, more earnestly. He had already begun to do this in *Oedipus*, by designating Hades as 'hell', the sphinx as 'songstress' and Apollo as 'the god of the plague', all these names redolent of a certain infidelity, indeed, of an infernal betrayal. Yet in *Antigone*, on which Hölderlin worked especially diligently in 1803, the gods' names are almost always transliterated.[12] As we have heard, Zeus is often transliterated as 'lord' or 'father' of time and the earth. Ares is 'spirit of battle', Nike 'victory'. Hades is 'the future site of the dead', 'the world of the dead', 'the god of hell', 'the god of the dead', or quite simply, 'the Beyond'. Dike is 'conscience' (*Gewissen*), Olympus 'the heaven of my fathers'. The Erinyes are 'rage', 'the mockers' and 'the women who judge'. Eros is 'the spirit of love and peace', Aphrodite 'divine beauty', Persephone 'a wrathful-compassionate light' (*zornigmitleidig . . . ein Licht*). Bacchus is 'the god of joy', Iacchus 'the jubilant lord' (3: 439–40). Finally, Deo, or Demeter, is 'the impenetrable' (*Undurchdringliches*).

Many of these transliterations appear in the sixth choral song (2: 359–60), which opens with the apostrophe *Nahmenschöpfer*, πολυώνυμε, 'Creator of names', 'God of many names', as Elizabeth Wyckoff has it. The god in question is the new Zeus, Dionysos, the jubilant lord, the god of joy. Is Dionysian polynomy related to betrayal, oblivion and categorial reversal? Could it be that all these things, and every tragedy, invoke the sufferings of the god Dionysos? Could it be that every strange house and every strange family of tragedy is the house of Semele and Zeus, the house of the moon and the earth? Among these lively translations of the names of the gods, perhaps the two most uncanny ones are those of Persephone and Demeter. Persephone, who is both dark and light, is *zornigmitleidig*, as furious as Oedipus and as compassionate as Jocasta. Perhaps *Persephone* is a name for the monstrous coupling and separation of gods and mortals, a name for the intense pleasures of κάθαρσις as such? And the mother of Persephone, Demeter? Why are the Eleusinian plains of Demeter, Mother Earth, where the polynomial gods gather, more vitally translated as 'the impenetrable'? Has not the famous second choral song already defined human beings as the creatures who tirelessly plough the earth, irritating and scratching open her surface? Δηοῦς ἐν κόλποις, 'Gathering in the bosom of the goddess', sings Sophocles' chorus, whereas Hölderlin reads that bosom as *Undurchdringliches*. Κόλπος is the bosom or lap upon which a child or a domestic animal lies. For Aristophanes, in *The Birds*, τὰ ὑπὸ κόλπου means all things aphrodisiac; in medical literature the phrase means the vagina or the hollows of the womb; in poetry it is a metaphor for the tomb, 'the body concealed in the loins of the earth'. Impenetrable at last.

If not outright betrayal and infidelity, Dionysian polynomy and treachery (Dionysos to Pentheus: 'Would you like to *see* the women?') do seem to retain something of categorial reversal. As Creon slips off into the Hesperian west, to a more humane time, a time of 'firm opinion born of divine destiny', and as the play *Antigone* becomes more political, depicting a conflict of persons who have been stylised or formalised – by Hegel, among others – to represent a certain status or role, only an echo of Greek tragedy proper remains. Hölderlin calls the characters of Greek tragedy proper 'ideal configurations in struggle for the truth'. The dialogues and choruses of Hesperian tragedy become more relentless (*unaufhaltsamer*) and more significative (*deutend*), while those of Greek tragedy as such remain more violent (*gewaltsamer*) and more interruptive (*haltend*). Yet in both cases, if I understand Hölderlin aright, the dialogues and choruses of tragedy 'give to infinite strife the direction or the force to be the *suffering* organs [*leidende Organe*] of the divinely wrestling body [*des göttlichringenden Körpers*] (2: 374). The polynomial words of tragedy, whether factically murderous or mortifying, are *organs*. We should understand these organs as organisational factors, attuned to διάνοια, yet solicited by the more aorgic realm of nature. These dianoetic organs, the dialogues and choruses of any given tragic drama, flesh out the body of the suffering godhead, Dionysos. They dare not go missing, 'because even in the tragically infinite configuration the god cannot communicate himself to the body absolutely immediately'. Rather, the god must be 'comprehendingly grasped', or 'gotten under control by the intellect' (*verständlich gefaßt*); or, better, he must be 'appropriated in a living way' (*lebendig zugeeignet*). How does such appropriation take place? The factical word permeates the play from beginning to end, not so much in any particular utterance, but in the very nexus (*Zusammenhang*) of characters and incidents, under the influence of a certain form of reasoning (*Vernunftform*). The latter may not be the διάνοια to which we are accustomed; nor will it be the familiar and reassuring intellectual intuition of the philosophers. It will 'take shape in the frightful muse of a tragic time' (2: 375).

We have already heard something about that higher nexus – in the Aristotelian context of the aporia of law, equity and justice. Yet what about the nexus of the godhead, of the suffering organs of the god? What are we to make of the incapacity of the god to communicate himself to the body absolutely immediately? What can such an incapacity mean in our more humane time, the time of a more appropriate human and mortal temporality? If it belongs to the essence of Zeus to reverse the tendency toward eternity to an earthbound drive, does a more appropriate and genuine Zeus become less like himself, reverting to the sky, or does he become more authentically earthbound than ever? One might interpret the mystery Christologically, as the problem of an incarnate son who has need of a mediating word, a holy spirit. However, in a more violent time, a time of incessant interruption (and I leave it to my readers to weigh the time we share on these Hölderlinian scales), one may be cast back to the dungeon in which Danaë ticks off the hours for the father of time. Zeus needs her to dispense his gold. She is the *Es* of *Es gibt Zeit*. His struggling body does not have every organ it needs. Well, he was *there*, with her, and for reasons that were *not* arbitrary. Presumably, the god dreams of Danaë in the way Oedipus dreamed of Jocasta, the way the chorus of Theban elders dreamed of Antigone, the way Empedocles dreamed of Panthea and Pausanias, and the way Dionysos dreamed and fumed above the smouldering grave of impenetrable Semele.

And what way is that? Let us agree to call it *excessive*. *Zu innig, zu einzig*, 'too intense, too singular', as Hölderlin says of Empedocles. Here the word *zu* carries the force – the excessive force – of life itself: ζωή, Ζεύς, Ζάς, ζα-.[13]

*   *   *

An obsessive micromaniac reading such as this one – rummaging through a few houses in the universe of tragic being – clearly must respond to the diametrically opposed difficulties of reading Aristotle and Hölderlin. The Aristotelian corpus seems so familiar that we manipulate its concepts and texts with scarcely a thought, Hölderlin's so utterly strange that we grasp at straws, accepting any motif that promises to get us through the text. If this has all been a big mistake, I can be pleased; if I have made a few little errors here and there, that will not be enough.

Aristotle assures us that chance (τύχη) must be subaltern to both mind and nature. Chance nevertheless disrupts both νοῦς and φύσις, as though in counterrhythmic interruption of entelechy. The subaltern position of chance only aggravates its impact on a universe where neither mind nor nature was clever enough to exclude it. (Recall that even Plato's δημιουργός was not so clever.) If nature built houses, says Aristotle, she would proceed precisely in the way that intelligent art proceeds. Nature builds no houses, though she helps to form families and households. Some of these, perchance, build very special houses, houses in which, as Aristotle also says, 'mistakes are possible' (199a 35). They are the houses that spawn tragedy.

In a more violent time, a time in which the body is once again factically seized, divinity and mortality collide, then draw apart. Yet the father of time and the earth inherits mortality from his children; from hence his will be a time for the body and for words. In a more human time, divinity departs, and there is a certain nostalgia for its return. Yet that return will always be a turning toward the earth, time and mortality. 'The fire of spirit will mount toward the heights, but love and pain [*l'amour et la douleur*], which are the lot of mortals, bend that flame back to the earth [*courbent la flamme vers la terre*].'[14]

David Farrell Krell

Once installed, soon enthralled, divinity will learn mortality, will achieve the supreme consciousness that is finitude. The suffering god – not altogether without organs, yet never with all the organs – will be ineluctably *en famille*. Whenever gods need families and households, someone somewhere tolls a bell, sounds a deathknell (*glas*), counts the strokes of the hours for all divinity. We may rest assured that, whether in golden orgasmic ecstasy or the throes of death, divinity will always have zeroed in on a small number of houses. Divinity will never quit those mortal houses, will never survive that small number of houses in a universe of tragedy. At least, that is what the stories of the tragedians and the thoughts of thinkers have always told us.

Notes

1 For the Greek text of Aristotle's *Poetics* I have used the Oxford Classical Text, *Aristotelis De arte poetica liber*, edited by Rudolf Kassel (Oxford: Oxford University Press, 1965); I have also used English translations by Richard Janko (Indianapolis: Hackett Publishing, 1987) and Ingram Bywater, in Richard McKeon, ed., *The Basic Works of Aristotle* (New York: Random House, 1966), 1455–87, along with the French translation by Michel Magnien, Aristote, *Poétique* (Paris: Livre de Poche, n.d.). For the Greek text of Sophocles I have used the Loeb Classical Library edition, translated by F. Storr (Cambridge, MA: Harvard University Press, 1981), and the translations in the University of Chicago series edited by David Grene and Richmond Lattimore, first published in 1954. On the Hölderlin edition I have used, see note 3, below.

2 Kevin Thomas Miles, *Razing Ethical Stakes: Tragic Transgression in Aristotle's Equitable Action*, PhD dissertation, DePaul University, 1998.

3 Friedrich Hölderlin, *Sämtliche Werke und Briefe*, edited by Michael Knaupp, 3 vols (Munich: Carl Hanser, 1992) 2: 54–5, cited henceforth in the body of my text.

4 *Physics* 8: 9, *Metaphysics* Λ: 6, *On the Soul* 1: 3, and elsewhere. See also Jacques Derrida, 'Ousia and Gramme', in *Margins of Philosophy*, translated by Alan Bass (Chicago: University of Chicago Press, 1982), 29–67, esp. 52–3:

> This is what will not budge from Aristotle to Hegel. The prime mover, as 'pure act,' . . . is pure presence. As such, it animates all movement by means of the desire it inspires. It is the good, and the supremely desirable. Desire is the desire of presence. Like movement, Hegel calls the *telos* that puts movement in motion, and that orients becoming toward itself, the absolute concept or subject. The transformation of parousia into *self*-presence, and the transformation of the supreme being into a subject thinking itself, and assembling itself near itself in knowledge, does not interrupt the fundamental tradition of Aristotelianism. The concept as absolute subjectivity itself thinks itself, is for itself and near itself, has no exterior, and it assembles, erasing them, its time and its difference in self-presence. This may be put in Aristotle's language: *noesis noeseos*, the thought of thought, the pure act, the prime mover, the lord who, himself thinking himself, is subjugated to no

114

objectivity, no exteriority, remaining immobile in the infinite movement of the circle and of the return to self.

It will not be possible for me to show here how the structure of the trace, writing and *différance* disturbs the continuity of the metaphysical tradition. Allow me only to suggest that such a disturbance reveals a deeper continuity than that represented by metaphysics, namely that of *tragic thinking*, extending perhaps from the time of Gilgamesh to our own era. To be sure, that continuity is all about counterrhythmic interruption.

5 The 'Notes' are to be found after the respective translations in Knaupp's edition at 2: 309–16 and 2: 369–76. Because the 'Notes' involve so few pages, and because my own reading will proceed rather directly through these dense pieces, I will cite pages only rarely. While I am grateful for Thomas Pfau's translation of these pieces, I have worked only with the German text. See Friedrich Hölderlin, *Essays and Letters on Theory*, edited and translated by Thomas Pfau (Albany: State University of New York Press, 1988).

6 The editors refer us to two of Hölderlin's letters, one to Schiller dated 4 September 1795, the other to Niethammer dated 24 February 1796 (2: 595–6, 614–15). The letter to Schiller is particularly illuminating: 'My displeasure with myself and with what surrounds me has driven me into abstraction. I am trying to develop for myself the idea of an infinite progression in philosophy. I am trying to show that the relentless demand that must be made on every system, namely, the unification of subject and object in an absolute – in an ego or in whatever one wants to call it – is possible aesthetically in intellectual intuition. Theoretically it is possible only through an infinite approximation, as in the squaring of the circle. I am thus trying to show that in order to realize a system of thought an immortality is necessary – every bit as necessary as it is for a system of action. I believe that I can prove in this way to what extent the skeptics are right, and to what extent not.' See also the important statement in 'Seyn, Urtheil, Modalität', 2: 50.

7 For a discussion of Hölderlin's *Empedokles*, see the first two chapters of my *Lunar Voices: Of Tragedy, Poetry, Fiction, and Thought* (Chicago: University of Chicago Press, 1995), entitled 'The Sensuality of Tragedy, the Tragedy of Sensuality' and 'Stuff · Thread · Point · Fire: Hölderlin's Dissolution'. These two chapters also discuss the secondary literature on Hölderlin and tragedy in a way that these brief notes will not. Allow me here only to express my pleasure that Françoise Dastur's wonderful work *Tragédie et modernité* has been reissued: see Dastur, *Hölderlin: le retournement natal* (La Versanne: encre marine, 1997), 25–96.

8 In the corrections that Hölderlin made to the first edition, *wem* is changed to *wenn*. I have nevertheless preferred the first version, because of the parallel with *er* in the next line.

9 Pasolini's script to his magnificent film reads at this point as follows:

Jocasta draws close to him, and presses his hand in hers. In that moment, he would seem almost to have triumphed over destiny.
JOCASTA: *You see? Don't think any more on these atrocities which have obsessed you these last few days . . .*

115

David Farrell Krell

OEDIPUS: *Yes, but there is one thing more which terrifies me . . . The idea of mak-*
ing love to my mother . . . This still horrifies me . . .
JOCASTA: *But why? Why? We are at the mercy of fate, and no one can ever fore-*
see what is going to happen next! The wisest course is to pin our faith on for-
tune, and live as we can . . . And why does the idea of making love to your
mother hold such terror for you? Why? Think how many men must have made
love to their mothers in their dreams!

These words drip into the silent assembly as a revelation. The councillors look
with shocked expressions at Jocasta and Oedipus; but there are some amongst
them who are smiling: a faint, derisive smile born of the realization that here is
something very much out of the ordinary, a scandal in fact.

JOCASTA: *Who has not dreamt of making love to his mother? And does he live in*
horror of his dream? Of course not, unless he wants to clutter his life with use-
less suffering.

Pier Paolo Pasolini, *Oedipus Rex*, translated by John Mathews (London: Lorrimer
Publishing, 1971), 92.

10 Danaë's own father, Acrisius, had imprisoned his only daughter in a dungeon, for
she had already been seduced by his twin brother Proetus. The oracle had told
Acrisius that Danaë's future son, Perseus, would kill Acrisius – very much in the
way that Io's father, and Zeus himself, had been warned about Io's race or stock,
which many generations down the line would produce Zeus-destroying Heracles.

11 It will be clear from the above that I disagree with the judgement of Philippe
Lacoue-Labarthe, followed in this regard by Françoise Dastur, that in Hölderlin's
view *Antigone* is the 'most Greek' of tragedies. I believe that all the evidence, early
and late, shows that in Hölderlin's view *Oedipus the King* is the most profoundly
Greek of Greek tragedies. Perhaps Lacoue-Labarthe and Dastur are confusing the
character of Antigone with the play itself. To the extent that the time of Creon follows upon the time of Antigone, she is of course an utterly Greek character,
whereas Creon is more Hesperian. Yet the properly Hesperian play is *Oedipus at
Colonus*. And the properly Greek play is *Oedipus the King*, whose word is mediate,
but also murderously factical. See Philippe Lacoue-Labarthe, 'La césure du spéculatif', in *L'imitation des modernes: Typographies II* (Paris: Galilée, 1986), 52–3 (translated by Robert Eisenhauer as 'The Caesura of the Speculative' in *Typographies:
Mimesis, Philosophy, Politics*, edited by Christopher Fynsh [Cambridge, MA: Harvard
University Press, 1989]); see also Françoise Dastur in *Hölderlin: le retournement natal*
(cited in note 7, above), 26, 66, 93–6.

12 This may in fact be a part of that 'emphasis on the Oriental', which the Greek
world wanted to deny, but which Hölderlin insisted on emphasising (2: 925).
Indeed, one of the ways of defining those special households of tragedy more specifically is to note their thoroughgoing 'Orientalism'.

13 See D.F. Krell, *Daimon Life: Heidegger and Life-Philosophy* (Bloomington: Indiana
University Press, 1992), 14–16, on the 'excessive' prefix.

14 Dastur, *Hölderlin: le retournement natal*, 51.

6

Hölderlin's theatre[1]

Philippe Lacoue-Labarthe

The very simple hypothesis which I am forming, the justification for which I want to sketch out here, is that when Hölderlin tries to write of theatre (and on theatre), it is actually a matter of *theatre* itself.

In order to develop this hypothesis, it is clearly necessary to dispel the myth (or myths, but I am thinking of the most powerful amongst these, which is the one put about by Heidegger); that is to say, one must not deny the obvious.

Hölderlin's career – if indeed there is any 'career' – lasts near enough fifteen years: from 1791, the date of the first journal publication of his poems, to 1806, the date of his incarceration at the Autenrieth clinic at Tübingen. During this period Hölderlin, who had, upon leaving the Stift in 1793, refused (like Hegel and Schelling) to take up the ministry, lived chiefly by his wits: the little family money that his mother grudgingly allowed him, the disastrous private tutelages. His only chance of freedom, and that is to say his only chance of avoiding being a minister, lay in 'living by his pen'. Yet even if he was recognised as a great poet from very early on (from 1799 by August Wilhelm Schlegel, who was then one of the authorities of the critical 'avant-garde'), and even if he was published by Schiller, poetry was not enough to support him. Barring his obtaining a university position – Schiller, then all-powerful, refused to support his application for a post in Hellenics at Jena – Hölderlin had no choice but to practise the only two forms which could at that time guarantee economic survival, granted that one would meet success: the novel and the theatrical drama. The only two books he published during his lifetime were *Hyperion* (1797 and 1799) and the translations of Sophocles (1804).

However, the success of *Hyperion* was one of esteem, nothing more. And everything leads us to believe that it was for this reason that Hölderlin turned to the theatre, with the hope, certainly, of being performed in Weimar (Schiller, again). In 1798 he began drafting a 'modern tragedy', *Empedocles*. All told, until the publication of this work in 1804, he spent six years busying himself with theatrical drama. This is not altogether negligible.

But it is not enough to dispel the myth or to re-establish a rudimentary truth. One still has to read, and with a minimum of probity, the texts. All of them.

And insofar as it is a matter of theatrical drama, there are thus two 'groups'.

The *Empedocles* group, first of all – which is always privileged under the pre-text that Hölderlin is its 'author' and that it includes, in itself or in its margins, some of the most important of his 'poetological' essays (all, moreover, incomplete): the two first versions of the play and, with respect to the third version, a draft of the opening act, plans, a sketch of the rest, not to mention, of course, the letters from the two years which span this attempt (1798–1800).

Then the 'Sophocles' group – which, of course, also holds our interest, but above all due to the 'novel' experience of translation to which Hölderlin is committed (not, it needs to be said, exclusively of Sophocles: he also tries his hand at translations of Lucan, Euripides, Pindar), and to the philosophy of art and history – they are entirely inseparable – which he elaborates during this period: the two tragedies with their 'Remarks' (a preface to which Hölderlin alludes was either lost or never written), brief commentaries on the Pindar fragments, very close to the 'Remarks', some letters.

But there is, as we know, a link between these two groups: it is because of the failure of his own 'modern tragedy' that Hölderlin undertakes, quite deliberately, to translate Sophocles and these two tragedies in particular: *Oedipus Tyrannus* and *Antigone*. In Hölderlin's eyes, these two tragedies are models – an idea which comes from Aristotle, who held Sophocles to be the greatest and most perfect of tragedians: the first, *Oedipus*, is a model of modern tragedy; the second, *Antigone*, a model of properly Greek tragedy. It is, moreover, in order to bring out this trait – the innately 'Western' character of Greece – that Hölderlin twists the translation of *Antigone* in an extremely violent way, it being understood that his general concern is to wrest tragedy from its neo-classical translation–adaptation–interpretation. Although he hopes to get 'himself' staged at Weimar – that is where he sends the two works as soon as they are published by Wilmans – the principal villain of the piece is Goethe, or the Schiller of *On Tragedy*, and that is to say of the French (Corneillian) and moral (Kantian) interpretation of tragedy. (It is pointless to insist, I think, upon the 'reception' the work received in Weimar.)

Now, although everyone knows that this is the link which leads from *Empedocles* to the translation of Sophocles, no one, or nearly no one, has wanted to take account of it. Which means: no one has seen, although it is glaringly obvious, that within an identical project of theatrical drama (Hölderlin uses the word *modern* to describe this tragic drama), this so-called 'link' is a rupture, a radical rupture, first of all, and very simply, in that it opens onto the very root of theatre, and that is to say onto Attic tragedy. The 'return to Sophocles' does not, for Hölderlin, mean some sort of 'nostalgia for Greece'. It means: a return to the ground of theatricality.

It is none the less clear – and Hölderlin himself says as much – that what wrecks *Empedocles* is its lack of theatricality. And it is here that things begin to come together.

In what is essential, there are, it seems to me, two reasons for this lack of theatricality (I am gathering together, somewhat brutally, the result of lengthy analyses which it would be impossible to reconstruct here):

- The first is that, despite his desire for genuine drama, Hölderlin is immediately disposed only to an Idea of tragedy. Idea is taken here in the strictest sense, the sense which speculative Idealism has given to the word. This Idea – such, at least, is the formula in which, for Hölderlin, it is condensed – dictates that tragedy, in its essence, is 'the metaphor of an intellectual intuition' (*Essays*, 83). Which means, first of all, in the language of the time: the sensible presentation (*Darstellung*) of the Absolute. This definition owes much to the brief but decisive analyses of Sophocles' *Oedipus* put forward by Schelling four years earlier in the last but one of the *Letters on Dogmatism and Criticism*: for the Greeks tragedy was the conciliatory presentation of contradictions of Reason in the Kantian sense (and that is to say in the meta-physical sense), and the promise of a liberation from Necessity (the tragic hero accepts punishment for a crime which he has not committed and, in succumbing, thus affirms his inalienable freedom). Equally, this definition anticipates the meaning that Hegel, a few years later in his article on natural law, will attribute to Aeschylus' *Eumenides*, at that time emblematic for him (later on, it will be *Antigone*): tragedy is the presentation of 'the eternal tragedy that the Absolute plays with itself'.[2]

It is clear that this interpretation has two distinguishing features:

(1) Tragedy is the work of art absolutely speaking, the absolute *organon* (the *opus metaphysicum par excellence*, Nietzsche will say much later *à propos* Wagner's *Tristan*[3]), because it is the presentation of the very tragedy of the Absolute, and that is to say of the Absolute as the contradiction and, indissociably, necessity of its presentation or of its manifestation, which, dialectically, is its death. A brief note of Hölderlin's indicates that in tragedy, 'the sign . . . $= 0$' (*Essays*, 89). The sign is understood here as the sign of the Absolute: the hero. That it equals zero means that he dies, and dies from the very fact of what he is: the sign of the Absolute or, more exactly, the Absolute as sign. Nothing presents the presentation of the Absolute better than tragedy.

(2) If this is what tragedy is as such, then this is because its very structure is contradictory. At least the suspicion begins to arise, in the

119

Schlegels in particular, that the opposition of the stage and the choral space is not unimportant, if only with regard to the opposition between the two principles constitutive – and emblematic – of the Greek 'moment' or 'spirit': the future opposition between the Apollinian and the Dionysian. But it is, above all and in truth almost exclusively, because the tragic schema, Aristotle's *muthos*, is the straightforward development of a structuring oxymoron: Oedipus, a guilty innocent. On this same note, Hölderlin states that 'the significance of tragedies is most easily explained by way of paradox' (*Essays*, 89).

• Whence the second reason for *Empedocles'* lack of theatricality: its schema is *this* same schema, which has nothing of the schema about it, and that is to say what Aristotle calls the *sunthesis ton pragmaton*, the composition of actions. *Empedocles'* scenario is nothing other than a speculative scenario in Greek-Platonic mode, which means: its hero is the philosopher-king (*basileus*). It is enough to read the synopsis of the start of acts I and V in the so-called *Frankfurt Plan*:

> Empedocles, his temperament and his philosophy long since dis-
> posed to the hatred of civilisation, to contempt for all determined
> matters, all interest directed to this or that object – – – – – –
> – a
> mortal enemy of all one-sided existence, and thus also unsatisfied,
> edgy, long-suffering even in really beautiful relations, because they
> are particular kinds of relations, ones that are felt only in the great
> accord with all living things which truly satisfy him, simply
> because he cannot live in them and love them with an
> omnipresent heart, like a god, and freely and expansively, like a
> god, merely because, as soon as his heart and his thought embrace
> anything at hand, he is bound to the law of succession –
> Empedocles takes particular offence at a festival of the
> Agrigentians <. . .>.
>
> . . . .
>
> Empedocles prepares himself for his death. The contingent
> causes of his decision have now fallen from him and he looks upon
> it as a necessity of his innermost being . . . <etc.>
>
> (*WB*, 567, 568)

One cannot make theatrical drama with this sort of 'action', which is, at the very most, a sort of lyric 'drama' or oratorio without music, an assuredly sublime genre, as Kant had suggested, but one hardly conducive to the stage. Besides, Hölderlin himself looked to define a 'tragic ode', pure generic monstrosity.

Hölderlin felt it so strongly that all the revisions he attempted were essentially directed toward the construction of a schema: the introduction of an 'adversary', for example, unfortunately understood as an adverse principle, in order to introduce a little antagonism to the proceedings. But nothing comes of this: it remained a quasi-monologic and static exercise in eloquence, a sort of politico-metaphysical demonstration (the renunciation of royalty as pure sovereignty, as aspiration to the Absolute – or visitation of the Absolute – right up to death) in the style of Jacobean or Directoire aesthetics. (Michel Deutsch clearly recognised this when he wrote his *Thermidor* on the basis of *Empedocles'* framework.[4])

• Finally, there is a third reason, but one which is of a piece with the two others: the only attention that Hölderlin does pay to the conditions of theatrical representation is subordinated to the Platonic interpretation of *mimesis* (*Darstellung*) as a mode of dramatic statement (*lexis*), and that is to say, from the exclusive viewpoint of the speaker – in this case the tragic author – as a mode of indirect statement through an interposed person. Which Plato condemned without hesitation, as everyone knows.

It is precisely such an attention which manifests itself and exposes itself, in dialectical mode, in the first part ('General Ground') of 'The Ground for Empedocles'. None the less, one quickly sees there that it is his own difficulty – and it is immense – as a poet which Hölderlin is seeking to regulate on this basis: the indirect statement alone allows the most profound interior, the interior most fully alive to the divine – but for precisely this reason 'inexpressible', too infinitely submerged, too empty or gaping and, Hölderlin adds, 'at the limits of nefas', of impiety (this, as he is perfectly well aware, is the danger which awaits him) – to express itself concretely, as Hegel will say, in an analogic or symbolic 'foreign matter'.

It would be necessary to comment on this text at length. I will restrict myself to citing a few lines, which would merit being left to resonate in their own language:

> It is the deepest intensity <*die tiefste Innigkeit*> which expresses itself in the tragic dramatic poem. The tragic ode presents inwardness [*das Innige*] also in the most positive differences, in actual oppositions, although these oppositions are present merely in form and as the immediate language of sensation. The tragic poem veils intensity still more in the presentation, expresses it in more marked differences, because it expresses a deeper intensity, a

more infinite divinity. The sensation no longer expresses itself immediately, it is no longer the poet and his own experience which appears, even though every poem, and thus also the tragic poem, must have come from the poetic life and actuality, from the poet's own world and soul, because otherwise the right truth will everywhere be lacking. <. . .> In the tragic dramatic poem the divine, which the poet experiences in his world, also expresses itself, the tragic dramatic poem is also an image of living things, of that which is and was present in his life; but to the extent that this image of intensity denies and must deny its ultimate ground insofar as everywhere it must increasingly approach the symbol, the more infinite, the more unspeakable, the more at the limit of *nefas* is the intensity, the more rigorously and coldly must the image of man and the element of his sensation be differentiated in order to fix the sensation within its limits, the less can the image immediately express the sensation, it must deny form as well as matter[:] matter must be a bolder and more alien analogon <*Gleichnis*> and example, form must instead take the character of opposition and separation. Another world, alien events, alien characters, but like every bolder analogy, all the more intensely [*inniger*] adapted to the basic matter, heterogeneous only in outer form, for if this intense [*innige*] affinity of the analogon with the matter, the characteristic intensity in which the ground of the image lies, were not visible, then its distance, its alien form, could not be explained.

(*Essays*, 51–2)

And I will simply add two brief remarks:
(1) The situation which Hölderlin is describing here as being that of the poet – infinite enthusiasm, *die unendliche Begeisterung*, suffocating *and* blasphemous – is precisely the situation he recognises in Sophocles, as the essence of tragic *hubris*, immoderation and transgression. This is particularly the case with Antigone.
(2) Under the principle of oppositions, and in the name of 'foreign matter', Hölderlin does indeed evoke 'another world, alien events, alien characters' (all elements, consequently, proper to an effective dramaturgy); but this 'similitude', he adds immediately, this analogical or symbolic similitude, is 'heterogeneous only in outer form'. The 'composition of actions', in other words, ought to remain simply formal for – and this is the explanation he gives – 'if this intense affinity of the symbol with the matter, the characteristic intensity in which the ground of the image

lies, were not evident, then its distance, its alien form, could no longer be explained'.

And therein lies the impasse: how to construct a theatrical drama from the mere representation of the destiny of poetic creation?

It is in order to make the move to theatre, as I have indicated, that Hölderlin moves to Sophocles. But if he moves to Sophocles, and not, for example, to Aeschylus or even to Euripides, translations of whom he had already sketched out – and if, in Sophocles, it is *Oedipus* or *Antigone* which he chooses as models or examples, this time in the strong sense, of tragedy – this decision comes from Aristotle, and that is to say from the only document that the Greeks bequeathed on the subject, if one can say this, of *tekhne tragike*. The move to Sophocles is *also* a move to Aristotle.[5]

Which in no way means that Hölderlin renounced the speculative – or in any case theological – interpretation of tragedy. Nothing of the sort, as we shall see. In his eyes, tragedy remains a mystic drama, or rather – the nuance is peremptory – the drama of the mystical. Which is just as much to say, as I will try to indicate, the drama of the theologico-political or, if you prefer, of speculative politics. But no more does this mean, conversely, that under the (more or less anti-Platonic) authority of Aristotle, which is a philosophical authority all the same, Hölderlin still persists in making tragedy a (or the) philosophical genre, and in making the tragic figure a hero of philosophy. Schelling inaugurates the lengthy and persistent tradition of philosophical hero-isation, of Oedipus or of Antigone (thus: Hegel and Kierkegaard, Nietzsche, Heidegger, even – negatively – Deleuze). Hölderlin does not write himself into this tradition. If he does address himself to Aristotle, it is because he finds in him the resource of a question which he admittedly formulates in a philosophical (in this case, transcendental) style, but which is *also* a technical question: on what condition is tragedy possible? Which immediately translates as: how to go about tragedy? Through this, Hölderlin arrives at the problematic of theatricality.

This is what is brought to the fore, under the light of a specifically modern preoccupation, in the opening of the 'Remarks on Oedipus':

> It will be good, in order to secure for today's poets, also at home, an existence in the city, to elevate poetry, also at home, given the difference of times and institutions, to the level of the *mekhane* of the Ancients.
>
> When being compared with those of the Greeks, other works of art too lack reliability; at least, they have been judged until today according to the impression they produce rather than according to

123

their lawful calculation and to the other methodical modes through which the beautiful is engendered. Modern poetry, however, lacks especially training and craftsmanship; indeed, it lacks a way of calculating and teaching its mode of operation, which, once learned, may always be capable of being repeated reliably in practice. As men, we must first of all come to realise that it is something, that is, that it is something which can be known by means (moyen) of its manifestation, that the way in which it is conditioned may be determined and learned. Such is the reason why – to say nothing of higher reasons – poetry is in special need of secure and characteristic delimitations.

(Essays, 101)

I suggested just now that Hölderlin makes the move to Sophocles when he realises that the poet (or the thinker, the philosopher) himself cannot make a tragic figure. Which does not simply mean: when he realises that, in order for there to be theatrical drama, the figure or the figures must be absolutely exterior to the author. It *also* means: when he realises that, essentially, a tragic figure only exists through a fault, in the sense of *hubris*, a crime – the transgression of an interdiction, if not of interdiction itself. That this fault is revealed through a *hamartia*, an error or a lie, is what Hölderlin learns from Aristotle. (I will come back to this in a moment.) It is this indication which guides his reading of the *muthoi* – of the 'fables', in Brecht's translation – of *Oedipus* and *Antigone*. But what it is that constitutes such a fault, what the fault is in its essence, Hölderlin does not learn from Aristotle. And, as paradoxical as it might seem, no more does he learn it from Sophocles. He *recognises* it in Sophocles – and only in the two tragedies that he considers exemplary – with a stunning operation in which it is the theologico-speculative or even religious interpretation of *katharsis* which allows the essence of the fault, and, by the same stroke, the finality of the tragedy, to be known.

In attacking things on this basis I am referring to the third part of each set of 'Remarks', where Hölderlin defines the essence of tragedy, and that is to say of tragic (re)presentation (*Darstellung*). Two formulations of this are proposed, one in terms of *Oedipus* and one in terms of *Antigone*. I recall these in order to recall the very precise terminology, before going on to try to describe this operation:

The presentation of the tragic rests above all on the fact that the monstrous[6] – how god and man are coupled, and how the power of nature and man's innermost being limitlessly become One in fury – can be conceived on the basis of the fact that the limitless becoming-one is purified through limitless separation.

(Essays, 107)

As has been hinted at in the remarks on *Oedipus*, the tragic presentation stems from the fact that the immediate God, all at One with man
(for the God of an apostle is more mediate, is the highest intellect in
highest spirit), that the *infinite* enthusiasm/possession by spirit, in separating itself saintly, conceives of itself infinitely, that is, in oppositions, in the consciousness which cancels consciousness, and that the
God is present in the figure of death.

(*Essays*, 113)

In what, therefore, does the operation consist? I will decompress these
remarks very schematically:

(1) The tragic fault, *hubris* or, as Hölderlin says, *nefas*, that same fault that
'The Ground for Empedocles' (almost) attributed to the tragic poet – and from
which the tragic poet had hoped to shield himself or to deliver himself in objectivity (tragedy in this case operates as a sort of *autokatharsis*) – this fault, then,
is *recognised* as the fault of the tragic figure – which is such, namely tragic, only
by itself.

In *Empedocles*, the fault was the poetico-speculative and meta-physical allure:
the infinite aspiration to the All-One, the metaphysical desire for death (or for
a metaphysical death), the affirmation of a sovereignty beyond all royalty. It was
a fine and great fault wherein, despite (or because of) his suffering, the poet's
complacency with regard to his situation and a sort of *delectatio morosa* un-
problematically find their bearings. The scenario of *Empedocles* was that of a
'melancholic' tragedy and, despite Hölderlin's best efforts, *Trauerspiel* ceaselessly
turned into *Trauergesang*, if I can use this word to translate the Greek elegy.

On the other hand, what Sophocles reveals, crucially, is that this fault is a
fault through and through, without grandeur or beauty – if not, all the same,
without sublimity: it is a sacrilege. Ideally metaphysical, the fault becomes concretely religious, and that is to say, since for the Greeks the two are indisso-
ciable, politico-religious. The fault lies not only in the self-importance of
self-affirmation (proper, as one knows, to tyranny), but in the dementia of self-
divinisation, in the madness of enthusiasm, in the *ungeheuer* (monstrous) coupling with God. Beginning with Antigone, tragic figures are mad. And that
which they act out, in the sense of *praxis*, that which their madness dictates, is
literally catastrophic.

(2) This is what explains, I indicate in passing, that *hamartia*, the mistake or
error of appreciation, is each time politico-religious in nature. Oedipus adopts
the posture of the priest-king, he 'interprets the oracle too literally' (where,
in coded language, the oracle suggests simply 'establishing a severe and precise
justice' and 'maintaining a good civil order', he takes things according to the
letter and enters into sacrificial logic: he seeks an expiatory victim). As for

125

Antigone, her error is to oppose *her* Zeus – on this point, Hölderlin deliberately alters the text – not to that of Creon, but to the Zeus of the City, to the legal Zeus, under whose authority Creon 'too formally' places himself. This is why her fault is instead to identify or to *compare* herself to the divine: descending into the tomb, she evokes the destiny of Niobe.

(3) According to this understanding, as we have seen, the fault is purified, and that is indeed what tragedy (re)presents: a *katharsis* of the fault.

In the case of Oedipus, a more Western or less Greek tragedy in Hölderlin's eyes – thus corresponding less to the destiny of modern *knowledge* (Oedipus/*oida*) – the *katharsis* lies in the form of a slow atonement, first of all 'insane quest for a consciousness', then 'wandering under the unthinkable': a-theistic exile, if one recalls line 661 of Sophocles' play. In contradistinction to the properly Greek tragic word, which is 'murderous' (*tödtlichfaktisch*), the modern tragic word is 'deadly' (*tödtenfaktisch*), touching not the body but the spirit. In *Antigone*, which is *antitheos*, 'the God is present in the figure of death' (*Essays*, 113).

Contrary, then, to what happens in Aristotle, where *katharsis* is a *function* of the tragedy, and a properly political function – it purges, more than it purifies, the two originary passions of the political or of its destruction (piety, which is the passion of association, but which always risks being that of fusion; and terror, which is the passion of dissociation; this is what practically the whole of the philosophico-political tradition has repeated) – contrary, then, to the functional interpretation of *katharsis*, Hölderlin interprets *katharsis* as the purification of tragic *pathos*. Basically, in his consideration of tragedy, he is uninterested in the spectator. Rather, *katharsis* is for him, in a certain way, the effect of *mimesis* (*Darstellung*), but it is an internal effect of (re)presentation, which is not the effect *of* representation. In the auditorium, if you like (and that is to say, in a more modern language), *katharsis* is transferred onto the stage. At least this appears to be the case.

(4) This final precaution is necessary because Hölderlin insists just as strongly, on the other hand, on the political significance of the two tragedies that he examines. For *Oedipus*, this is self-evident: it is the condemnation of tyranny (not forgetting that, against the whole of an already ancient tradition, and one which will survive him, Hölderlin restores to Sophocles' play its real title). A single term suffices to explain it ('It is precisely this excess in the search, this excess of interpretation, which finally throws his spirit <that is, Oedipus' spirit> to the raw and primitive language of those who obey him') (*Essays*, 107). For *Antigone*, the whole of a detailed development is necessary – but it is true that in 1804, in Stuttgart, this is politically more risky – in order to demonstrate that the 'form of reason which takes shape here tragically is political, and more precisely republican' (*Essays*, 115).

It will be objected: these indications envisage nothing other than the 'lesson', even the 'morality' (in the sense of the fabulists), that one can draw from the tragic 'action'. And what clearly predominates, in the name of the significance of tragedies, is the onto-theological (the 'categorical' turning away of the divine; the faithful – or treacherous – infidelity of the human; the installation of a limit, which is that of finitude) or historico-ontological (the vaterländische turning back, the Greek insurrection [Aufruhr] and the 'Hesperian' measure, etc.) interpretation, all of which is relatively well known, even if only on the basis of Heidegger's extremely slanted reading – to which, obviously, I cannot return here.

But things are not so straightforward: when he speaks of the 'republican form' of Antigone, Hölderlin adds the following: 'because, between Creon and Antigone, between the formal and the counter-formal, the equilibrium is kept too equal. This is particularly evident at the end, when Creon is almost abused by his servants' (this is the motif, a topos, of the punished tyrant). Equilibrium, then: Gleichgewicht. This is exactly the same word that Hölderlin used in what one can call the 'technical' opening of the 'Remarks on Oedipus' when he was explaining what he called the Kalkul, the law or the rule (Gesetz) of the work, in this case of tragedy.

Here is what Hölderlin says:

> The law, the calculation, the mode according to which a system of receptivity, man in his entirety, insofar as he is under the influence of the element, develops, and according to which representation, sensation, and reasoning appear in various successions yet always according to a law which is certain, exists in tragedy more as a state of balance than as mere succession.
>
> (Essays, 101)

One really ought to pause at this point. For it is here that Hölderlin approaches head on the question of the conditions of tragic Darstellung, of theatricality.

What is described here is the mode of composition (sunthesis) of the mimesis ton pragmaton which defines the two genres, epos (narrative) and tragedy (theatre). This description is formulated in Kantian terms: man is defined as a 'system of receptivity' (representation, sensation, reason), and the tragic Darstellung is the presentation of the praxis of such a 'system' insofar as man is under the 'influence of the element' (which, in Hölderlin, denotes at the same time both the divine and nature, as necessity and as power). Tragedy thus presents the course (der Gang), under these conditions, of a praxis: a succession of acts 'under influence'. And in contradistinction to the epos, where this succession is 'pure sequence' or pure succession, in tragedy there is equilibrium.

127

It is here that Hölderlin introduces the famous *'caesura'*. It is necessary to read attentively:

The tragic *transport* is actually empty and the least restrained.

So, in the rhythmic sequence of the representations wherein *transport* presents itself, there becomes necessary *what in poetic meter is called caesura*, the pure word, the counterrhythmic rupture, namely in order to meet the onrushing change of representations at its highest point in such a way that very soon it is not the change of representations which appears but representation itself.

(*Essays*, 101–2)

This crucial text has been subjected to so many commentaries and, because it is, to say the least, enigmatic, so many dissimilar and contradictory commentaries, that it is difficult to resume reading it. Let me try anyway.

Just before this, and from a basically methodological point of view, Hölderlin distinguishes two things: the calculation of the law of the composition of the work – that is what I have already evoked – and the 'content', the 'particular content' of each work, in relation to the general calculation, which is itself incalculable. He says, in a very precise manner:

Next <once the calculation of the law of composition has been considered> one has to see how the content is distinct from this . . . and how the course <*der Gang*> and that which is to be fixed, the living meaning which cannot be calculated, are put in relation with the calculable law.

(*Essays*, 101)

It is clear that it is this with which we now have to deal: the living meaning, the incalculable, is the 'tragic transport' itself; that to which it is bound, in a 'composition of actions' which the tragedy (re)presents, is an equilibrium or, more exactly, an equilibrial or stabilising *caesura*. And it is bound to it because it is 'empty'.

One can unpack things in the following manner:

(1) If tragedy – let us say as *structure*, that will be simpler – is equilibrium, and not sequence, this is because it unfolds in the dialogic form of the pure *agon* (and that is to say, from the logical point of view, in the form of an antagonism or of a contradiction without conciliation or resolution). As Hölderlin says with regard to Oedipus, 'all is discourse against discourse, each suppressing <*aufheben*> the other' which, reciprocally, suppresses itself (*Essays*, 107). Which also means, very simply, that tragedy is without issue or without result,

that it produces nothing – no meaning, if you like. In the paragraph with which we are concerned, Hölderlin speaks of 'the exchange <or the alternation, *Wechsel*> of representations' (*Vorstellungen*, here, are the thoughts or the points of view of figures which confront each other), an exchange which exacerbates itself, which rises to extremes, to a summit or 'highest point'.

(2) In this insane *agon* there is, none the less, that which the tragedy presents (*darstellen*), which is its meaning, the truth of that which it shows – the incalculable. Hölderlin continually seeks to offer a properly transcendental account of what allows for the manifestation of what he is here calling 'representation', *Vorstellung*. His question is: what is the *structural* condition of possibility for the manifestation of *Vorstellung*? In Kantian terms: what is the *a priori* form – in dialectical terms: what is the necessary means or mediation – of the manifestation of *Vorstellung*?

(3) The tragic *Vorstellung*, that of which the tragedy is the *Darstellung*, *the tragic*, then, as Hölderlin always calls it, is the 'transport' – by which he translates into French, and by a word which belongs to the lexicon of classical tragedy, the Greek *metaphora*. The tragic is the enthusiastic transport, which, moreover, allows us now to see that when Hölderlin earlier defined tragedy as the 'metaphor of an intellectual intuition', he wanted also to speak of intellectual intuition as metaphor, as transport. The tragic is, or rather originates in, the meta-physical transgression pure and simple – which, and this is the clearest 'lesson' of the Transcendental Dialectic of the *Critique of Pure Reason*, only opens itself onto the contradictions of reason going beyond the limits of finite experience.

This is, moreover, very exactly what Hölderlin will re-elaborate a few pages later under the name of the 'categorical turning away of God'.[7]

(4) In tragedy, the transport is 'empty' – and it is in this that it is properly tragic. The tragic is not the transport, but the *empty* transport – Hölderlin said beforehand: the sign = 0. This emptiness is nothing other than the 'purification' or the 'infinite separation' of the 'infinite becoming-one' of the transport itself. This emptiness is the place of *katharsis*, the point of *katharsis*. And it is there, precisely, that the meaning of tragedy, *Vorstellung*, manifests itself, insofar as it is wrenched from antagonism, from the endless battle of contradictions, from the indefinitely 'binary' rhythm of conflict.

Equally, it is in this way that the tragic effect is produced: when *mimesis*, as Aristotle says, produces *mathesis*: gives it to be thought and understood.[8] That is its function. On this point, as on others, Hölderlin is absolutely faithful to Aristotle: the theatre is an exercise in thinking.

If the *agon*, the alternation of representations, is thought, in its own rhythmicality, according to the rules proper to the calculation of poetic rhythm – that is to say, according to metrics – then the emptiness of the tragic transport corresponds structurally to the *caesura*, to the 'counterrhythmic inter-ruption', on the basis of which rhythm (and consequently meaning) is organ-ised into a whole, into a signifying totality: the entire verse or tragedy; the phrase which is the work. The *caesura* is the condition of possibility for mani-festation, for the (re)presentation (*Darstellung*) of the tragic.

Such is the law or, if you prefer, the principle of its theatricality.

* * *

I will leave it at that. But I cannot end without handing over to, without cit-ing once again, the few lines in which Hölderlin describes the moment – null, out of time – of the *caesura*. Since I first read these lines, exactly thirty years ago, I have thought that it is precisely there that the *lesson* of theatre lies:

> In both pieces, it is the speeches of Tiresias which form the *caesura*.
> He enters the course of destiny as the custodian of the power of nature which, tragically, tears man from his own life-sphere, the mid-point of his inner life, transporting him into another world and into the eccentric sphere of the dead.
>
> (*Essays*, 102)

Addendum: Faithful infidelity

In note 7 of the preceding text, with respect to the 'categorical turning-away' of the divine, I alluded to a work-in-progress which, under the (provisional) title of 'The All-forgetting Form of Infidelity', concerns the whole of the Hölderlinian interpretation of Sophocles and which harks back to two previ-ously published essays in order to amend and amplify what was said there.[9] As a complement to the preceding text, it does not seem to me entirely pointless to extract here some indications from this work-in-progress.

* * *

In the third part of the 'Remarks on Oedipus', after having deduced the antag-onistic or conflictual structure of tragedy (a structure which accounts for the formula: 'Everything is discourse against discourse, each suppressing the other') from a general definition of the 'presentation of the tragic' (*Darstellung des Tragischen*), Hölderlin adds the following:

> . . . <all this> as a language for a world where under pest and con-fusion of senses, and a spirit of prophecy everywhere exacerbated, in a time of idleness, the God and man *express themselves in the all-forget-ting form of infidelity* – for divine infidelity is what is best to retain –

so that the course of the world will not show any rupture and *the memory of the heavenly ones will not expire.*

At such moments man forgets himself and the God and turns around like a traitor, naturally in saintly manner. — At the most extreme limit of suffering <*Leiden*>, there exists nothing but the conditions of time and space.

At this limit, man forgets himself because he exists entirely within the moment, the God because he is nothing but time; and either one is unfaithful, time because it is categorically turned-away at such a moment, no longer fitting beginning and end; man because at this moment of categorical turning-away he has to follow and thus can no longer resemble the beginning in what follows.

Thus Haemon stands in *Antigone.* Thus Oedipus himself at the heart of the tragedy of *Oedipus.*

(*Essays*, 107–8)

This text is difficult not only because it is elliptical; nor, moreover, because the references or allusions to Kant ('conditions of time and space', 'categorical turning-away') remain completely obscure insofar as the exact measure has not yet been taken of the use, to apparently poetic ends, that Hölderlin made of Kant — 'the Moses of our nation', he says in a letter to his brother (and — this would warrant attention — he knew exactly what he was saying when he said this). This text is also difficult because what it in fact sets out is a theology, and because this theology is entirely singular, without example in the tradition. It is not a 'negative theology' or a theology of the *Deus absconditus*; and no more is it, as in Hegel or Nietzsche — albeit in different ways — a post-Lutheran theology of 'God (himself) is dead'. It is an 'other' theology. None the less, this is not, as has too quickly been believed, a matter of an 'unprecedented' theology; rather, it is an attempt to restore — or to 'invent' — the theology of the Greeks, which they themselves — in any case, those before Plato and Aristotle who 'inclined' a little too far in the direction of instituted Christianity — never took the trouble to explicate as such.

For Hölderlin, Sophoclean tragedy does not simply belong to theatre (of which it is none the less exemplary); it is *also* the document or the monument of this theology. Or, if you prefer: *Oedipus Tyrannus* and *Antigone* are the *testament* of the Greeks: what they attest to is the Greek experience of the divine, which, according to the law of History that, long before the Christian (re)foundation, it institutes, rings out to us.

In order to understand this we must think back to the initial definition that Hölderlin gives of the tragic, of the 'presentation of the tragic', at the start of the third part of the 'Remarks'. As I have already suggested, we can see here, and without too much difficulty, the major categories of Aristotle's *Poetics*: *hubris* and *katharsis*, categories that, in some way, Hölderlin 'defunctionalises'. I will not return to this except to emphasise that he does so in order to submit them to a properly metaphysical or theologico-speculative re-elaboration. Although he still interprets tragedy in terms of *mimesis* (*Darstellung*), this is no longer the (re)presentation of *pragmata*, but that of the tragic itself in its essence; that is to say, of the experience or the ordeal of the divine as *hubris*. Consequently, *katharsis* is no longer a functional category. It is the outcome, in religious, ritual and sacrificial mode, of *hubris* (which accounts for the fact that it is internal to *muthos*, to fable, and that it impinges upon the significance of tragedy).

In what does *hubris*, transgression, consist? Hölderlin expresses it bluntly: in the coupling (*sich paaren*) of man and the God. This is, literally, the experience of enthusiasm, of *unendliche Begeisterung*, as is said in the 'Remarks on *Antigone*', of 'infinite possession by spirit'. Long before Nietzsche, but around about the same time as Friedrich Schlegel, Hölderlin suspects amongst the Greeks, in their original nature (the Eastern element, he says), a mystical savagery and violence, a mystical fury – we would probably say today: enrapture. Greek madness, the *mania* of which Plato spoke, is the madness of God. Which just as easily means, and it is in precisely this way that Hölderlin himself also understands it, meta-physical madness itself. *Hubris* is in-finite, un-limited transcendence, in the active sense of the word 'transcendence': it is, indeed, the transgression – of the finite (which, moreover, begins to clarify the persistent reference to Kant).

Now, such a transgression is the impossible itself. In the brief commentary which accompanies 'The Supreme', one of the nine Pindar fragments that he translates in the same period, Hölderlin expresses this with absolute clarity. The fragment says:

The law <*das Gesetzt*>
King of all, both mortals and
Immortals; which thus leads
for this reason powerfully
The justest justice with the highest hand.

And Hölderlin comments:

The immediate, strictly called, is for mortals impossible, as for immortals <. . .> But the strictly mediated is the law.

(*Poems*, 639)

In the language which is thus already that of dialectic-speculative onto-theology (then in the process of being formed), this unswervingly supports the unconditional affirmation (the Law or, in Kantian language, the categorical imperative) of the necessity of the limit – or of the measure, as is repeated in so many of the poems. So that if, in the properly theological register of tragedy, *hubris*, the 'limitlessly becoming-One in fury', is neither more nor less than sacrilege or impiety, the Law of the mediated commands purification: 'limitless separation'. Tragedy, in other words, is the presentation of the Law. The commandment of impiety by the very obligation of fidelity. Hölderlin calls this *Revolution*, insurrection (*Aufruhr*), even, and this is still the situation we are in.

Hölderlin thus gives two versions of such a presentation (of the Law). I would like to cite once again the second, the one which concerns *Antigone*, structurally identical to the first but markedly different as to the 'result': it allows us to clarify what happens with Oedipus:

> As has been indicated in the remarks on Oedipus, the tragic presentation rests on the premise that the immediate God is wholly at one with man (for the God of an apostle is more mediate, is highest intellect in highest spirit), that the *infinite* possession by spirit *infinitely* grasps itself by sacredly separating itself, that is, though oppositions, in consciousness which cancels <*aufhebt*> consciousness, and that the God is present in the figure of death.
>
> (*Essays*, 113)

This version of tragic purification is properly Greek: violent and brutal, since in Greek the word is, as we have seen, 'murderous', *tödtlichfaktisch*, and not simply deadly, *tödtenfaktisch*. It is a sacrificial purification: it operates within the annihilation of the hero: as 'the God present in the figure of death'. Now, things are very different with the tragedy of Oedipus; already it is no longer entirely Greek, and it prefigures, in contrast to the dazzling brevity of Greek destiny, the lingering *catastrophe* which comprises Western or, as Hölderlin says, 'Hesperian' destiny. There, in the questioning of this destinal difference which underpins History in its entirety, the enigmatic thought of faithful infidelity – or of pious impiety – is elaborated.

The reason for this difference is very simple: in *Oedipus Tyrannus*, Oedipus does not die; and if he does die in *Oedipus at Colonus*, then it is, as we know, in a mysterious – but completed – manner after his long 'wandering under the unthinkable'. The fact that Oedipus does not die does not simply mean that the God does not present himself 'in the figure of death', but that, in a particular way, he does not present himself at all. Or else, in an absolutely paradoxical fashion, he presents himself only by his very retreat: what Hölderlin calls his turning-away (*Umkehr*), his shift or his volte-face (*Wendung*), his infidelity (*Untreue*). I have risked defining the paradox that is put to work here as a 'hyperbologic', a logic suspensive of the dialectic (antagonistic) process which governs the tragic mechanism.[10] It lies in the augmentation – in infinitely inverse proportion – of opposites or of contraries. In this instance: the more the God manifests himself, the more he turns away – and vice versa; or else, and this, strictly speaking, amounts to the same thing: the more unfaithful he is, the more faithful he is. Which means what, precisely?

It is important, first of all, to understand properly that the manifestation or presentation of the God – if indeed he manifests or presents himself other than according to his retreat, which leaves the hero *atheos*, or other than in the death that he inflicts – is a *moment*, in truth extracted or abstracted from time: a pure syncope – not without relation to the *caesura* which structures tragedy – 'at the extreme limit of *pathein*' or in that instant 'of the highest state of consciousness' when the soul 'evades consciousness' (*Essays*, 111). This moment, so far as Oedipus is concerned, comes in the middle of the tragedy of Oedipus (*in der Mitte der Tragödie von Oedipus*) (*Essays*, 104). It is a moment of reciprocal forgetting: man forgets himself and forgets the God, 'because he exists entirely within the moment'; the God forgets 'because he is nothing other than time' (*Essays*, 107), and that is to say, the law of irreversibility: the 'this is irretrievable' of tragic destiny. Or, at the *limit*, (the possibility of) death. Indeed, at such a moment there *remain* no more than *conditions* – that is to say, in Kantian language, finitude itself; and what comes about (taking place without taking place) is the impossible itself: the experience of the 'conditions of experience', these 'pure' or 'empty' forms, as Kant has it, of time and space (from which beings, in general, can appear). The tragic 'moment' is the experience of the no-thing [*le né-ant*] – of being – dazzling by the very fact that it presents the condition of all presence: of time itself as *a priori*, since this is what Hölderlin emphasises. Or of the God himself, whose turned-away face, whose volte-face, *is* time. The tragic moment could be given the title not of *Sein und Zeit* but rather, according to its final reversal, *Zeit und Sein*.

And, in fact, the reversal is what, secondly, needs to be considered: this is infidelity. Man does not decide upon it; he is obedient to its law – which is, therefore, the Law in general. The pious treachery of man is a response, the only way in which he can maintain a 'communication' with the categorically turned-away God and, as such, hold him in memory. The God, in his essence, is revolt and imposition of revolt. Or, to put it differently, history is revolution. It is, finally, through the fact 'that the course of the world will not show any rupture and *the memory of the heavenly ones will not expire*', that 'divine infidelity is . . . to be retained <*zu behalten*>' (*Essays*, 108). The tragic moment, in its very nullity, is not historical: it is the condition of history. Which is nothing else than the submission – faithful infidelity – to the prohibition of transgression or, what amounts to the same thing, of meta-physical desire. The 'Remarks on *Antigone*' are totally clear on this:

> For us, given that we live under the reign of the Zeus who is more properly himself, this Zeus who not only establishes a limit between this earth and the ferocious world of the dead, but also forces more decisively towards the earth the wave of panic eternally hostile to man, the wave always on route towards the other world . . .
>
> (*Essays*, 113)

Or again:

> In a way that is more or less determined, it is really Zeus who must be said. In all seriousness, rather: Father of time or: Father of earth, for it is his character, opposing the eternal tendency, to reverse <*kehren*> the desire to leave this world for another world into a desire to leave another world for this one.
>
> (*Essays*, 112)

Infidelity – fidelity itself – is thus metaphysical impiety; that is, piety toward the metaphysical Law (a sort of pure *noli me tangere*) which has been destining us, us 'Westerners', ever since, as is announced in the elegy 'Bread and Wine' – which is dedicated as much to Dionysus, the son of the God, as to Christ – 'the Father turned his face away from men' (*Poems*, 271). An elegy is, in Greek, a mourning song; just as tragedy, in German, is a 'mourning play': *Trauerspiel*. Our destiny is, therefore, to endure or to suffer (*pathein*) mourning for the divine. Or our experience, and this amounts to the same thing, is melancholic. It is not certain that, from Hegel to Nietzsche and to Freud, the full force of this has been grasped or its measure taken.

Translated by Simon Sparks

Notes

1 *Translator's Note.* The German text used throughout is Friedrich Hölderlin, *Werke und Briefe*, edited by Friedrich Beißner and Jochen Schmidt (Frankfurt am Main: Insel, 1982), *WB* where cited in the text. Although translations of Hölderlin have been prepared for this volume, I have tried also to be faithful to the inflections given by Lacoue-Labarthe, *particularly* in those instances where he deviates in determined manner from the standard French translations in the Pleiade edition of Hölderlin's *Oeuvres*, edited by Philippe Jaccottet (Paris: Gallimard, 1967). Equally, when Lacoue-Labarthe silently presents multiple translations of the same passage, thus layering the meaning he exposes in Hölderlin's text, I have sought

also to reflect this. References are provided to the following English editions: *Friedrich Hölderlin: Essays and Letters on Theory*, translated and edited by Thomas Pfau (Albany: SUNY, 1988), henceforth cited in the text as *Essays*; and Friedrich Hölderlin, *Poems and Fragments*, translated by Michael Hamburger (London: Anvil, 1994), henceforth cited in the text as *Poems*. Remarks in square brackets ([. . .]) have been added by the translator, those in angled brackets (<. . .>) are Lacoue-Labarthe's own.

2 *Translator's Note*. Cf. 'Über die wissenschaftlichen Behandlungsarten des Naturrechts' in G. W. F. Hegel, *Werke*, edited by Eva Moldenhauer and Karl Markus Michel (Frankfurt am Main: Suhrkamp, 1970) II: 494.

3 *Translator's Note*. Cf. *Unzeitgemäße Betrachtung* Viertes Stück: 'Richard Wagner in Bayreuth' § 8, in Friedrich Nietzsche, *Kritische Studienausgabe*, edited by Giorgio Colli and Mazzino Montinari (Munich: Walter de Gruyter, 1988) I: 479.

4 Michel Deutsch, *Thermidor* (Paris: Christian Bourgeois, 1988).

5 On this point, I subscribe unreservedly to the recent analyses developed by Jacques Taminaux in his *Théâtre des philosophes* (Grenoble: Jérôme Millon, 1995).

6 The word 'monstrous' is an attempt to render *das Ungeheure*, that is to say, in its strictest and strongest sense, the in-habitual.

7 I have sketched this analysis in a forthcoming work entitled 'The All-Forgetting Form of Infidelity'.

8 Aristotle, *Peri Poietikes* 4.

9 'La césure du spéculatif' and 'Hölderlin et les grecs' in *L'imitation des modernes: Typographies II* (Paris: Galilée, 1986), 39–84; translated by Robert Eisenhauer as 'The Caesura of the Speculative' and by Judi Olson as 'Hölderlin and the Greeks' in *Typographies: Mimesis, Philosophy, Politics*, edited by Christopher Fynsk (Cambridge, MA: Harvard University Press, 1989), 208–47. [*Translator's Note*. A small part of this work has recently been published under the title *Metaphrasis* (Paris: PUF, 1998). See also the author's translations of the plays in Hölderlin's 'Sophocles' group: *Oedipe de Sophocle* (Paris: Bourgeois, 1998) and *Antigone de Sophocle* (Paris: Bourgeois, 1998).]

10 *Translator's Note*. See 'La césure du spéculatif', 64ff.; 'The Caesura of the Speculative', 231ff.

Part III

Nietzsche

Aesthetically limited reason: on Nietzsche's *The Birth of Tragedy*

Günter Figal

We moderns know the feeling of looking back over our shoulder. Thus, we watch the way we live, and look at what we are. We see, as Ernst Jünger put it, the 'signal of an inner point of view': a signal with which 'a second, more refined and impersonal consciousness'[1] comes forth. Here, it is not merely isolated actions that are questioned from within a fundamentally secure context. Rather, it is the whole of life that becomes the object of a questioning, searching and comparative scrutiny. This robs the present of its self-evidence, but compensates for this by way of an intensified dynamic and a heightened readiness for experimentation.

It is not that reflexivity or self-examination by itself constitutes something new, something distinctly modern. Without reflexivity there is no practical reason; the latter consists, among other things, in making present to oneself one's own comportment, along with its circumstances. And the *confessio*, the care for oneself and beyond oneself, has always been a self-examining. The focus on the way life flows and flows away is also not specifically modern, but belongs to our basic experience. What is modern, however, is the radicality of reflection and above all the overlapping of reflexivity and transience: the always recommencing attempt to withdraw from one's life in order to understand it, to interpret it, and give shape to it, and, along with this, the experience that this attempt belongs to the very flow of life and that one will never gain the sovereignty that the reflective distance from life appears to promise. Instead, we discover that the possibilities of articulation granted by reflection are bound up with a developing, changing and even for this reason alone unfathomable speech. We find instead that articulated self-examination is carried away by the stream of life and that what just a moment ago constituted the reflective actuality of life returns as something past.

We moderns are thus certain that reason is limited – not from outside, on account of something which would necessarily withdraw from reason, or surpass its power of comprehension. Rather, the so-called 'other' of reason lies within reason itself. Since reflection always takes place differently, depending on the historical constellations, and the varying points of view, at times broader, at times narrower; since reflection always articulates itself differently, according to the becoming and the passing away of modes of speech, reflection must continually overtake and surpass itself. Where, just a moment ago, we believed ourselves to have grasped life in its nexus, we now have a discarded mask before ourselves, a worn-out attempt to shape and interpret ourselves. If the observing consciousness is thus carried away by the stream of the observed life, the limits of reason prove to be the conditions of its possibilities: it has possibilities only because of that which limits it. In the passage of time, the second, more refined and impersonal consciousness becomes aware of its own experiences, its representations and images, and discovers how it has always already been temporal. For reason, temporality is not merely a darkening which prevents it from seeing in full clarity that which it sees. Rather, reason lives out of temporality, because it itself belongs in the very happening of the life that is reflected upon.

Yet reflection cannot really take all of this in. In reflection one is after all cut off from the flow of life; having left for an observing, searching and comparative distance, one can maintain this distance only by ignoring the fact that reflection is itself a life-event. While living, one takes up a standpoint outside of life.

*   *   *

In the search for self-understanding that belongs to modernity, a paradigm soon emerged in which, it seemed, the specificity of self-limited reason could be shown particularly clearly, namely aesthetic experience. The latter has indeed the character of a distanced involvement or a participatory distance. This becomes immediately clear in a process that virtually amounts to the primal scene of the aesthetic comportment:[2] when Petrarch climbs Mount Ventoux, he frees himself from the world so that it can be experienced as landscape. But the path does not actually lead him out of the world, for each vantage point from which a landscape displays itself belongs to the world in which one moves about. The vantage point can itself become an object of aesthetic contemplation and thus be integrated into the very landscape from which it stands out as a vantage point.

That the two moments of distance and entanglement, of involvement and standing apart, belong together in aesthetic experience allows us to determine their relationship as play. In play, one is concerned with something, without taking it seriously with regard to how one orients oneself in one's life and conducts it. A killjoy is whoever pursues a matter with dogged determination, or falls into the other extreme – a lack of interest – and thus in both cases does not hit upon the delicate middle of distanced involvement.

Aesthetic experience can be understood as play also given the fact that the two moments of involvement and distance never settle down in a relationship that is the same at all times. They interplay, which means: they hold each other in motile freedom. Their relationship has a free interplay: it is characterised by an openness, which can always express itself in a new form.

However, aesthetic experience is not yet sufficiently determined by such characteristics. The decisive question remains: how is one to think the interplay of involvement and distance in its essence? What character is one to attribute to it? There are basically two possibilities here. One can represent the balance of reflection and life-events as the *reconciliation* of both. In this case aesthetic experience would be the liberating of self-limited reason from its limits: where the limiting finds a unity with the limited, the limitation is dissolved and the full actuality of rational life, of living rationality, steps forth.

A chiastic structure such as this refers us to the most influential representative of the reconciliation thesis in aesthetics. In his *Letters on the Aesthetic Education of Man*, Schiller proves himself to be the master at such formulations, as he interprets the aesthetic, with ever-changing conceptual pairs, as the happy medium of oppositionality, as yet another situation over against the fighting out of opposites. If one takes the ordinary conception of comedy as a production in which everything comes out well in the end, against expectation or according to an artful design of deferral, and in which the contenders again or for the first time are in harmony, then one could say that in his aesthetic letters Schiller has described the comedy of the aesthetic.

Like any *mise-en-scène* of reconciliation, comedies are sustained by the fact that the conflict is not forgotten. Only the conflict allows us to be happy to see the reconciliation; even more, it alone makes the reconciliation understandable. The untensed unity is sustained by the tension, and it is only what it is when it presents the previously conflictual moments in a new relation that nevertheless preserves the conflict. As happens in the best comedies, the untensed unity holds the conflict in suspense and often doesn't conceal the fact that it can break out anew; one is reminded of the conclusion to *The Marriage of Figaro* or *Cosí fan tutte*. As we see there, the reconciliation is sustained by *strife*, which suggests that reconciliation is nothing other than a particularly successful working-through of strife, a momentary standing still, through which alone the conflicting moments appear distinctly as such.

This is how Nietzsche thought, and in his treatise on the birth of tragedy he conceived the aesthetic without the thought of an overarching unity. He thus opposed Schiller's aesthetic of reconciliation and the succeeding aesthetic of German Idealism, which is even more insistent on the readiness

141

for reconciliation. But Nietzsche also assimilated Schiller's thought and radicalised it: the aesthetic is indeed no longer the realm in which the rift of life and reason vanishes; rather, it remains, as for Schiller, what sets the standard for the self-understanding of modernity and its limited reason. The aesthetic becomes for Nietzsche the realm in which self-limited reason/the in itself limited reason [die in sich begrenzte Vernunft] becomes transparent. Furthermore, the aesthetic allows us to recognise the one-sided realisations of this reason as such: whether it be the autonomisation of reflection, or the no less problematic attempt to bring reason back into a new immediacy in the completion [Vollzug] of life. The aesthetic is the counter-weight to the one-sidedness of supposedly objective thought and, likewise, to the immersion and the desire for dissolving in the becoming and passing away of life. For in the realm of the aesthetic, the strife of reason and life cannot be resolved. Rather, it intimates how far more problematic conflicts may arise if one attempts to evade or to overcome it: the chaining up of life in forms which have become rigid and independent, or the break-out into a supposedly immediate form-despising anarchy. The forms of an aesthetically limited/delimited reason have here no solving power, but they do indeed have a purifying power. On this presupposition – that tragedy is the open fighting through of a conflict and so can also bring about an open relation to it – one can therefore say that Nietzsche wrote the tragedy of the aesthetic. The tragedy of the aesthetic is what also peaks through in the temporary suspension of apparent reconciliation.

To understand Nietzsche's tragedy of the aesthetic, one must pursue the way he precisely developed the strife of reason and life. Only in this way can one grasp why he let himself be guided by the aesthetic in order to understand this strife. Thus the precarious and complex relations of an aesthetically limited/delimited reason can finally gain clearer contours.

*   *   *

At the heart of the strife of reason and life lies a traumatic experience. It appears when one pulls down the edifice of a culture 'brick by brick', 'until we glimpse the foundation'.[3] What shows up there is the insight into the nothingness of human life: humans are the 'poor ephemeral race, the children of chance and misery', for whom the best would be 'never to have been born, not to be, to be nothing' – their being is already shot through with non-being, with mutability and passing-away. And so, since humans can never truly be, but also are incapable of disavowing their defective and fragmentary being, the next best thing for them is 'to die quickly' (I: 53).

What is here given out as 'folk wisdom' and transmitted as the word of the wisdom of Silenus, he who was imprisoned by King Midas, is for Nietzsche in another formulation – without the pointed denial of existence at the conclusion – also the quintessence of the meditation of a temporally informed philosophy. The existence of humans, we read in the second *Untimely Meditation*, 'On the Advantage and Disadvantage of History for Life', is 'an uninterrupted having-been [*Gewesensein*]', 'a thing, that lives in order to deny itself and use itself up, to contradict itself' (I: 249).

Certainly, a closer examination indicates that it would be precipitous to regard transience as the essence of human existence. Even if it were to be an essential trait of that existence, as such an essential trait it can make itself felt only in another arrayed over against it. Nietzsche alludes to this when he says that human existence sustains itself by 'contradicting itself'.

What this means is elaborated in Nietzsche's philosophical meditation on time at the beginning of the essay on the advantage and disadvantage of history for life. Nietzsche shows here that passing-away needs the present in order to appear, and indeed the present of remembrance, for if that which passes away were not held fast in remembrance, then it would not be experienced as passing-away and hence as past. Memory works against time and its passing away, thereby giving it a presence which time, taken by itself, does not have. It is the presence of a holding firm that is only possible by a distanciation from the passing-away of time.

That which is remembered, and the existence stamped by remembrance, has in truth another side. As passing-away first appears in the presence of the ability to hold firm, so is, on the other hand, a determinate present first shaped through this appearance. The present of existence is indeed not merely an infinitely quick passing moment. It is a *while*, which always already endures and swings back. What belongs to the present is not just what one has immediately before the eyes, but also what even now already was/has been and is yet to come. The present is thus, by virtue of the presence of the ability to hold firm, a present-space [*Gegenwartsraum*], an open expanse, in which life has its factical nexus and its perspectives. Nietzsche names this present-space of life its 'horizon' (I: 251). To live means: shaping a horizon and always shaping it anew. This means: finding a life form that arrests passing away. As so shaping and understanding, rational life is an uprising against time.

This uprising is just as successful as it is unsuccessful: passing-away and holding-firm, time and presence, interplay, and this interplaying is precarious. What comes to presence is indeed the temporal, and it remains experiencable *as* temporal even when it shapes, with its presence, a present-space. The open expanse of the present can suddenly become a sign of transitoriness, and when this happens with particular intensity, one is faced, as Nietzsche foresaw, with the 'most extreme example' of a human being, who 'would be condemned to see everywhere a becoming: such a one no longer believes in his own being, no longer believes in himself, sees everything dissolve into moving points and loses himself in this stream of becoming' (I: 250). Here becoming has gained superior power over being, while for whoever who can forget transitoriness, becoming is domesticated in the being of a determinate present. The forgetting of transitoriness is equivalent to the security of he who does not look into the abyss. Here a glance is enough to lose that security.

The unstable balance in the interplay of time and presence, of becoming and being, arises from the circumstance that the two moments have equal right. They need each other and yet call each other into question. They will not let themselves be dissolved into one another, and yet they are so closely related to one another that each wants to make itself felt at the cost of the other. The interplay of becoming and being is a strife – the strife, without which becoming and being would not be experienced. It is the strife of self-limited reason/of reason limited in itself, which can only be temporal in an atemporal manner, and atemporal only in a temporal manner.

The strife of time and presence, of becoming and being, has its unrest in the fact that the two moments are never finally determined in their mutual relation. The experience of strife is therefore open to various degrees of intensity; its moments can appear with variable acuteness. Yet it is always a matter of degrees of intensity and acuteness of the same, which makes time and presence, becoming and being, fleeting life and reason show up against the foil of one another. They show themselves as what they are each time in reference to the other, yet this other is not the other of them themselves; it is not derivable from that which stands opposed to it; it is not a manifestation or emanation of the latter, but must, as it were, step over to that which stands opposed to it as its other. Both moments are exterior to each other, and yet they make themselves felt only through one another.

Such a relation is a relation of presentation [Darstellungsverhältnis]: in Darstellung, something manifests itself in something else, in something which does not belong to the very essence of that thing. A circle can be drawn with pencil on paper, chalk on the board, or with foot in the sand. Yet none of these belong to the essence of the circle. Admittedly, becoming may always make itself felt – present itself – only through being, and being through becoming. The contingency that is operative in the relation of presentation does not reveal itself in the fact that there are very diverse media of presentation. Rather, this contingency stems from the fact that there are very diverse modes of representation, very diverse constellations of representation. And, in turn, of particular importance are those constellations of presence in which both of the mutually conflictual moments can make themselves felt – that is, so that we have neither time in the overflow of presence or conversely being in the forgetting of becoming. Constellations of representation of this type are aesthetic. It is the business of art to accomplish the strife of being and becoming so as to remain faithful to both moments if possible.

*   *   *

Since this is the conception of art Nietzsche aims at, much is indeed gained for 'the science of aesthetics, once we perceive not merely by logical inference, but with the immediate certainty of intuition, that the continuous development of art is bound up with the duplicity of the Apollinian and the Dionysian' (I: 25). Were one here to stay on the side of 'logical inference', one might take the distinction which Nietzsche makes in the first sentence of *The Birth of Tragedy* merely as an attempt at a typology of art, one in which the distinction is made between the Apollinian 'art of sculpture', or the rationally stamped form, and the Dionysian, vital, 'imageless art of music' (I: 25). Now such a typology does indeed play a role in Nietzsche's thought, but not a decisive one. What is much more decisive is the fact that there is a Dionysian art only as Apollinian, and an Apollinian only as Dionysian.

Nietzsche develops this idea first of all as the fundamental lineaments of a philosophy of culture, whose point is that a culture can only endure when it does not exclude that which is menacing to it. Where a culture succeeded at granting a place in life to Dionysian celebrations through an art form, this was, on the one hand, equivalent to 'taking the destructive weapons from the hands of his powerful antagonist, by a seasonably effected reconciliation' (I: 32). The Dionysian is domesticated insofar as it takes shape as an art form; in fact, only within these limits can it be expressly experienced. This entails, on the other hand, an opening of the Apollinian form to the Dionysian and thereby an alteration of that very form; the Apollinian form first effectively comes into clarity when what previously would only be struggled against in order to make it disappear is now allowed to be. The 'reconciliation' of the Apollinian with the Dionysian does not therefore imply that a unitary art form can be developed out of the Apollinian and Dionysian moments, nor that out of two originary art forms a third should arise. The reconciliation turns out to be much more a productive outcome of a strife in the manner of exhibition: the Apollinian is presented in Dionysian vitality, while the Dionysian can be presented in Apollinian images.

Nietzsche sharply illustrated both modes of presentation, and thus, insofar as this is possible in an essay, took account of the 'immediate certainty of intuition' over and above 'logical inference'. For the representation of the Apollinian in Dionysian vitality he referred to Raphael's *Transfiguration*: the scene with the possessed boy in the lower half of the painting is, in Nietzsche's words, 'the reflection [*Widerschein*] of eternal contradiction [*Widerspruch*], the father of things' (I: 39). This is the imaginal presentation of undivided life, where life breaks through the shape. The image points to the breaking down of the limits of consciousness and perception, to the collapse of being into becoming.

With the transfiguration of Christ in the upper half of the picture arises now out of this appearance 'a new visionary world of appearances, invisible to those wrapped in the first appearance – a radiant floating in purest bliss, a serene contemplation beaming from wide-open eyes' (I: 39). With this 'apparent world' of undimmed presence, the art of images celebrates itself. In the painting image-making presents itself as transfiguration, and this in turn is possible only insofar as the life which leaves behind its own limits is set forth in the painting: only thus does the signification of the transfigurative movement that is constitutive of image-making become manifest.

This structure, which Nietzsche works out in his interpretation, deserves a closer look. It is characterised by two distinct concepts of appearance [Schein]: with regard to the representation of de-limited life, Nietzsche uses the term Widerschein, reflection, and with regard to the transfiguration, he speaks about a 'visionary world of appearance [visiongleichen Scheinwelt]'. A 'reflection' is a mirroring, and thus the inverting impression or expression of something. The 'visionary world of appearance' is a unitary sight, a self-enclosed representation [Vorstellung], and thus a meaningful manifestation inscribed in the image.

The painting also points to the 'eternal contradiction' in this apparent world, and correspondingly the reflection of life is here not immediately experienceable. It has come to imaginal form and so is concealed in the imaginal form. Imaginal form is thus also appearance in the sense of deception: it deceives about its springing forth/emerging from life. And yet, the imaginal form, as this deception, is still transparent: as appearance [Schein] the image is equally manifestation [Erscheinung]. It can show what was a reflection, its world of appearance can reflect the reflection [den Widerschein reflektieren]. In itself, in its form, the painting brings the untransfigured life to its transfigured appearance. Thus the art of images as a whole amounts to that which Raphael's painting announces in its title: Transfiguration.

Precisely how one is to read the manifestation of images, how one is to decipher in the transfiguration the reflection of life, cannot easily be gleaned from the painting itself. To do so, the merely reflected vitality in the painting must be able to be experienced immediately. Only in this way can one know what is recognisable in the showing of images and their signs.

The immediate experience of vitality belongs to another art form: music. Nietzsche was even more interested in its lyrical form, for in lyrical art, music comes into a relation to imaginal form. Lyrical art is essentially music: the lyricist a Dionysian artist who lets himself be pulled along by the flow of life, by its motility, and who articulates life in its motility. As articulation, lyrical art is

already more than mere life; indeed, it is, on the one hand, immediate oscil-
lation, but, on the other hand, has already pulled itself up out of life. In the
sounding of tone and of speech, something quite distinct takes place, something
which Nietzsche designates a 'repetition of the world', as the 'imageless and
conceptless reappearance of life' (I: 44).[4] Furthermore, lyrical art is, in its very
occurrence, already a reflection – yet not in the sense of an inverting impression, as in painting, but in the sense of an inverting expression. In its expressive character, lyrical art can make life be felt immediately, but not
unbrokenly. On account of this brokenness, lyrical art is also already, as pure
music, 'redemption in appearance' (I: 44).

Insofar as the rhythm and sound of music find their words in lyrical art, this
appearance is doubled. The reflection of music 'produces now a second mirroring, as a specific symbol or example' (I: 44). The expression presents itself
in images and representations; it objectifies itself. But unlike in imaginal art,
the images and representations do not become independent. Their being
remains bound up with the unfolding of musical articulation. The image is 'produced' in the imageless and conceptless reflection of music; with lyrical art,
one must listen to the speaking, let it sound, in order to understand its meaning *qua* representation. Thus the reflections are not appearances alongside which
one can linger, but rather objectivations in the movement of expression.

In this respect, lyrical art, it seems, is superior to imaginal art. The reflection of life in expression is not concealed in some imaginal form, but the image
remains itself fluid and transparent. As opposed to imaginal art, lyrical art has
to do with an incessant transfiguring, rather than with a completed transfiguration, the latter being able to show what it was before only by way of images.
Thus Nietzsche appears with good reason to be able to interpret lyrical art as
the authentic self-presentation and self-knowledge of life. The lyricist is, as he
says, 'at once subject and object, at once poet, actor and spectator' (I: 48). In
lyrical art there appears to be a reconciliation of life and reflection.

But this reconciliation is bound up with a condition that is never fulfilled:
'Only so far as the genius in the fact of artistic production coalesces with the
originary artist of the world', thus becoming one with the innermost foundations of life, does he become 'like the weird image of the fairy tale which can
turn its eyes and behold itself' (I: 47). Only thus, when the artist collapses in
the 'expressionless and imageless medium of life, is the rift of life and reflection closed. But art itself thereby would collapse. It would annihilate the
appearance, which none the less sustains it, and which alone gives content to
what is meant by the phrase 'self-intuition of life'.

On the other hand, appearance in art also cannot remain unquestioned and
unqualified. Without interrupting the world of appearance, without protest
against appearance, art would be a glossy mirroring surface. A moment of

147

presentationlessness [*Darstellungslosen*][5] belongs together with the presentory presence [*Darstellungspräsenz*] of art. It is characteristic of the experience of the
'truly aesthetic spectator' that he 'must see at the same time that he also longs
to transcend all seeing' (I: 150). The truly aesthetic spectator 'shares with the
Apollinian art sphere the complete pleasure in appearance and in seeing, yet at
the same time negates this pleasure and finds a still higher satisfaction in the
destruction of the visible world of appearance' (I: 151). Life is presented only
in reflection, and yet every reflection is insufficient, precisely because as reflection it only grasps life in a broken manner.

The protest against appearance, on the other hand, first allows appearance
to come into its own. No manifestation is convincing without pointing beyond
itself, and whoever experiences the appeal of a manifestation never stops with
mere manifestation. But at issue here is not the possibility of getting closer to
something which might be found behind manifestation and which would itself
be without presentation. The step beyond manifestation leads only deeper into
presentation and to the presentory – to life in its inarticulatedness and undi-
videdness. Not in what is presented, but in the presenting itself do we find the
promise of that higher satisfaction that is said to lie in the 'annihilation of the
visual world of appearance'. Manifestations do not suffice, but vitality, as it is
experienced beyond manifestations, shows an impulse towards manifestation in
order to make itself present.

*   *   *

In the interplay of life and reflected appearance the self-presentation of a limited reason occurs. Unfolding and objectifying have always already penetrated
one another and cannot be without one another, and yet they do not make
themselves felt in the same manner. What has been shown in the distinction
between lyric and imaginal art holds generally: either being comes to expression by becoming or becoming comes to manifest itself by being. Oriented by
the formal determinations of being and becoming, we can understand and
describe all forms of life in their singularity. Cultures, institutions, even the
tonality of individual characters first give shape to themselves in the occurring
and leading of life. The determinateness of life, the free space in which it is
to be determinately lived, is moreover found only in these forms. To live in
such and such a way means to *exist* in forms, to *be* in the very presentation of
forms. To live is to exist in free spaces which are forms and, as determinate
forms, have been shaped or reshaped in the living-through of life. The genetic
view, oriented to becoming, and the structural view, aiming at being, will not
let themselves be played off against each other as alternatives, for only by alternating one's point of view does one do justice to the matter.

This alternating viewpoint can never be so radical that the other view would completely vanish. Bare perspectives and new illuminations always take place: structures always appear only as a result of alterations which as such recede the more sharply one sees the structures; alterations occur as determinate and graspable only in the play-space of a life form, whether the latter modifies another form or whether it is transposed into another. Yet the alteration can never be completely grasped in the light of form alone; every alteration has a radically formless moment, a moment that cannot be domesticated by any form.

Now this is precisely what comes to fruition in art. As has become manifest through our discussion of Nietzsche, the exchange of glances between being and becoming in aesthetic impression is always bound up with an inverted manifestation of what is dimmed down in direct experience. Therein lies, so to speak, the cunning of aesthetic representation. To its essence belong the recurrence of what has been forgotten, the recurrence of what had to be forgotten in order to set free a particular experience. Through the cunning of aesthetic presentation the essence of presentation in general first appears. It is remarkable that nothing that must present itself can be present without another, and that its presence depends upon what stands over against it as other and alien. Thus in the process of presentation, tribute is paid to the very possibility of presentation: where the other of a self-presenting presence itself comes to reflective presence, presentation lets its possibility become manifest at its very limit; the delimiting, which the presence of the self-presenting carries with it, appears in the measure of the delimited. Thus that which manifests itself in its limitedness accounts for that which provided the ground for its manifesting.

Nietzsche is convinced of the paradigmatic character of art for modernity. Art has fully reached its pre-eminent medium of articulation and has contributed more to the self-understanding of the epoch than philosophy; at least it has, in Nietzsche's words, opened up possibilities of an 'immediate assurance of intuition', which have surpassed in every way isolated 'logical inferences'. Art's manifold, ever newly posited attempts at presentation testify to a reason which can be self-transparent in its limiting binding to life, in its limited reflective separation from life.

That Nietzsche grants a paradigmatic meaning to art in his thought has often been understood as an inadmissible aestheticisation of life. It would actually be impossible to claim that every life form is determined exhaustively, wherever one discovers in it traits of art or wherever one attempts to grasp art as its ideal. Correspondingly, one should not grasp the orientation to the paradigm of art as an exclusive generalisation of art, but should find in it the realisation that all life comportments are comportments of presentation. Seen in this way the aesthetic is, in its distinction from life, precisely its appropriate presentation; no presentation can be identical with that which in it makes itself felt. There as well rests the manifoldness of the possibilities of exhibition, the irreducible plurality of forms of presentation. Not everything that is is art, but what everything is is shown in art.

This holds naturally as well for philosophy. In view of the paradigmatic character of art, philosophy must not become art, or accentuate its artistic aspects – which it more or less explicitly has – to the point where its own specificity would disappear. Rather, one should attempt to bring to the fore philosophically that other which art has always been for philosophy. Where this happens and philosophical thought reflects the model of aesthetically limited reason, thinking can discover how it itself is presentation in general, and how it is thus referred to an other which has, as it were, encroached upon it. One can remain faithful to the other only where one conceives of the other not as the other of thought, but as that reason which has manifested itself and has not quite yet reached itself. Where thinking wishes to grasp the encroaching, it will have to do so reflectively, presenting within itself the corresponding thought of what the other was.

A thinking that knows itself to be conditioned by what limits it and that will not let this conditioning be overlooked can be called 'hermeneutic'. A hermeneutic thinking is one which brings to language that which escapes it as its cause, but which none the less sustains its articulations. In a thinking which carries its own quality of presentation within it, the trace of the other is preserved.

Translated by John Protevi and Peter Poellner

Notes

1 Ernst Jünger, 'Das abenteuerliche Herz: Erste Fassung', in *Sämtliche Werke* (Stuttgart, 1978–83) IX: 33. Cf. my *Für eine Philosophie von Freiheit und Streit. Politik – Ästhetik – Metaphysik* (Stuttgart, 1994), 92–110. See also my essay 'Ästhetische Individualität: Erörterungen im Hinblick auf Ernst Jünger' in G. Boehm and E. Rudolph, eds, *Individuum: Probleme der Individualität in Kunst, Philosophie, und Wissenschaft* (Stuttgart, 1994), 151–71.
2 See Joachim Ritter, 'Landschaft: Zur Funktion des Ästhetischen in der modernen Gesellschaft' in *Subjecktivität: Sechs Aufsätze* (Frankfurt, 1974), 141–63.
3 All references to Nietzsche are to the *Kritische Studienausgabe*, edited by Giorgio Colli and Mazzino Montinari (Berlin, 1988), cited in the text by volume and page number without further designation. Here, the reference is to *Birth of Tragedy*, I: 34.
4 That we read here 'reappearance [*Wiederschein*]', while in the interpretation of Raphael's *Transfiguration* the talk is of 'reflection [*Widerschein*]' should not cause a great deal of irritation, for the sense of the two expressions is the same. It is possible that the writing of 'reappearance' is to be interpreted as a complement to the 'repetition' that had shortly before made its appearance (I: 44 n2). *À propos* the two citations, the edition of Karl Schlechta reads 'reflection', a choice I find persuasive.

Cf. Friedrich Nietzsche, *Werke in drei Bänden*, edited by K. Schlechta, (Munich 1966) I: 33, 37.

5 With this concept I indicate a modification of the 'expressionlessness [*Ausdrucklosen*]', as understood by Walter Benjamin in his essay 'Goethe's Wahlverwandschaften'. Cf. Walter Benjamin, *Gesammelte Schriften*, edited by Rolf Tiedemann and Herman Schweppenhäuser (Frankfurt, 1974) I.1: 180–2.

8

Zarathustra: the tragic figure of the last philosopher

Walter Brogan

> The coast has vanished, now the last chain has fallen from me,
> the boundless roars around me, far out glisten space and
> time; be of good cheer, old heart.[1]

Nietzsche says often that he is the disciple of the philosopher Dionysus. After the death of God and the exhaustion of Socratism and philosophy, suddenly just at this moment Dionysus, the god of tragedy, becomes a philosopher. My aim in this essay is to explore the character of this tragic philosopher who wears the mask of the god whom, Nietzsche claims, was unmasked by Socrates and remained thus disempowered by this Socratic exposure even up until the time of Nietzsche.

As a Dionysian disciple, Nietzsche positions himself as a satyr in the retinue of Dionysus; thus a he-goat, a tragic sacrificial figure who is destined to go under, to be surpassed, to perish. He is a manifestation of Dionysus himself since the distinction between the god and his devotees is surpassed in the frenzy of the Dionysian rites. The inadequacy of the distinction between disciple and god is evident in Euripides' *Bacchae* where Dionysus in fact appears in the disguise of his followers. One of Dionysus' favourite activities as the wearer of masks is in fact just this sort of self-mirroring disguising of himself. We might then conclude that Nietzsche, as the disciple of Dionysus, is the manifestation, the image, of Dionysus, the figure of this god; that Nietzsche's name is a substitute for that of Dionysus. So when towards the end of his life Nietzsche at times signs his letters 'Dionysus', this is a confusion that is characteristic of devotees of Dionysus and of tragic theatre.

But why does Nietzsche call Dionysus a philosopher? Is it not Nietzsche who has absorbed the death of God and the end of philosophy, and the one who announces the rebirth of art, the victory of music *over* philosophy? Thus Nietzsche speaks in *The Birth of Tragedy* of the shipwreck of Socratic logic which speeds to the border of its own horizons only to witness in horror how logic coils up at these boundaries and finally bites its own tail; and then suddenly out of this collapse of the philosophical voyage, a new form of insight breaks through, *tragic insight* which needs not philosophy but art in order to be endured. What does it mean that Nietzsche reinstates philosophy as a Dionysian pathway? And how is Nietzsche's philosophy the traversing of this new path?

In *Beyond Good and Evil*, after arguing that philosophers should be ranked according to *laughter*, Nietzsche suggests that even gods can be ranked in this way, and he mentions specifically Dionysus, whom he here calls 'the great ambiguous one'.[2] Then, in continuing the thought of this juxtaposition of philosophers and gods, he says:

> I the last disciple and initiate of the god Dionysus – and I suppose I might begin at long last to offer to you my friends a few tastes of this philosophy. . . . Even that Dionysus is a philosopher, and that gods, too, thus do philosophy, seems to me a novelty that is far from innocuous, and might arouse suspicion precisely among philosophers.
>
> (BGE, § 295)

This suspicion is aroused nowhere as strongly as it is by Nietzsche's own work. Even as early as *The Birth of Tragedy*, Nietzsche says: 'Believe with me in Dionysian life and the rebirth of tragedy. The age of the Socratic man is over; put on wreaths of ivy. . . . Only dare to be tragic beings.'[3]

If philosophy finds itself reinscribed by Nietzsche as the Dionysian life and the rebirth of tragedy, then we might rightly wonder whether Nietzsche is not himself undermining his narrative of the overcoming of the metaphysical tradition. But there are, of course, many indications that the philosophy that is paired by Nietzsche with Dionysus cannot be understood as the same philosophy he calls Socratism.

At the end of *Ecce Homo*, Nietzsche says: 'Have I been understood? Dionysus *versus* the crucified.'[4] So the philosophy of Dionysus is a philosophy of the *gegen*, the versus, the *polemos*, precisely a philosophy in opposition to the form of Socratism associated with the cross.

Among the several descriptions of 'the last philosopher' contained in Nietzsche's notes is the one where Nietzsche calls the last philosopher the philosopher of tragic insight:

> He masters the uncontrolled knowledge drive, though not by means of a new metaphysics. He establishes no new faith. He considers it *tragic* that the ground of metaphysics has been withdrawn, and he will never permit himself to be satisfied with the motley whirling

game of the sciences. . . . One must even *will illusion* – that is what is tragic.⁵

The insight envisioned in this rebirth of tragedy and tragic philosophy does not lie in the discovery of a new ground. To think this tragic event of the vanishing ground is to think *Schein* untethered from the definition of illusion upon which metaphysics is based. Nietzsche calls this freed sort of illusion 'Apollinian *illusion* whose influence aims to deliver us from the Dionysian flood and excess' (*BT*, 129). But then Nietzsche cautions: 'at the most essential point, this Apollinian illusion is broken and annihilated' (*BT*, 130). The non-metaphysical, Apollinian vision projects out of the pain and excess of the Dionysian, not for the sake of dissolving its broken, fragmentary force, but for the sake of allowing us to live more faithfully in its midst. Thus Nietzsche says: 'In the total effect of tragedy [which includes dislocation and fragmentation], the Dionysian predominates' (*BT*, 130).

In the reconciliation of tragic art and philosophy that the term Dionysian philosopher promises, the Dionysian predominates. Tragic knowledge remains the kind of knowledge and insight that Nietzsche speaks of in analysing *Oedipus Tyrannus* in *The Birth of Tragedy*. Indeed, Oedipus is one of the signatures of the last philosopher in Nietzsche's notes. Oedipal, tragic knowledge violates lineages, exposes incestuous genealogies, disrupts the natural order. It is true that a reconciliation and unification is accomplished through Oedipus' riddle-solving knowledge. But it is far from the harmony and beauty of Hegelian dialectic in its culminating moment. It is a violent, monstrous reconciliation, a grotesque violation.

In part, the monstrosity of a philosophy that is Dionysian is indicated by the *figure* of Oedipus, who as both husband and son, father and brother, foreigner and citizen, is an inherently dis-figured philosopher, a double figure like Dionysus and, in fact, like Nietzsche himself in *Ecce Homo*:

> . . . the good fortune of my existence, its uniqueness perhaps, lies in its fatality: I am, to express it in the form of a riddle, already dead as my father, while as my mother I am still living and becoming old. This double origin [*doppelte Herkunft*] . . . explains that neutrality, that freedom from all partiality in relation to the total problem of life that distinguishes me. I have a subtler sense of smell for the *signs* of ascent and decline than any other human being before me; I am the teacher *par excellence* for this – I know both, I am both.
>
> (*EH*, 678)

But it is Dionysus above all who is the prototype of the double figure who is both masculine and feminine, as is again made evident in the *Bacchae* where Dionysus appears as a woman.

In a fragment about Oedipus written in 1872, Nietzsche writes:

> I call myself the last philosopher because I am the last human being. No one talks to me other than myself. . . . For my heart refuses to believe that love is dead, cannot bear the terror of the loneliest loneliness: it compels me to talk, as though I were *two*.[6]

The figure of the last philosopher is that of an utterly solitary, yet bifurcated being. In *Ecce Homo*, Nietzsche says: 'My whole *Zarathustra* is a dithyramb on solitude' (*EH*, 690). The fact that *Zarathustra* is dithyrambic-like indicates that Nietzsche views this work as a Dionysian, tragic poem. At another point in *Ecce Homo*, Nietzsche declares: 'Perhaps the whole of *Zarathustra* may be reckoned as music; certainly a rebirth of the art of *hearing* was among its preconditions' (*EH*, 751). Thus the aesthetic *listener* is also reborn with the rebirth of tragedy. He says of the period in which *Zarathustra* was written: 'the yes-saying pathos *par excellence*, which I call tragic pathos, was alive in me to the highest degree' (*EH*, 752). Of *Thus Spoke Zarathustra*, he says:

> My concept of the 'Dionysian' here becomes a *supreme deed*. . . . In every word he [Zarathustra] contradicts, this most Yes-saying of all spirits; in him all opposites are blended into a new unity.
>
> (*EH*, 760–1)

The connection between the figure of Zarathustra and that of Dionysus, the god of tragedy, is made most explicit at the end of Book Four of *The Gay Science*, where Nietzsche quotes the first lines of *Zarathustra* and entitles the section: 'Incipit Tragoedia'. At the end of *The Gay Science* he says that it is only with Zarathustra 'that the real question mark is posed for the first time, that the destiny of the soul changes, the hand moves forward, the tragedy *begins*'.[7] Thus we are to understand that *Thus Spoke Zarathustra* is the rebirth of tragic art and Zarathustra is the prototype of the tragic philosopher. Zarathustra, Nietzsche says, is 'the soul in which all things have their sweep and countersweep, and ebb and flood – Dionysus' (*EH*, 761–2).

In a reference to what he calls in *Birth of Tragedy* the new tragic aesthetics of the sublime, Nietzsche says that the task of Zarathustra is to say yes to the point of justifying, of redeeming even all of the past, of overcoming the *nausea* of abysmal thinking (through comic, parodic laughter, as we will see later). And in 1889, at the end of *Twilight of the Idols*, Nietzsche says:

155

And herewith I again touch that point from which I once went forth: the *Birth of Tragedy* was my first revaluation of all values. Herewith I again stand on the soil out of which my intention, my ability grows – I, the last disciple of the philosopher Dionysus – I, the teacher of the eternal recurrence.[8]

Thus, in various ways, Nietzsche repeatedly suggests that the rebirth of tragedy that he called for in his earlier work is accomplished in *Thus Spoke Zarathustra*. We can sustain this claim through an examination of various aspects of *Zarathustra*, culminating with an interpretation of the eternal recurrence as the tragic insight that Nietzsche refers to in *The Birth of Tragedy*. But it would be too limited to suggest that *Zarathustra* is only a tragic work. It is also important to examine part IV of *Zarathustra*, which resembles a satyr play[9] and allows the work to pass from tragic literature over into comedy and, finally, to close the gap between this division of literature.

If *Thus Spoke Zarathustra* is a work of *tragic* philosophy, then it must have already experienced the death of Socratism, for during the reign of Socratic philosophy, Nietzsche says, a tragic work was not possible. The first part of *Zarathustra* is about Zarathustra's or the tragic figure's relationship to Socratism.

One aspect of Zarathustra's speeches is their attempt to ferret out and make clear the sin against life involved in Socratism. Given Nietzsche's description of tragedy as having its origin in life itself where art is life's metaphorical self-expression, this critique of Socratism as a crime against life is in effect an analysis of it as both anti-life and anti-Dionysian, that is, anti-tragic. If we are to take Nietzsche's claim seriously that with *Zarathustra* tragedy begins, then *Zarathustra* can be seen to begin with the overcoming of Socratism. In a sense, then, *Zarathustra* begins at the time of and with the announcement of the death of Socratic philosophy. This is a kind of double overturning: it is the death of the death of tragedy. Zarathustra begins his Odyssean journey as the prophet and precursor of this overcoming, but comes to realise that he himself must undergo this double dying in order to be reborn as the tragic *Übermensch*.

This double dying that involves a tragic rebirth is replicated in Zarathustra's relationship to God. The story of Zarathustra is the story of one who comes after the death of God. In *The Gay Science*, there is the well-known passage on the madman where the madman, who cries 'Whither is God?', and continues:

I will tell you. *We have killed him* – you and I. All of us are his murderers. But how did we do this? How could we drink up the sea? Who gave us the sponge to wipe away the entire horizon? What were we doing when we unchained this earth from its sun?

(*GS*, § 125)

Apollinian sun imagery also pervades the text of *Zarathustra*. In the Prologue, we find that the sun has entered the underworld; it moves and is no longer fixed in the sky. The fixity of metaphysical principles has given way, entering into the movement of a sun that moves *into* the earth. Zarathustra says: 'For I must descend to the depths as you do in the evening when you go behind the sea and still bring light to the underworld, you overrich star. Like you, I must *go under*' (*TSZ*, 122). In a sense, I want to argue that the task of Zarathustra is to follow the downward plunge of the sun. If one learns to enter into this plunge in the right way, then what occurs is the birth of a dancing star out of and within the chaos one has in oneself. Zarathustra, unlike the madman, no longer seeks a transcendent God. This is the significance of his encounter with the saint in the forest who has surprisingly not yet heard of the death of God. Zarathustra has already absorbed this event before his story begins. Thus *Zarathustra* is not essentially about the experience of nihilism but about a new possibility, a new beginning; not about the death of God but about the rebirth of tragedy after the death of God.

The rebirth of tragedy occurs because the archimedean point of reference has shifted out of centre. Plato's fixed supreme point of reference comes unchained. The chains through which human beings were enchained in Plato's cave have been broken. In contrast to the closure and conservation of energy at the heart of metaphysics, this unchaining unleashes the Dionysian excess once again. All talk of containing the multiplicity of the earthly in a primal unity or metaphysical *will* must now be suspended.

In place of will, Nietzsche calls for us to 'remain faithful to the earth and not to believe those who speak to us of otherworldly hopes' (*TSZ*, 125). The earth unchained from the sun is no longer the earth that is there to be sacrificed for our use. Rather, Nietzsche calls for human beings to sacrifice *themselves* for the earth. The earth as the realm of mere appearance and deception, whose meaning is imposed from beyond, has disappeared with the death of God. With the destruction of the metaphysical, with the advent of nihilism, the earth is set free. In trying to rethink tragedy after the end of metaphysics, this may be important. The human confrontation with the gods that was the central issue of Greek tragedy gives way to the question of our relationship with the earth. But this does not necessarily imply the victory of the tragic hero – an unbridled Oedipus or a new triumphant Prometheus. There may after all still be a god to deal with in the new tragic age, not the god of metaphysics but the goddess earth, Gaia. Thus Zarathustra says: 'Once the sin against god was the greatest sin. But god died and these sinners died with him. To sin against the earth is now the most dreadful thing' (*TSZ*, 125). Being faithful to the earth after having killed god means living in an age where, according to Nietzsche, all ladders with which to escape are gone: 'There is no longer any path behind you. . . . Your own foot has effaced the path behind you' (*TSZ*, 265). Nietzsche describes this new faith in terms that make clear that the required fidelity is not to an order that would impose meaning on the earth from outside:

> O my brothers, is not everything in flux now? Have not all railings and bridges fallen into the water? Who could cling to 'good' and 'evil'? Woe to us, hail to us, the thawing wind blows! . . . Exiles shall you be from all father-and-forefather lands.
>
> (*TSZ*, 313/316)

To remain faithful to the earth is a tragic posture precisely because it requires of us that we undergo the refragmentation of the past, the reopening of the accidental and multiple character of the it was. The tragic age is an age that permits itself to experience this Dionysian event of being torn to pieces. Thus, in contrast to parables of permanence, Zarathustra says in 'Upon the Blessed Isles': 'It is of time and becoming that the best parables should speak. Let them be a praise and a justification of all impermanence' (*TSZ*, 198–9). In the same passage, we find the metaphor of the past as a stone, to be shattered by a hammer blow, thus releasing the images contained and imprisoned there and, with them, one's creativity and poetic capacity.

This philosophy of fragmentation and multiplicity also has implications for the modernist attempt to replace a theistic conception of reality with humanism. In contrast to parables of equality, Zarathustra says in 'On the Tarantulas': 'Men are not equal. Nor shall they become equal. What would my love of the overman be if I spoke otherwise? On a thousand bridges and paths they shall throng to the future' (*TSZ*, 213). This is one of those passages where Nietzsche's anti-humanism comes out most strongly. On one level, it is a critique of one of the pillars of modernity and an apparent return to a classical model of political inequality. But I would suggest Zarathustra's political stance here is more a kind of anarchistic politics of multiplicity after the breakup of all politico-metaphysical systems.

All of these themes and implications come together in the passage 'On Redemption', where Zarathustra encounters the cripples and speaks of inverse cripples. He begins to find disciples among those who are misfits in the marketplaces of the last man. This is especially evident in the case of the higher men in part IV of *Zarathustra*.

Zarathustra says:

> I walk among humans as among the fragments and the limbs of human beings. . . . And when my eyes flee from now to the past, they always

find the same: fragments and limbs and dreadful accidents – but no human beings.

(TSZ, 250)

Zarathustra goes on to call himself a cripple on the bridge to the future and says:

> I walk among humans as among the fragments of the future – that future which I envisage. And this is all my creating and striving, that I create and carry together into one what is riddle and dreadful accident.

(TSZ, 251)

The question of the political in tragic times begins as a politics of fragmentation. This is evident in Zarathustra's many discourses on friendship and solitude. Nietzsche's preoccupation with the solitude of Zarathustra seems to be related to the experience of utter abandonment and forsakenness after the collapse of metaphysics and the death of God. In § 367 of *The Gay Science*, Nietzsche says: 'For the pious, there is as yet no solitude; this invention was made only by us, the godless.' Solitude is a prerequisite for entering into the movement of Nietzsche's most radical thought: the thought of eternal recurrence. In the passage entitled 'The Return Home', Nietzsche is said to return to his home, his solitude, where his solitude says: 'You were more forsaken among the many, being one, than ever with me' (*TSZ*, 295). In this solitude, the idle chatter that fails to communicate what is essential vanishes. Nietzsche says: 'Here the words and word-shrines of all being open up before me: here all being wishes to become word, all becoming wishes to learn from me how to speak' (*TSZ*, 296). Zarathustra's solitude is not an absence of communication but the discovery of one's poetic being that prepares one for the communication of the eternal recurrence.

Nietzsche says that in the solitude of the return home, what comes home is myself to myself and what of myself has long been in strange lands and scattered among all things and accidents. But this is not another version of Cartesian solipsism. Like Descartes, Nietzsche is addressing the experience of a vanishing world and the loss of structures and ladders necessary to climb out of ourselves. But the self that is returned to Zarathustra is the one that remains dispersed and scattered over the landscape. It is because the accidental belongs to this very being that he is able to see himself as the shattered one when things become fragmented.

When in tragic art, Dionysus is torn to pieces and reborn, this means also that the world is torn to pieces and reborn. It seems to me that Nietzsche's

159

discourse on solitude is not an attempt to find a non-shattering ground of self as the basis for a belief in the unity and permanence of the being of all beings. Rather very much the contrary. It is a declaration that being itself, so to speak, is essentially fragmentary.

Zarathustra's loneliness is broken by the next passage, called 'The Vision and the Riddle', where the solution to the Sphinx-like riddle is the first pronouncement of the eternal return, which is here expressed as the *insight* that all things are knotted together so firmly that the moment draws after it all that is to come. The thought of eternal recurrence is not the thought of one who has concluded that to will *all* means in effect to be unable to commit oneself forcefully to any *one* life perspective. If anything, the opposite conclusion would be closer to the truth. Namely, what is required of us by this thought is precisely that we ourselves become creative. The ass festival in part IV is all about this question. Eternal recurrence is not the affirmation of the ass who brays Yeah to everything indiscriminately.

And yet the difficulty of this question is not easily resolved. Even more strongly, part IV concludes that the affirmative will affirms all things, even the last men. So perhaps it is really a question about what it means to be an affirmer. How Zarathustra can affirm the higher men and yet let the lions' roar scare them away from his cave. On the one hand, Nietzsche indicates that the thought of eternal recurrence is tragic insight. On the other hand, in significant ways, this thought of the circulation of all that is overcomes tragedy. Or perhaps eternal recurrence is a way of thinking at the limits of tragedy. For the thought of eternal recurrence destroys the very distinctions that would allow us to call something tragic – the distinction between God and humans for example, or even the distinction between parent and child. And of course most of all it blurs the essential distinction between life and death. So in some sense eternal recurrence is beyond tragedy. Just one indication of this is that the notion of a tragic hero is thoroughly undermined by Nietzsche's treatment of the higher men, as we shall see.

But this means that my thesis has been undermined. I have been unable to sustain the claim that *Zarathustra* is a tragedy. I have only been able feebly to walk through the text up to the point before the thesis collapses upon itself. The claim that *Thus Spoke Zarathustra* is about the rebirth of tragedy cannot be sustained. Perhaps even tragedy cannot redeem us from the nihilism and nausea of our times. Perhaps rather a certain overcoming of tragedy is required. In fact, it should have been clear from the outset that tragedy would not work for us as a central notion around which to rally Nietzsche's most essential thinking. For all great tragedians know that the culmination of tragedy is not tragic theatre but comedy. The great tragedians followed their trilogy of tragic plays with a fourth satyric comedy.

This epilogue of tragedies, this excessive tragedy that spills over into comedy, must of course throw into question our traditional separation of these two art forms. Perhaps the eternal recurrence somehow blurs the distinction between tragedy and comedy as it does the Apollinian–Dionysian distinction and, in fact, all oppositional dualisms, not by evading the opposition but by entering into it more fully. Perhaps this is why it is not said to be the cry of distress of the higher men that would lead us to the vision and insight of eternal recurrence. Rather it is the piercing laughter of Zarathustra. In other words, the shortcoming of the higher men, as well as their resemblance up to a point to Zarathustra, may lie in the fact that the higher men are mired in a tragic vision that they cannot surpass.

On this reading, the soothsayer (of great weariness) would represent a response that Nietzsche in *Will to Power* calls incomplete nihilism: 'Its forms: we live in the midst of it. Attempts to escape nihilism without revaluating our values so far: they produce the opposite, make the problem more acute.'[10] The soothsayer says: 'All is the same, therefore nothing is worthwhile. The world is without meaning. Knowledge strangles' (*TSZ*, 353). In *Will to Power* § 55 (1887), we read: 'Nihilism appears at that point, not that the displeasure at existence has become greater than before but because one has come to mistrust any "meaning" in suffering, indeed in existence.' Then he adds:

> Let us think this thought in its most terrible form: existence as it is, without meaning or aim, yet recurring inevitably without any finale of nothingness: '*the eternal recurrence*'.
>
> (*WP*, § 55)

For the nihilist soothsayer, the prophet of doom, the eternal recurrence of the same is the final stage of nihilism, that is, it is complete nihilism, the *amor fati* of nihilism, the embrace of the wisdom of Silenus. That would explain Nietzsche's comment after a passage on nihilism where he says: 'In sum this constitutes the tragic age' (*WP*, § 37).

Nietzsche refers to the soothsayer as *another* shadow, that is, not his own shadow. Remember that Zarathustra calls him the soothsayer of great weariness and mentions that they shook hands in a desperate effort to recognise themselves in each other. So the two spirits are not the same, the tragic spirit of nihilism and Zarathustra's spirit. You will recall that it is the devil who takes Jesus to the highest mountain and offers him his final temptation and sin. So the soothsayer is the devil who admits that he has come to seduce Zarathustra to *his* final sin, which he acknowledges will not be material possession of an earthly kingdom – this would not be appropriate – but rather pity for the tragic call of distress of the higher person.

161

Now several questions might be raised here: why is Zarathustra concerned about the higher one in particular? Is it because the higher one has attempted to go through nihilism and overcome it and because the cry of distress is the inevitable failure of all attempts to heed or practise Zarathustra's teachings? And why does Nietzsche explicitly note that Zarathustra's response to this cry is dread? Zarathustra seems especially concerned that this cry of distress has been sounded in his realm rather than in the blessed isles. In other words, melancholy and distress still belong to Zarathustra.

This is made clear in the final lines of discussion with the soothsayer, where the soothsayer warns that he cannot escape him, that he will be waiting for him in his cave. And then Zarathustra says: 'So be it! . . . And whatever is mine in my cave belongs to you too, my guest. . . . And you yourself shall dance to my songs' (TSZ, 356). So the weariness and spirit of melancholy is transfigured but does not vanish at the end of Zarathustra's journey. That is perhaps why the old magician says:

> Zarathustra sometimes seems to me like a beautiful mask of a saint, like a new strange masquerade in which my evil spirit, the melancholy devil, enjoys himself. I love Zarathustra, it often seems to me, for the sake of my evil spirit.
>
> (TSZ, 409)

We should perhaps pay some more attention to the various characterisations of Zarathustra that are given by the higher ones. The old magician here says that Zarathustra is a mask and producer of masquerades. The magician himself is of course a trickster who can appear in many forms, who is his disguises. He is the ultimate game-player and riddle-maker — a caricature, a facet of Zarathustra himself whom the soothsayer says cannot be found, not even by one who could come to his mountain. There we are told we would look in vain for 'that' man: 'caves we would find, and caves behind caves, hiding places for those addicted to hiding, but no mines of happiness' (TSZ, 355).

The song of melancholy is the cry of distress of the would-be suitor of truth who is unmasked as only a poet: 'Only screaming colourfully out of fools' masks, climbing around on mendacious word bridges' (TSZ, 410). It is a song that mocks the longing of the spirit for truth, even the truth of abysses, which the magician compares to the eagle who swoops and soars and plunges downward but in order to prey on the lambs, 'tearing to pieces' the god in man and laughing while tearing.

So the magician sings an ode to Zarathustra even though Zarathustra is absent. It is Zarathustra who tears to pieces by his poetry, whose longings are under a thousand masks. In the actual passage on the magician, Zarathustra calls

162

him the great deceiver and counterfeiter. His complaint is not this, however, but rather that there is neither enough truth nor enough falsity in what he says. In other words, the magician has seen only the collapse of truth and concludes all is mere deception; he has not seen the liberation of appearance, the affirmation and truth-saying dimension of Zarathustra's teaching. Thus he remains a sophist and nihilist, a trickster rather than a Zarathustrian game-player.

If everything is false, then there remains for us the possible task of seeking truth. The old magician says that he is 'seeking' Zarathustra as the truth, one who is genuine, right, simple, unequivocal, a vessel of wisdom, and so on. Ironically, Zarathustra does not reject these accolades but merely sends him to his cave, warning him though that only fools succeed. The limitation of the magician, we are told, is that he has harvested nausea as his one truth. But that he strives to overcome the nihilism that says 'all is false' is admired by Zarathustra. In his cave, the magician will learn what is necessary to overcome this last temptation of nausea. It will of course be laughter.

We might note a similar redemptive quality in the case of each of the other higher ones. Take, for example, the kings: their complaint is that the age of kings has been overturned, that now the peasant rules. They remain as kings but no longer rule. They are in other words *mere* representation. They say: 'we are not the first and yet must represent them; it is this deception that has come to disgust and nauseate us. . . . What do kings matter now?' (*TSZ*, 357). They like Zarathustra's talk about warriors because it reminds them of their forefathers who had power. So the kings too are detached from the past and yet defined by it. They too share the problem of deception that plagued the magician. But Zarathustra admires their dissatisfaction with the role of empty representation and their ability to wait for their kingdom to return.

In a similar way, the pope is a higher man precisely because he held on to his piety, that is, he did not conclude that since God is dead, everything holy has become profane. And the ugliest man did not conclude that the death of the great witness who looked over and saw all things forgave him in any way from the further task of repelling the pity of the left-over Godlovers who also loved to witness him in this way. In other words, the ugliest man refused to conclude that with the death of God everyone is pitiful. Thus we are told that the ugliest man made room in his life for great failure, presumably even for the failure of Zarathustra, a failure that avoids the pitfall of pity.

In the beginning of the parody of worshipping that pervades part IV, we see in the voluntary beggar one who preaches to cows in order to be faithful to the earth. But it is a parody of Zarathustra, as Zarathustra makes clear:

Are you not the voluntary beggar who once threw away great riches [the squanderer]? Who was ashamed of his riches and of the rich, and

fled to the poorest to give them his fullness and his heart? But they
did not accept him.

(TSZ, 381)

So what the voluntary beggar has recognised is that Nietzsche's anti-
Christianity, which condemns the spiritually of weakness and poverty, does not
lead one to conclude that one should become a supporter of the rich.

In a sense all of this is summarised for us in the discussion of Zarathustra
with his shadow. The shadow has become untethered. Zarathustra talks of run-
ning away from his shadow, but the shadow has longer legs and always overcomes him. The shadow complains that he has been decimated by travelling
with Zarathustra. The homelessness of the shadow becomes the central theme
of this section 'O eternal everywhere, O eternal nowhere, O eternal – in vain!'
(TSZ, 386). Zarathustra calls him a free spirit and wanderer and warns him not
to search to be imprisoned again.

Let's go back now to the problem of interpreting this part of Zarathustra in
the context of the question of tragedy. We were suggesting that part IV forces
us to reconsider our claim that Zarathustra is the rebirth of tragedy. Minimally
we would, I think, have to acknowledge that if this were so, then each of the
higher men could be tragic figures in their own right and the story would revolve
around their tragic vision. To a certain extent of course this is true. But the cry
of distress that would represent the high moment in a tragedy turns out here to
be disseminated amongst all of the contenders and all together constitute the
tragic figure. Each individually falls short of the heights of a tragic experience.
So at the rebirth of tragedy, one conclusion we might draw is that the tragic
hero is a disseminated, fragmented self that can no longer be contained in one
voice. But when all of these criers get together, it is not of tragic proportions
but of comic proportions, a mutual parodying, ironic caricature, an ass festival.
And then there is also the shrill of Zarathustra's laughter throughout.

In Genealogy of Morals, Nietzsche says: 'Every artist arrives at the ultimate
pinnacle of his greatness only when he comes to see himself and his art beneath
him – when he knows how to laugh at himself.'[11] If this is so, then Zarathustra
is the pinnacle of Nietzsche's artistic greatness.

So is Nietzsche then laughing at himself here, at the Zarathustra he has written, at his own child, his authorship? Part IV, then, would be self-referential
irony, ridiculing his attempt to make sense of life and our attempt to make
sense of his life and work. Does part IV function in a way that displaces any
attempt to settle on a doctrine of Zarathustra or of Nietzsche, any attempt to
secure a new truth on the basis of his work? (So, for example, the doctrine of
eternal recurrence is not a redemption from nausea but the ultimate philosophical joke.)

This posture of self-parody in Zarathustra may be Nietzsche's final word on his challenge that we behold the man. For if Nietzsche would desire that we write his autobiography by achieving some level of identity for him and closure for his work, this would hardly be in keeping with his own remark on interpretation:

> 'Everything is subjective,' you say; but even this is interpretation. The 'subject' is not something given; it is something added and invented and projected behind what there is – Finally, it is necessary to posit an interpreter behind the interpretation? Even this is invention. . . . [The world] has no meaning behind it, but countless meanings. – 'Perspectivism'.
>
> (WP, § 481)

The self as ego and substrate is a fiction, a mask, a representation. In a sense this was the last hold that held back each of the higher men. They refused to unmask the mask of their identities. They wanted to hold onto their self. Zarathustra recognised this greatest of all temptations, this desire to be witnessed as a self. Indeed if Nietzsche had not had this temptation, would he have written Ecce Homo? Zarathustra seems to admire this desire to secure for oneself a self. But this desire to be authored is the greatest of metaphysical dangers. Therefore only with pseudonyms and indirect discourse and self-parodying irony and self-transgressive reversals does he risk the adventure of authorship.

In the end we are also left, as is the ending of Zarathustra itself, with only signs that the children of Zarathustra are at hand. This tragi-comic theatre has achieved its effect. Cathartic pity has been undergone and overcome. The day of Zarathustra is breaking open. The musical dissonance that Nietzsche says in The Birth of Tragedy will accompany the rebirth of tragedy has been heard in the songs of part IV. In the end, Zarathustra announces that his work is about to begin.

Notes

1 Nietzsche, Thus Spoke Zarathustra in The Portable Nietzsche, translated by Walter Kaufmann (New York: Viking Penguin Inc., 1982), 342. Henceforth TSZ.
2 Nietzsche, Beyond Good and Evil (henceforth BGE) in Basic Writings of Nietzsche, translated by Walter Kaufmann (New York: Random House, 1968), § 295.
3 Nietzsche, The Birth of Tragedy, translated by Walter Kaufmann (New York: Random House, 1967), 124. Henceforth BT.
4 Nietzsche, Ecce Homo (henceforth EH) in Basic Writings of Nietzsche, 791.
5 Nietzsche, Philosophy and Truth: Selections from Nietzsche's Notebooks of the Early 1870s,

translated by Daniel Brezeale (Atlantic Highlands, NJ: Humanities Press, 1990), 11–12.

6 Cited by David Farrell Krell in *Postponements: Women, Sensuality and Death in Nietzsche* (Bloomington: Indiana University Press, 1986), 39–49.

7 Nietzsche, *The Gay Science*, translated by Walter Kaufmann (New York: Vintage Books, 1974), § 382. Henceforth *GS*.

8 Nietzsche, *Twilight of the Idols*, in *The Portable Nietzsche*, 563.

9 Gary Shapiro offers an insightful account of the interpretation of part IV as a satyr play in 'Festival, Carnival, and Parody (Zarathustra IV)' in *Nietzschean Narratives* (Bloomington: Indiana University Press, 1989).

10 Nietzsche, *Will to Power* (henceforth *WP*), translated by Walter Kaufmann (New York: Random House, 1967), § 28.

11 Nietzsche, *Genealogy of Morals*, in *Basic Writings of Nietzsche*, 535.

Part IV

Heidegger

9

A 'scarcely pondered word'. The place of tragedy: Heidegger, Aristotle, Sophocles

Will McNeill

Der Mensch ist jenes Nicht-bleiben-Können und doch nicht von der Stelle Können.

Man is that inability to remain and is yet unable to leave his place.[1]

In his 'Letter on "Humanism"' (1946), Heidegger pointed unequivocally to the fundamental significance of Greek tragedy from the point of view of his own thinking of being. 'The tragedies of Sophocles,' he stated, ' – provided such a comparison is at all permissible – shelter the *ethos* in their sayings more primordially than Aristotle's lectures on "ethics".'[2] The more original Greek meaning of *ethos* – more original than that of the 'ethical' and of 'ethics' – is one's abode, one's place of dwelling. Heidegger goes on to indicate this by reference to Heraclitus' saying *ethos anthropoi daimon*, which he translates: 'The abode (of the ordinary) is, for human beings, the site that is open for the presencing of the god (of the extra-ordinary).'[3] To say that Sophocles' tragedies shelter in their sayings and in their telling the *ethos* of human beings, of their thinking and of their actions, is thus to say that these tragedies shelter – and thus also may bring to light – the very meaning and truth of human dwelling, that is, of our being. For already in *Being and Time* (1927) Heidegger had identified the primary meaning of our being-in-the-world as dwelling:[4]

Being-in does not mean a spatial 'containedness' of things lying present before us, nor does the word 'in' originally signify a spatial relation of this kind. 'In' comes from *innan-*, to dwell, *habitare*, to have an abode; 'an' signifies: I am in the habit of, familiar with, I tend to something;

169

it has the signification of *colo* in the sense of *habito* and *diligo*. We characterised this being, to which being-in in this sense belongs, as the being that I myself in each case am [*bin*]. The expression *bin* is connected with *bei*; *Ich bin* [I am] means in turn: I dwell, I have my abode in the presence of [*bei*] . . . the world as something familiar to me in such and such a way. Being [*Sein*] as the infinitive of *Ich bin* . . . means dwelling in the presence of . . ., being familiar with. . . .[5]

Dwelling, in this sense, does not refer to a 'physical' place that could be located in mathematical terms; it is precisely that which resists any mathematical (or scientific) localisation. Being in the world in the sense of dwelling means being in the presence of (*bei*) other beings, and thus also always being situated in a particular context; it means being an open site, not just or primarily for beings, but for beings in their presence and presencing. To exist as such a site is also to be an exceptional presence in the midst of other beings – exceptional because although it is the site of disclosure of other beings as a whole, this site itself is never fully disclosed as such. The site of unconcealment is equally, indeed even more so, a site of concealment, itself concealed in its innermost essence.

What the tragedies of Sophocles shelter and may reveal to us is not so much the 'essence' of this site in the sense of what it is, but the site itself in its very prevailing and occurrence, in its worldly happening and unfolding. In other words, the tragedies shelter the 'essence' of dwelling not in the philosophical-Aristotelian sense of *Wesen* (of the *to ti en einai*), but in the verbal sense of *Wesen* as the 'essential happening' or enduring self-showing and self-concealing of something.[6] Yet the latter is unveiled – if it comes to be unveiled at all – not as an already existent ground, but in a historical, or, as Heidegger would also say, in a destinal and epochal manner; and such unveiling occurs, if and when it occurs, not in a descriptive *logos* that contemplates (*theorein*) that which is in its permanent form (*eidos*), but poetically, in a telling and saying that is poetic and that in its very happening not merely discloses, but enacts and thus accomplishes the 'poetic dwelling' (to use Hölderlin's word) of human beings upon this earth.[7] To say that it *enacts* and *accomplishes* human dwelling means that the poetic telling of Sophocles' tragedies is itself originary *praxis* or 'action'. Such telling does not, on Heidegger's readings, merely 'depict' or 'portray' human action. The 'Letter on "Humanism"' indeed begins by inviting us to rethink the essence of action or *praxis*: to act, Heidegger indicates, does not mean to cause or bring about an effect; rather, 'the essence of action is accomplishment'. To accomplish, *vollbringen*, means to unfold something into the fullness of its 'essence', to *bring it to its full unfolding*. But if this is so, then we can bring to its full unfolding only that which in some way already 'is':

But what 'is' above all is being. Thinking accomplishes [*vollbringt*] the relation of being to the essence of the human being. It does not make or cause the relation. Thinking brings this relation to being solely as something handed over to thought itself from being. Such offering consists in the fact that in thinking being comes to language. Language is the house of being. In its home human beings dwell. The thinkers and poets are the guardians of this home.[8]

The poetic saying of Sophocles' tragedies thus accomplishes the being of human beings as dwelling. It does so in thoughtfully enacting, that is, bringing to full disclosure, the unfolding of such dwelling in its own time and situation. The thinkers and poets, Heidegger goes on to say, 'guard' or tend the homestead of human dwelling in accomplishing the manifestness of being, in bringing such manifestness to its full unfolding, and this occurs as their thoughtful saying and telling of being. When such telling happens, being itself comes to the fore and is 'preserved' in language.[9] Human beings become manifest in their relation to being, which is to say, in the manner in which they dwell in the midst of beings as a whole.

What kind of thinking and thoughtfulness is it that here accomplishes human dwelling? Why is such thinking itself originary action or *praxis*? Does this imply that for Heidegger only the action of the professional thinker or philosopher, of the Greek tragic poet such as Sophocles, or of the German poet of the homestead, Hölderlin, is authentic action – as is often claimed – and that all other kinds of action (ethical and political) are of lesser status and importance? Is this just one more instance of philosophy's traditional and well-documented denigration of the political? Not at all. The action of a great thinker or poet is indeed exceptional; its greatness lies precisely in its reaching into the realm of the extra-ordinary, bringing the latter into being in its 'work'. Yet this does not mean that other kinds or instances of action are of lesser status. For Heidegger's claim is not, strictly speaking, a philosophical one; nor is there any claim to a principle upon which such a hierarchical ordering could be made. Precisely the 'destinal' happening of being's unfolding or 'history', as the destinal manner of poetic and thoughtful unveiling, precludes and refuses any such principle and any transcendent ground. And this is why, ultimately, the very comparison between the telling of Sophocles' tragedies and that of Aristotle's lectures on 'ethics' is problematic. More precisely, what would be problematic would be any straightforward comparison between the two tellings of *ethos* that would claim one to be 'more original' than the other, implying the continuity of an order of founding between the two. And this implies that Heidegger's claim of a 'more primordial' (*anfänglicher*) telling in Sophocles should not be taken as a purely historical claim. For between these two ways of telling of the *ethos* of human beings a fundamental transformation in telling itself (and thus also in the nature of *ethos*) has occurred, namely from the poetic telling of *muthos* to a primarily apophantic *logos*, such that there *is* no common measure (if being itself indeed finds its unfolding and completion in the saying of language). Yet far from precluding any comparison, it is this very event that not only first invites, but indeed necessitates a recollective thinking of this transformation. Thinking itself must first take the measure – that is, find the measure in first bringing it to being – of that which it has been invited to ponder: the measure of action itself. In the words of the statement that opens the 'Letter on "Humanism"', 'We are still far from pondering the essence of action decisively enough.' Heidegger's essay itself is nothing other than an attempt to take the measure of this historical event.

Yet why, then, does Heidegger claim that the telling of Sophocles' tragedies shelters the *ethos*, the dwelling and abode of humans, in a more primordial manner than do Aristotle's lectures on 'ethics'? And what can be meant by 'more primordial' (*anfänglicher*) here? Are we invited to ponder the essence of *ethos* and of action in relation to Aristotle and to Sophocles purely as a matter of historical interest and significance? Or is something else at stake? Heidegger's remark occurs in the context of his addressing Jean Beaufret's question of the relation between ontology and a possible ethics. Must not ontology – in particular the fundamental ontology of Dasein presented in *Being and Time* – be supplemented by an ethics? In reply, having indicated the sense of Heraclitus' saying in Fragment 119, Heidegger, on the contrary, affirms that

> If the name 'ethics', in keeping with the basic meaning of the word *ethos*, should now say that ethics ponders the abode of the human being, then that thinking which thinks the truth of being as the primordial [*anfängliche*] element of the human being, as the one who eksists, is in itself originary [*ursprüngliche*] ethics.[10]

The context makes apparent right away what is problematic not only about Aristotle's lectures on ethics, but also about the account of being-in-the-world as dwelling presented in *Being and Time*. Heidegger begins his response by addressing the relation between ontology and ethics in terms of the historical emergence of these disciplines. 'Ethics', along with 'physics' and 'logic', arose for the first time, he recalls, in the school of Plato, at a time when 'thinking was becoming "philosophy", philosophy *episteme* (science), and science itself a matter for schools and academic disciplines'.[11] Four significant factors are named here: the transformation of thinking into 'philosophy'; the further reduction of philosophy to *episteme* or 'science'; its becoming a scholastic affair; and, concomitant with these changes, the emergence of 'disciplines' of thought.

Each of these factors is significant for understanding the claim that Aristotle's lectures on ethics fail to attain the more primordial telling of *ethos* that resonates in Sophocles' tragedies.

(1) The transformation of thinking into philosophy marks the shift from a way of speaking and saying that simply and directly brings to presence what is, a telling that is thus in a certain harmony with being itself as appearing (*Erscheinen*),[12] to a *logos* that, inquiring into the essence of what truly 'is', begins to assert its radical independence from being *qua* appearing. This *logos* of the philosophers thus severs itself from the immediate appearing and self-presentation of things; appearances, it says, may deceive. The result of this different way of saying being, of this different claim? Speaking, saying and telling, itself loses the immediacy of its authority.[13]

(2) Nevertheless, one must recognise that the power and persuasiveness of this claim derive from the fact that this transformed thinking and saying – precisely in its most powerful form, the philosophy of Aristotle – does not institute difference between being and appearing, but remains in proximity to phenomena themselves in their self-showing. Yet rather than saying and thus itself bringing to being this self-showing of phenomena, the *logos* of the philosophers simply seeks what is most permanent and enduring in and throughout the self-manifestation or appearing of phenomena. It seeks to designate the underlying form (the *eidos*) that endures and in advance determines the entity in its being, as long as the entity remains what it is: its primary *ousia*, its 'substance' or 'essence'.

This second consideration marks the shift of philosophising into secured knowledge, or *episteme*. In this shift, something further comes to be concealed, and this is indicated indirectly by the very term that Aristotle uses to designate the primary *ousia*: it is *to ti en ainai*, that which already was in being. Despite the fact that it remains oriented toward the truth or true being of the particular entity in its 'thisness', the *logos* of *episteme* can designate only that which has already been, and in so doing conceals the singular appearing and coming into being of phenomena themselves. This apophantic *logos*, aimed at solely pointing out and revealing that which already is, relates to itself primarily *qua legomenon*, as that which has been said, that is, in terms of the meaningful content of discourse, thereby tending to conceal the *logos qua legein*, as incipient speaking and saying. The meaning or 'definition' (*horismos*) of the *logos*, as Aristotle himself says, here *is* the *eidos* or *ti to en einai* and thus, as he reminds us, it is possible for the *logos* to be true and for us to have 'scientific' knowledge (*episteme*) *without* our accomplishing a genuine beholding (*theorein*) and unveiling of things in their being.[14] For it lies in the nature of such *theorein*, as itself a *praxis*, that it is in each case singular and unique, and thus must be accomplished anew on each occasion by the individual concerned. By contrast,

I can learn and thus 'know' the truth in a purely formal way, indeed having the right *logos*, but without any insight into the grounds of its truth. For these 'grounds' lie in the phenomenon of appearing itself. Precisely the formal nature of epistemic knowledge thus enables and prepares the severing of truth from the ethical. As a scientist, I can be 'in the truth' without this truth making any ethical claim upon me.

(3) The third factor mentioned by Heidegger, philosophy as 'science' becoming a scholastic affair, is no less significant, and can be understood only in the context of the first two points. For the emergence and development of epistemic knowledge is possible only on the basis of a *withdrawal* on the part of the philosopher or 'scientist' from being involved in and claimed by the immediate affairs of life, and in particular from the activities of speaking and acting concerned with the ultimate freedom of human beings in their worldly community and plurality, namely the affairs of the *polis*. Epistemic or 'scientific' knowledge, like philosophical knowledge itself, arose only when humans not only had leisure (*schole*) or time free from the necessities of life, but when they used this time not for direct involvement in truly human affairs – the affairs of the *polis* – but for contemplation (*theorein*) of the world and of its divinity. The philosophy of the schools first emerged on the basis of this use of *schole*.

(4) Fourthly and finally, the development of the 'disciplines' that accompanied the rise of epistemic knowledge can likewise be understood in its fundamental significance only in relation to the first three points. For it was only on the basis of taking this time and distance from immediate involvement in human affairs, and only through the emergence of a *logos* that itself marked this very distanciation, that the philosophers could make epistemic knowledge a matter of 'disciplines'. The development of disciplines of knowledge becomes possible only on the basis of a withdrawal from the immediate and pressing affairs and activities of daily life, such that one's being is no longer a dwelling *in* the world but increasingly becomes a standing before the world as something to be contemplated and investigated.[15] The dividing up of being into various regions, each to be investigated by a regional science or 'discipline', is in the first instance the result of a *decontextualising* of one's being in the world, of dwelling in the midst of other beings as a whole that press upon one and address one in their immediacy. The phenomenon of worldly *context* and situatedness becomes increasingly formalised. In dividing the being of the world (of beings as a whole) into regions, what presses to the fore are the specific *differences* between beings and their different ways of being; the primordial element of their original belonging together – the phenomenon of world itself – recedes. In place of the original phenomenon of the world, we find in the history of philosophy and science only retrospective attempts to (re)construct a world that has already been epistemically dissected, not to say decimated.[16]

These remarks on some of the issues surrounding the emergence of 'ethics' as a discipline perhaps let us see better what is at stake in Heidegger's claim concerning the distance between Aristotle and Sophocles. In each of the four factors we have commented on, what comes to the fore is a *withdrawal from the immediacy of dwelling in the world and from a* legein *or saying that itself dwells in this proximity to appearing.* What appears problematic or less 'primordial' about Aristotle's ethics is, on the one hand, that his inquiry remains an inquiry into a restricted region of being, and that this regional character of the inquiry – despite the greatness with which Aristotle integrates it into the study of political life and indeed into the subjects of his other investigations – is problematic, because symptomatic of a certain loss of worldly dwelling. On the other hand, as a theoretical and epistemic inquiry, it seeks formal knowledge of *praxis*, that is, of that which, by Aristotle's own admission, can in its very accomplishment never be reduced to or grounded in purely formal knowledge.[17] Furthermore, however, while Heidegger's own fundamental ontology of Dasein in *Being and Time*, on account of its preliminary and non-regional character (which also make it prior to any anthropology), thinks the realm of the ethical or of dwelling more originarily than the history of philosophy hitherto – precisely because it seeks to avoid any splitting up of being-in-the-world by insisting on the 'equiprimordiality' of being-in as being in the presence of other beings (the present-at-hand; ready-to-hand equipment; nature; other Dasein-like beings) – it too nevertheless remains problematic, not least, as Heidegger himself points out here, because of its 'inappropriate concern with "science" and "research"'.[18] For it still speaks the language not only of philosophy, but of philosophy with – at least in part and in its preliminary self-understanding[19] – a 'scientific' orientation.

Yet Heidegger's remark concerning the more primordial sheltering of *ethos* in the telling of Sophocles' tragedies should not be read as a dismissal of Aristotle's inquiries into 'ethics'. Aristotle's works on ethics have their own greatness, and this greatness lies in large part in their very proximity to the pre-philosophical presentation of action and of the essence of human dwelling through tragedy. While we may strive for *eudaimonia* in and through our own actions, of which we are to some extent an origin, and in particular through the action of philosophising, in which we strive to contemplate (*theorein*) the divinity of the world, whether we achieve *eudaimonia* or not ultimately depends on the gods, on fate and fortune, on the forces of destiny that exceed our powers. Indeed, in the *Nicomachean Ethics* Aristotle in advance situates the possible human striving to bring about *eudaimonia* within the more encompassing perspective of fortune and misfortune, of possible reversals (*metabolai*) of fate and disasters – in short, *within* the realm of the tragic. Because *eudaimonia* concerns the story of a complete life (*biou teleiou*), Aristotle notes, we should heed the

counsel of Solon that only in retrospect, only at the end of a life, when someone is dead, should we venture to judge that someone was happy and blessed
during his or her lifetime. What we are judging is then that someone *will have
been* happy; the living present, by its very openness, eludes the time of con-
clusive human judgement. Indeed, Aristotle adds, even then, at the end of a
life, ancestors in a sense continue to be affected by the fortunes of their descen-
dants.[20]

Thus, Aristotle's *Nicomachean Ethics* is remarkable not least for its constant
reminders about the limitations of its own inquiry, that is, of a theoretical
inquiry into the general nature and truth of *praxis*, and for the emphasis it places
on the fragility of all human knowledge in the face both of the human contin-
gencies of action and of the element of fortune and destiny that lies in the
hands of the gods. The *Nicomachean Ethics* emphasises throughout that neither
ethical virtue formed by habit (*ethos*[21]), nor purely intellectual virtue, can on
its own ensure that we will act virtuously. What is decisive, rather, is the way
in which we dwell in the moment of decision itself (the *kairos*, which Heidegger
translates as *Augenblick*[22]), our response to the singularity of the given situation
as that which precisely cannot be known or 'seen' in advance by a philosophical *theorein*. Our dwelling in the moment of decision is itself determined by,
or, better, occurs as, *phronesis*, which, as the deliberative accomplishment of
dwelling, mediates in an altogether singular manner between ethical virtue of
character (formed by habit and by contemplation) and the arrival of the
unknown, of that which has yet to be decided: the being of one's dwelling in
the openness of a world. Recent publications of Heidegger's early lecture
courses have shown the importance of his interpretation of Aristotle's *phronesis* for understanding the analytic of Dasein in *Being and Time*. For what
Aristotle's account of *phronesis* – despite its being a theoretical inquiry – itself
brings to the fore is precisely the temporality and finitude of human dwelling
as being-in-the-world, a finite temporality that will become concealed through
the increasingly removed 'theoretical' discourse of subsequent philosophy.
Aristotle's *theoreia* itself thus orients *praxis* in advance toward the deliberative
accomplishment (*euboulia*), in *phronesis*, of its own excellence (*eupraxia*), and it
does so by first disclosing the world as the contextual whole and general horizon within which alone deliberative action can orient itself in advance toward
'living well as a whole' (*to eu zen holos*). Such *theorein*, which participates in an
originary manner in *bringing about* the guiding possibility of *eudaimonia* for
human beings, thus remains in close proximity to a *poiesis* that lets the finitude
of our being-in-the-world come to the fore, even if this bringing-to-the-fore
occurs here through the discourse of philosophy, and not through the sensuous
presentation of the theatre of Greek tragedy. Poietic accomplishment, as a
bringing to the fore of that which already presents and announces itself, remains

176

intrinsic to the very sense of *theoria*, even when the latter is no longer the immediate presentation of the sensuous, but its more withdrawn, more scholarly, more philosophical presentation.[23]

And yet – Greek tragedy itself already tends in this direction of the 'more philosophical'. The significance of Sophoclean tragedy cannot be fully appreciated without taking into consideration precisely this proximity of poetic presentation to a thinking that is at least proto-philosophical, centring as it does on a thoughtfulness and a giving-to-be-thought that occur in the time of the ancient *theoria* of Greek theatre. Heidegger himself reminds us of this very proximity when he alludes, in the same 'Letter on "Humanism"', to a statement made by Aristotle in the context of his discussion of tragedy in the *Poetics*: 'But Aristotle's words in the *Poetics*, although they have scarcely been pondered, are still valid – that poetising is truer than the exploration of beings.'[24] What Aristotle actually says is that poetising (*poiesis*) is 'more philosophical' (*philosophoteron*), as well as 'more serious' (*spoudaioteron*) – because it points to more grave matters – than historical inquiry (*historia*) (1451 b5).[25] Poetising, particularly that of tragedy, is more philosophical – it already dwells in proximity to philosophical inquiry, which is likewise distinct from a mere recounting of beings such as that found in historical inquiry. If Heidegger here writes 'more true' instead of 'more philosophical', it is perhaps to indicate the ambiguity in the Greek sense of 'truth' (*aletheia*) during precisely this period. But this ambiguity is inseparable from concomitant transformations in the meaning and sense of *theoria* as a mode of apprehending that which is; and to say that poetising is 'more philosophical' is hardly any less ambiguous, provided we do not straightaway associate the philosophical with the discourse or *logos* of *episteme*, but understand *theorein* itself, in its always ambiguous status, as the site of the necessary transgression of such a *logos*. For *theorein* is itself a mode of *aletheuein*, one that not only, to the extent that it became subservient to *episteme*, became the highest mode of disclosure for Greek philosophy, but one that, in exceeding what can be appropriated by the *logos* of *episteme*, also transgresses such epistemic disclosure in the direction of the finite, the extra-ordinary, and the divine. And thus also of the tragic.[26]

A brief recollection of what is at issue here in the context of Heidegger's appeal to this 'scarcely pondered' word of Aristotle's own testimony may help to clarify this point. According to Aristotle, the reason that poetic disclosure is more philosophical than historical inquiry is that 'poetry is oriented more toward the universal, while history recounts the particular' (1451 b6–7). Poetic disclosure is turned more toward universal or general 'truths', whereas history recounts particular facts and events. *Poiesis* is thus turned in a more philosophical direction, toward the realm of the *katholou*, which, according to Aristotle, it is precisely the task of philosophical contemplation or *theoria* to disclose and

177

thereby bring to language – language meaning now the *logos* of *episteme*. 'History', *historia*, by contrast, has the task of bringing into view and letting be seen particular deeds and events. And this means, as Aristotle points out, that it is concerned with what has happened, with that which has already come to be (*ta genomena*), and not, like poetic disclosure, with what may or could happen. Aristotle is here thinking of Herodotus' own testimony[27] at the beginning of his *History*:

> What Herodotus the Harlicarnassian has learnt by inquiry [*histories*] is here set forth: in order that the memory of the past [*ta genomena*] may not be blotted out from among men by time, and that great and marvellous deeds done by Greeks and foreigners and especially the reason why they warred against each other may not lack renown.[28]

The difference between a historian and a poet, writes Aristotle, is thus not that one writes in prose and the other in verse, since we could set the writings of Herodotus to verse, and they would still be a kind of history; rather, the difference lies in the different disclosure and telling of the word in each case. Yet it is important to note that *historia*, as a seeking to know and to have seen beings, did not mean inquiry into the past in the sense of modern historiography. For it did not imply investigation into something 'past' in the sense of no longer present, but was more a preservation of the great deeds that presented themselves and were deemed worthy of preservation. In particular, it did not imply research into uncovering a past, but was simply a recounting and recording of what had happened and had been seen to have happened.[29] It is important to recall this because the context in which Heidegger reminds us of Aristotle's *Poetics* – that of addressing Jean Beaufret's question 'How can we preserve the element of adventure that all research contains without simply turning philosophy into an adventuress?' – should not mislead us into simply identifying *historia*, 'exploration of beings' (*Erkunden vom Seiendem*), as Heidegger translates it, with 'research' (*recherche*) in the modern, scientific sense. Modern research, guided by scientific 'theory' in the form of a representational picturing (*Vorstellen*) of the world, is itself a particular historical transformation of the *theoria* that once commanded the attention of the philosophers. Indeed, Beaufret's association of philosophising with an 'element of adventure' suggests a problematically active sense of philosophical activity that Heidegger at once counters by pointing to the sense of advent and arrival (*l'avenant*) that adventure (*aventure*) implies, and by translating such arrival into the arrival and approach of *being* (not beings), to which thinking is destined and bound. Presumably, what is poetically disclosed in Greek tragedy has to do with this binding relation to the arrival 'of' being, that is, to being as itself futural. Presumably, this is what Aristotle's scarcely pondered word, mentioned by Heidegger only 'in passing', gives us to think.

While Herodotus' 'historical' inquiry is neither research not adventure in the modern sense, it none the less remains true that travelling and journeying into the foreign are inextricably bound up with his narration. And this is itself indicative of one of the transformations that the Greek *theoria* underwent during this period, prior to the emergence of philosophy. Herodotus himself, like Aristotle after him, recounts the travels of Solon to Egypt as the undertaking of a *theoria*, a seeing and experiencing of the foreign as a seeking of worldly knowledge.[30] Here, *theoria* does not appear to carry its more original connotation entailing an encounter with the divine, with the gods. In the theatre of Greek tragedy, by contrast, *theoria* not only preserves precisely this encounter with the gods; it is also the unveiling of the foreign at home, in the site of one's own worldly dwelling. It is the unveiling of the extra-ordinary in the midst of the ordinary, of the foreign *in the midst of one's own*. Like Nietzsche and Hölderlin before him, each of whom in his own way emphasises Greek tragedy as a presentation of the excess that attends the Apollinian, of the inevitable transgression that accompanies the worldly appearing of form, Heidegger too highlights Greek tragedy as enacting in human presence 'the struggle of the new gods against the old',[31] the struggle between the force of destiny that has been revealed and that which has yet to come. Such was the role of tragedy in the Classical age of the Greeks, when 'the arts ascended to the supreme heights of the revealing granted to them'. 'They brought to shine the presence of the gods, brought the dialogue between divine and human destiny.'[32] In bringing this dialogue to light (*Leuchten*), in illuminating it, they presented in the sensuous the worldly measure of human dwelling. In the tragedy, such presentation (*poiesis*) occurred *as* enactment (*praxis*), and such enactment (action itself in its full self-presentation and encounter with its own limits, the accomplishment of its own completion: enactment as supreme *energeia*) unfolded in and as a self-showing and coming to presence that was not merely 'for' an audience (as though the presentation of the action and the beholding of the spectators could be separated in reality, or exist in isolation), but *was* the *theorein* of the audience.[33]

Here, *theoria*, *praxis* and *poiesis* are *one* and inseparable: they unfold in their unity as the sensuous immediacy of human dwelling in the world, and are not yet analytically separated in the manner that becomes determinative for the remainder of Western philosophy, science and technology. It is perhaps no exaggeration to claim that the story of this separation is what has been the history of Western culture ever since. For the separation brings with it not only the reduction of meaningful human *poiesis* to a *techne* conceived instrumentally and in terms of utility, sidelining (as Heidegger remarks in this context of 'The

Question Concerning Technology') the *techne* of the fine arts, but also the concealment of *praxis* as the accomplishment of the human dwelling in its immediacy, a concealment that has as one of its consequences the contemporary 'homelessness', in the sense of uprootedness, of human beings across the Earth. 'Uprootedness' and 'homelessness', as Heidegger indicates in the 'Letter on "Humanism"', should not be understood simply as a loss of provincialism or of nearness to 'blood and soil', nor patriotically or nationalistically, but as a loss of 'nearness to being', of the proximity to presence that is the originary site of human dwelling.[34] Today, the near has become the far, the remote; technological presence is tele-presence and tele-presentation, 'virtual' presence, the global mediation of the technological Absolute. In the present era, being itself, as presence, becomes worthy of thought. 'Can thinking', asks Heidegger, 'refuse to think being after the latter has lain hidden so long in oblivion but at the same time has made itself known in the present moment of world history [*Weltaugenblick*] by the uprooting of all beings?'[35] Where human freedom no longer finds itself bound by the immediate presence of beings, where our response to beings is conceived in advance only along the lines of 'gathering and ordering all plans and actions in a way that corresponds to technology', there the desire for an ethics 'presses ever more ardently for fulfilment as the obvious no less than the hidden perplexity of human beings soars to immeasurable heights.'[36]

Yet precisely this desire for 'an ethics' remains in the thrall of the essence of technology itself, as the contemporary destiny of being, insofar as it seeks a measure, in the form of a set of rules or principles, that will be binding and in advance for all human action and self-presentation. It is the essence of technology to seek the orderability of all presencing in a manner that can be calculated in advance. It is in this context, and in the face of this predicament, that Heidegger is led to recall Sophoclean tragedy as disclosive of a more primordial human dwelling, in a recollective thinking that indeed provides a pointer and a directive (*Weisung*): 'Insofar as thinking limits itself to its task it directs the human being at the present moment of the world's destiny [*im Augenblick des jetzigen Weltgeschicks*] into the primordial dimension of his historical abode.' This directive calls for 'a descent into the nearness of the nearest'.[37] The 'moment' or *Augenblick* of the present world-destiny is not the objective time of an infinitely substitutable 'now' that could be ascertained by representational thinking as a picturing of the world from the distance of the Archimedean point occupied by science and technology, but the moment in which thinking is itself engaged in response to presence, the moment when it is itself looked upon by the face of the world and in which it attains insight (*Einsicht*) into that which is, into being itself as the configuration or constellation of presencing under the sway of technological ordering.[38] In such 'momentary' response to presence, at once finite and ek-static, thinking accomplishes and brings to the fore both the technological configuration of world-presencing and that which exceeds it, that which, beyond and within technological 'enframing' (*Gestell*), remains to be thought.

It is in this context, as we noted, and in the face of this world-destiny, that Heidegger's thinking recalls Sophoclean tragedy as disclosive of a more primordial human dwelling. Yet this recollection not only seeks to measure the distance between these two faces of dwelling, the Sophoclean and the technological, by a reminder of what is foreclosed in Aristotle's thinking of the ethical. Heidegger reminds us also, if only by way of a passing remark, that Aristotle's 'scarcely pondered word' is itself the site of a recollective thinking of human dwelling in the face of the incipient emergence of the present world-destiny through the transformation of philosophy into *episteme*. While Aristotle's account of *praxis* and of the 'ethical' in the *Nicomachean Ethics* proceeds from the outself precisely by distinguishing *praxis* from *poiesis* and from the *theoria* of the *bios theoretikos*, even while emphasising their ultimate inseparability and interwovenness in the activity of a human life, the *Poetics* recalls and preserves for us the thoughtful recollection of a more originary accomplishment of dwelling.

Aristotle's *Poetics* is thus a crucial resource in understanding how tragedy brings to light a sense of human dwelling in a manner more primordial than the 'scientific' discourse of his treatises on *Ethics*. We do not have the occasion here to present the sustained interpretation of the *Poetics* that would be necessary in order to help us fully appreciate Heidegger's own understanding of Greek tragedy, set forth most coherently in his two main commentaries on the famous 'ode to man' from Sophocles' *Antigone*. These commentaries are found in the 1935 text *Introduction to Metaphysics* and in the 1942 course *Hölderlin's Hymn 'The Ister'*.[39]

In the present context we must be content to provide merely a few pointers regarding tragic presentation as described in the *Poetics*, and to add a few remarks touching on Heidegger's readings of the *Antigone* chorus.

When in the *Poetics* Aristotle claims that poietic presentation is more philosophical than historical knowledge because it is oriented more toward the realm of 'universals', the 'universals' or 'wholes' (*ta katholou*) being referred to are nevertheless not identical to those disclosed by the *theorein* of philosophy. Nor does it mean that what tragedy presents is primarily universal 'character-types' or causal patterns of action. The nature of human action precisely exceeds prior determination by character or causal pattern that would have universal or general validity. The 'whole' that a particular tragedy discloses, rather, is the whole of *its story*, its *muthos*, the single and unified story that emerges from a sequence of actions and interactions on the part of the central character or hero of the tragedy. This point is brought out by Aristotle a little later in the *Poetics* when emphasising a certain similarity of tragedy and epic narrative. In epic as in tragedy, he remarks, the story or plot must be constructed around a single piece of action, whole and complete (*holen kai teleian*), and this is why it differs from historical recounting. Historical investigation reports and documents many diverse events and actions that happen within a certain time-period, but these events often have a merely incidental relation to one another; they do not coalesce into any one overarching end (*telos*) and thus do not form a single story or unified whole (Aristotle again cites Herodotus, who recounts two different battles that occurred on the same day, the battle of Salamis and the Carthaginian battle in Sicily[40]). By contrast, what is poetised by the tragic *muthos* is the inevitable interwovenness of a sequence of finite actions and interactions, their belonging together in a whole that came to pass by way of a certain *hamartia*, a failure to apprehend something important at the time a certain action was done.

What is important here is that the whole that is woven by the *muthos* itself is not foreseeable by the tragic hero. The world of the tragic hero cannot be foreseen and known by him in advance in the manner of a pure *theorein*, for the latter can disclose only that which already is and has been, but not that which has yet to happen. The protagonist's knowledge and understanding of the whole, of the situation and world within which he acts and in which he participates, is at best only partial; the finitude of his view of the whole, which guides his action in the moment, is what precisely comes to the fore as such in and through the mimetic presentation of tragedy. In this respect, the *theoria* of the spectators (who are not neutral observers in any modern sense of spectating, but participate in what is seen by way of 'fear' and 'pity') sees more: the audience anticipates and thus foresees the unfolding of a greater whole of which the protagonists are each but a part. But this 'foreseeing' again is merely intimative, and is carried by the *muthos* itself. It is not a having seen the whole in advance, for the whole story will have been seen only in retrospect. What thus becomes visible and is made manifest in and through the singular *muthos* of a tragedy is the fact that our relation to *eudaimonia* – which is, Aristotle claims, precisely what is presented in tragedy[41] – is never secured by knowledge alone, not even by the highest philosophical knowing, that of *theorein*. *Theorein* itself is shown to be finite, at least for human beings: it is itself implicated in a *poiesis* that is not merely human or within the control of the finite human perspective on the world.

The unfolding of human dwelling in and before a world that always exceeds it is thus not simply depicted poetically in the Greek tragedy, but is shown to be itself a poietic dwelling, accomplished in its being by the *poiesis* of a world that occurs in each case as *muthos* – as *muthos* that is at once singular, unique and worldly, bringing about a belonging to a whole that exceeds us. In the experience of fear and pity, the audience is precisely brought before the future of the tragic hero, a future that they also recognise to be potentially theirs: they are brought before the approach of something *deinon* which the hero is about to undergo or suffer.[42] The identification (through pity and fear) of the audience with the being and world of those involved will be all the greater, as Aristotle notes, if the tragedy presents the stories of a few families: not only or even primarily because their names will be known and thus already familiar to some, but because the tragic change in fortune threatens to rupture the belonging-together of those who are especially close to one another. It is not the *deinon* itself, but the approach and nearness of what is *deinon*, Aristotle notes in the *Rhetoric*, that arouses pity in us. And pity for others always implies fear for ourselves.[43] If the best tragedies are about a few families, and concern those 'whom it befell to suffer or inflict terrible things' (*e pathein deina e poiesai*),[44] it is because, as Aristotle indicates, the approach of the *deinon* has a special relation to *philia*, to the friendship and intimacy of those who are especially close to one another in their belonging together, in their dwelling in a world.[45]

If, for Heidegger, Sophocles' *Antigone* rather than *Oedipus Tyrannus* (to which Aristotle pays much more attention in the *Poetics*) was the greatest of his tragedies, and certainly the one that most drew his renewed attention and interpretive commentaries, the reason would seem to lie in the fact that whereas Oedipus' actions proceed from the beginning in a certain blindness or evasiveness toward the imminent approach of something *deinon*, Antigone's story begins with her taking knowingly upon herself the necessity of down-going, her relation to the *deinon*. Heidegger's 1942 commentary emphasises precisely the dangerous and grave counsel (*dusboulian*) that Antigone knowingly takes upon herself: *pathein to deinon touto*, 'to take up into my own essence *das Unheimliche* that here and now appears', as Heidegger renders it.[46] Heidegger's translation of *to deinon*, 'the decisive word',[47] as *das Unheimliche* – a German word normally rendered as 'the uncanny' – intends this word to be understood in the sense of *das Unheimische*, that which is 'unhomely', something 'not at home' that nevertheless belongs, in an ever-equivocal manner, to the worldly dwelling of human beings. 'This *pathein*', Heidegger comments, '– experiencing the *deinon* – this enduring and suffering, is the fundamental trait of that doing and action called *to drama*, which constitutes the "dramatic", the "action" in Greek tragedy.'[48] Antigone takes upon herself, in taking it up into her own essence, that being unhomely that becomes the 'all-determinative point of departure' of her actions, 'that against which nothing can avail, because it is that appearing which is destined for her (*ephane*, l. 457)'. What Antigone knowingly takes upon herself is her being-toward-death, the dying that is a belonging to being, and as such 'a becoming homely within and from out of such being unhomely'.[49] This 'becoming homely', or coming to be at home (*Heimischwerden*), is the poetic journey of her dwelling as a knowing exposure to and *pathein* of that which is not at home, the *deinon* as the proper being of man.

Yet what is it that thus decisively determines Antigone in her actions? What is the directive from which she takes counsel, that of which she herself says:

> It was no Zeus that bade me this,
> Nor was it Dike, at home among the gods below,
> who ordained this law for humans,
> And your command seemed not so powerful to me,
> That it could ever override by human wit
> The immutable unwritten edict of the gods.
> Not just now, nor since yesterday, but ever steadfast
> this prevails. And no one knows from whence it once appeared.[50]

What determines Antigone's actions is not only no mere human ordinance, but lies beyond the upper and lower gods, Zeus and Dike, even though it is both of the gods and 'pervasively attunes human beings as human beings'.[51] The all-determinative point of departure (*arche*) starting from which Antigone comes to be who she is has no simple origin, and is itself nothing determinate, and yet it prevails and even 'lives' (*waltet, zei*): it is that from which the time of human life first arises and comes to be. And 'this' is something that Antigone and the poet leave otherwise unnamed, but nevertheless point toward in these lines as the indeterminacy of that future that steadfastly belongs to being, and starting from which, in taking it upon herself (*pathein*), Antigone comes to be the one that she is. Heidegger intimates this in recalling the destined belonging of the one who is most *deinon*, the human being, to something inevitable, a belonging that is poetised in the famous chorus that begins '*Polla ta deina . . .*' (I cite Heidegger's 1942 translation[52]):

> *Vielfältig das Unheimliche, nichts doch*
> *über den Menschen hinaus Unheimlicheres ragend sich regt . . .*

> Manifold is the uncanny, yet nothing
> more uncanny looms or stirs beyond the human being . . .

and in its second strophe recollects this most *deinon* of beings back toward its ownmost essence:

> *Dem einzigen Andrang vermag er, dem Tod,*
> *durch keine Flucht je zu wehren . . .*

> The singular onslaught of death he can
> by no flight ever prevent . . .

'It is this One', comments Heidegger, 'to which Antigone already belongs, and which she knows to belong to being.'[53] In knowingly taking upon herself the *deinon*, Antigone first comes to be who she will have been, and the accomplishment of her dwelling, as the fulfilment of her potentiality for being, becomes the 'being unhomely in coming to be at home' that unfolds poetically as the *muthos* of the tragedy itself. Antigone knows neither the eventual repercussions of her actions, nor the particular finality of her own death: such things cannot be known in advance, for they first come to be poetically, through the *poiesis* of the *muthos* that accomplishes the belonging of finite, human dwelling to a greater whole. Remarks Heidegger: 'The human potential for being [*Seinkönnen*], in its relation to being, is poetic.'[54] But this poetic accomplishment of human dwelling, and thus the finitude of her actions (*praxeis*) as the accomplishment of *her* singular being, is precisely what Antigone knows and acknowledges in the *phronein* that guides her, the *phronein* of the heart (*phren*) that has taken upon itself the *deinon* as the all-determinative origin of her actions:

> Antigone herself *is* the poem of becoming homely in being unhomely. Antigone *is* the poem of being unhomely in the proper and supreme sense.[55]

This poetic dwelling and knowing, of which Antigone is the embodiment, the poem itself, is not only the story of Antigone herself. Rather, in and through the tragedy such a destiny is seen as such, raised into the clearing of the light and of the air by the chorus, and thus seen to be the kind of destiny (human, finite, wayward, poietic) to which we all belong in advance. But such a destiny is not only thereby manifested as an origin that is no determinate origin, a directive such that 'no one has seen from whence it once appeared'; it also becomes manifest in its unique singularity, as in each case *this* destiny, the journey and experience of this poetic dwelling. For this reason, notes Heidegger, the chorus, which is the 'innermost middle' and 'poetic gathering' of the work of tragedy itself, should not be understood as simply depicting a general or universal content. 'Poetising', rather, in this supreme form, 'is a telling finding of being.' It brings us before 'the nearest of all that is near'. What is misunderstood as the 'general content' of the chorus, he remarks, 'is the singularity of the telling of the singular *deinon*', which 'appears in the singular figure of Antigone'. 'She is the purest poem itself.'[56] The chorus itself is song, the harmony of a song that would not resonate without the singular voices that sustain it, but that raises into the light and the air a belonging to a world that will always have been more than the sum of its parts.

Poetic dwelling is thus at once indeterminate and determinate, unfolding as that which comes to be decided poetically, as the finite accomplishment of the singular poem that each human being will have been. While Heidegger's early work in *Being and Time* understood the fundamental attunement of *Angst* as first bringing us before the indeterminacy of our ownmost potentiality for being-in-the-world as such, before the *Unheimlichkeit* of our dwelling, his work from the mid-1930s onward, in constant dialogue with Hölderlin, Nietzsche and Greek tragedy, increasingly brings to the fore the poietic accomplishment of such being-in-the-world. In 1943, recalling the early account of *Angst* which – in bringing us before and attuning us to the 'nothing' that is other than beings – brings us before 'the veil of being', Heidegger relates this to the poetic destiny of beings, that destiny whose origins lie veiled in the completion of being, closing his Postscript with his own translation of the closing lines from *Oedipus at Colonus*, 'the last poetising of the last poet in the dawn of the Greek world':

> *Doch laßt nun ab, und nie mehr fürderhin*
> *Die Klage wecket auf;*
> *Überallhin nämlich hält bei sich das Ereignete verwahrt*
> *ein Entscheid der Vollendung.*

But cease now, and nevermore hereafter
Awaken such lament;
For what has happened keeps with it everywhere preserved a decision
of completion.[57]

Notes

1 Martin Heidegger, *Die Grundbegriffe der Metaphysik: Welt – Endlichkeit – Einsamkeit* (Gesamtausgabe 29/30) (Frankfurt am Main: Klostermann, 1983), 531 (henceforth cited as GA 29/30); translated by William McNeill and Nicholas Walker as *The Fundamental Concepts of Metaphysics: World, Finitude, Solitude* (Bloomington: Indiana University Press, 1995).

2 *Wegmarken* (Frankfurt am Main: Klostermann, 1967), 184; translated in *Pathmarks*, edited by William McNeill (New York: Cambridge University Press, 1998), 269 (translation slightly modified). References in *Wegmarken* are to the first edition.

3 *Wegmarken*, 187; *Pathmarks*, 271 (translation modified).

4 *Wegmarken*, 189; *Pathmarks*, 272.

5 *Sein und Zeit* (Halle a. d. S.: Niemeyer, 1927), 54.

6 Cf. 'Der Ursprung des Kunstwerkes' in *Holzwege* (Frankfurt am Main: Klostermann, 1950), 39; translated by Albert Hofstadter as 'The Origin of the Work of Art' in *Basic Writings*, edited by D. F. Krell (New York: Harper Collins, 1993), 175–6; see also 'Die Frage nach der Technik' in *Vorträge und Aufsätze* (Pfullingen: Neske, 1985); translated and edited by William Lovitt in *The Question Concerning Technology* (New York: Harper & Row, 1977).

7 The term 'poetic' should in the following remarks be taken in the broad sense of the Greek *poiesis* or the German *Dichtung*. It does not mean that we should be

186

concerned primarily with 'poetry' in the narrow sense, and thus might perhaps be better rendered as 'poietic'.

8 *Wegmarken*, 145; *Pathmarks*, 239 (translation modified).

9 'Being itself' here means being in its happening; for such preservation itself happens only when such telling happens, and the event of language is, as originary action, itself always finite, that is, singular and unique. On 'preservation' (*Bewahrung*), see 'The Origin of the Work of Art'.

10 *Wegmarken*, 187; *Pathmarks*, 271.

11 *Wegmarken*, 187; *Pathmarks*, 271. The following discussion should be compared to Heidegger's remarks on this issue in GA 29/30: §10.

12 This 'harmony' was, however, itself a *harmonious strife*, and was explicitly experienced as such precisely at the height of Greek tragedy. Thus, remarks Heidegger in 1935: 'The unity and strife of being and appearance [*Schein*] held sway in an originary manner for the thinking of the early Greek thinkers. Yet all this was presented in its highest and purest form in the poetising of Greek tragedy.' *Einführung in die Metaphysik* (Tübingen: Niemeyer, 1953), 81; translated by Ralph Mannheim as *An Introduction to Metaphysics* (New Haven: Yale University Press, 1959).

13 Cf. the effect of the Socratic *elenchos*.

14 *Metaphysics*, Book VII; *Nichomachean Ethics*, Book VI, 1139 b18f. Cf. Heidegger's commentary on this in *Platon: Sophistes*, Gesamtausgabe 19 (Frankfurt: Klostermann, 1992), 31ff. (henceforth cited as GA 19); translated by Richard Rojcewicz and André Schuwer as *Plato's Sophist* (Bloomington: Indiana University Press, 1997).

15 Of course, standing before the world as a realm for objective contemplation is still a mode of dwelling, but one that is everywhere and nowhere: dispersed in and through a historically determined 'everyday' dwelling, it remains oblivious to itself (to the 'unhomeliness' of its own dispersion) as such, to the truth of its own historical being.

16 Thus, in *Sein und Zeit*, Heidegger notes that the worldhood of the world has been repeatedly passed over (§ 14); in *Die Grundprobleme der Phänomenologie*, (Gesamtausgabe 24) (Frankfurt am Main: Klostermann, 1975), 234ff. (henceforth cited as GA 24); translated by Albert Hofstadter as *The Basic Problems of Phenomenology* (Bloomington: Indiana University Press, 1982), he remarks that the phenomenon of world has never yet been recognised in the history of philosophy.

17 This does not, of course, imply that Aristotle's inquiry is illegitimate; it simply emphasises his critical awareness of the limits of all theoretical inquiry.

18 *Wegmarken*, 187; *Pathmarks*, 271.

19 Cf. *Sein und Zeit*, § 7, and GA 24, § 22. I consider this issue in greater detail in *The Glance of the Eye: Heidegger, Aristotle, and the Ends of Theory* (Albany: SUNY, 1999).

20 *Nichomachean Ethics*, 1100 a1ff.

21 Cf. *Nichomachean Ethics*, Book II, 1103 a15f., where Aristotle states that the term *ethos*, the ethical, is derived from *ethos*, habitat.

22 GA 19: 164.

23 On the 'poietic' accomplishment of the philosophical *theorein*, to which Aristotle himself refers in the *Nichomachean Ethics*, see chapter 2 of my study *The Glance of the Eye*.

24 *Wegmarken*, 183; *Pathmarks*, 275.

25 References to the *Poetics* are from *Aristotelis De arte poetica liber*, edited by Rodolf

Kassel (Oxford: Oxford University Press, 1965). Translations are my own, or taken from the translation by W. Hamilton Fyfe (Cambridge, MA: Harvard University Press, 1932), modified where appropriate.

26 Cf. David Krell's remarks in 'A Small Number of Houses in a Universe of Tragedy', chapter 5 above.

27 Martha C. Nussbaum, in *The Fragility of Goodness* (New York: Cambridge University Press, 1986), rather oddly suggests that Aristotle must have Xenophon in mind (386, note). The context clearly suggests that he is thinking of Herodotus, to whom he has just referred a few lines earlier.

28 *Herodotus, Books I–II,* translated by A. D. Godley (Cambridge, MA: Harvard University Press, 1926).

29 On Heidegger's understanding of *historia,* see my remarks in *The Glance of the Eye,* part two.

30 For an account of this, and of the shifts in meaning of ancient *theoria,* see ibid., part four.

31 'Der Ursprung des Kunstwerkes', 32; 'The Origin of the Work of Art', 168–9.

32 'Die Frage nach der Technik', 38; *The Question Concerning Technology,* 34.

33 This perhaps helps one to understand why *theoria* retains such importance and primacy in Greek philosophy, why Aristotle continues to identify seeing and *theoria as* the highest form of *praxis,* and, as noted, even to insist that it entails a certain *poiesis,* participating in the bringing to presence of the world and of the human possibility of *eudaimonia* in the face of the divine and of the forces of suprahuman destiny. Apart from the other shifts mentioned in the sense of *theoria,* however, one can see that *theorein* has by then also become a more active beholding, entailing the difficulty and effort of philosophising, as contrasted with the simple apprehending of what shows itself in the theatrical presentation of tragedy.

34 *Wegmarken,* 168ff.; *Pathmarks,* 257ff.

35 *Wegmarken,* 184; *Pathmarks,* 268.

36 *Wegmarken,* 183; *Pathmarks,* 268.

37 *Wegmarken,* 182; *Pathmarks,* 267–8.

38 See the essay 'Die Kehre' in *Die Technik und die Kehre* (Pfullingen: Neske, 1985); translated as 'The Turning' in *The Question Concerning Technology.*

39 *Hölderlins Hymne 'Der Ister',* (Gesamtausgabe 53) (Frankfurt am Main: Klostermann, 1984) (henceforth cited as GA 53); translated by William McNeill and Julia Davis as *Hölderlin's Hymn 'The Ister'* (Bloomington: Indiana University Press, 1996).

40 *Poetics,* 1453 a22.

41 Ibid., 1450 a16–20.

42 Ibid., 1453 a22, 1453 b14ff.

43 *Rhetoric,* 1386 a24–9. References to the *Rhetoric* are from *Aristotelis Ars rhetorics,* ed. W. D. Ross (Oxford: Oxford University Press, 1959). Translations are my own, or taken from the translation by John Henry Freese (Cambridge, MA: Harvard University Press, 1926), modified where appropriate.

44 *Poetics,* 1453 a22.

45 Ibid., 1453 b14–22.

46 GA 53: 127.

47 Decisive, that is, not only for Antigone, but, as Heidegger remarks in the same commentary, in the sense of being 'the fundamental word . . . of Greek tragedy in general, and thereby the fundamental word of Greek antiquity' (ibid., 82).

48 Ibid., 128.
49 Ibid., 129.
50 *Antigone*, ll. 449–57. A later translation by Heidegger of the same lines renders the last sentences as:

> Not just today, nor since yesterday, but ever-enduring
> This arises (*ho nomos*, directive usage [*der weisende Brauch*]) and no one has seen
> from whence it came to appear.

This translation, from the essay 'Das Wort' in *Unterwegs zur Sprache* (Pfullingen: Neske, 1979), 219, identifies the Greek *tauta* as referring to *ho nomos*, the ethical 'directive' that Antigone takes upon herself, and emphasises the visual sense of *oiden*.
51 GA 53: 144.
52 Ibid., 71–2.
53 Ibid., 150.
54 Ibid.
55 Ibid., 151.
56 Ibid., 149.
57 *Wegmarken*, 108; *Pathmarks*, 238.

Part V

Benjamin

10

Fatalities: freedom and the question of language in Walter Benjamin's reading of tragedy

Simon Sparks

Während die Haltung der griechischen und der eigentlichen Tragiker der Welt und dem Schicksal gegenüber unbeugsam bleibt.

It is here that the stance of the authentic Greek tragedians toward the world and toward fate remains unbending.[1]

In his essay on Goethe's *Elective Affinities* of 1921, Benjamin stresses the importance of deciding on the place of truth with respect to myth. 'There is', he states, 'no truth, for there is no unambiguity and so not even error in myth' (I 1: 162; *SW*, 326). Rather, he continues, myth is essentially indifferent to truth. In this essential and destructive indifference – *seiner vernichtenden Indifferenz*, Benjamin writes – myth comes to be withdrawn from any relation to truth, so much so, in fact, that it altogether destroys the possibility of there even being anything like a truth of myth. 'As far as the spirit of myth is concerned,' Benjamin insists, 'there is properly only a knowledge of it.' And such knowledge is nothing other than that of myth's destructive indifference to truth. In this regard, 'authentic art, authentic philosophy – as distinct from their inauthentic stage, the theurgic – begin [*hebt . . . an*] in Greece with the closure [*Ausgang*] of myth, since neither is any more nor any less based on truth [*auf Wahrheit beruht*] than the other' (ibid.). To say that authentic art and authentic philosophy begin with the closure of myth thus means that this closure is *also* the opening of that upon which the very possibility of such art and such philosophy rests, namely truth itself. To the authentic artists and to the authentic thinkers falls, then, the task of safe-guarding truth against the threat of a disastrous turn back into myth.

In Benjamin's own plan for the essay, these few lines are titled 'Myth and

Truth' (I 3: 836). The title suggests a very simple schema, one which appears to be borne out by the text itself: myth comes to a close; then, from out of the close of myth and in opposition to it, something else begins to take place in the authentic art and philosophy of Greece, namely truth. In this regard, the authentic art and authentic philosophy of Greece would be the originary saying of truth, the saying which corresponds to the origin of truth itself. One could presume Benjamin's reading to fill out this schema by showing how it is that truth is given only with and as the closure of myth, and by considering what kind of art and what kind of thinking it is which shelters truth from an erroneous confusion with myth.

And yet, it is important that one *not* detach such a schema from these remarks on myth and truth, *not* employ it as a framework for reading Benjamin's text. Why not? Are these remarks not unequivocal in formulating this schema? Benjamin says that for art and philosophy to be authentic, they must be grounded on truth; only then can they be contrasted with the 'art' and 'philosophy' grounded upon myth which are, precisely, inauthentic. Could one possibly compose a more classical statement of metaphysical opposition, of the opposition constitutive of metaphysics as such? Is this not just one more expression of philosophy's founding and well-documented denigration of myth, that denigration in which myth comes to be located and defined only by way of the truth of a *logos* – a *logos* that defines itself precisely by way of a twisting free of myth – a truth which, by definition, would remain inaccessible to it? By no means. What makes Benjamin's grasp of the closure of myth more insightful than such a schema would suggest is his awareness that the peculiar nature of the relation of myth to truth puts seriously into question any hierarchical ordering of the two. What is placed in question is, in other words, the assumption that the pre-originary saying of myth – a saying prior to and hence indifferent to the original saying of truth itself – could be placed in opposition to the saying of truth as the saying of untruth. Benjamin writes: 'there is no truth, *for there is no unambiguity and so not even error*, in myth'. That truth does not take place in myth does not mean, then, that myth would harbour the opposite of truth: *Irrtum*, untruth or error. If, according to Benjamin, error cannot be set over against truth but must instead be understood as belonging essentially to it, then myth can no more be regarded in terms of the errancy of untruth as it can in terms of truth itself. The destructive indifference of myth with respect to the essence of truth, and that is also to say to error, means that there can be no possibility of a founding measure on the basis of which the two could come to be contrasted in terms of the opposition of truth to untruth, any such principle or measure being precluded both by myth's essential and destructive indifference to truth as well as by the essence of truth itself. Between these two kinds of saying an essential turning – here Benjamin calls it a closure, *Ausgang* – has taken place. An essential turning, that also means: a turning in essence. Between the essence of myth and the essence of truth, there can be no common measure.

Yet, far from precluding the possibility of a thoughtful encounter with the relation of truth to myth, this lack of measure actually invites us to ponder the nature of this turning or this closure. In order for this encounter to take place, however, it must first be possible for the site of this closure to show itself. There must be some common ground, some point of coincidence where truth and myth can be brought together in their very separateness. And although in this context Benjamin does not indicate what such a site would look like or how it might come to show itself, just such an indication is made elsewhere – in the section of the *Origin of the German Mourning Play*, his failed *Habilitationsschrift* of 1925, called 'Tragedy and Legend':

> The Greek, decisive confrontation [*die griechische, die entscheidende Auseinandersetzung*] with the daimonic world-order [*der dämonischen Weltordnung*] gives to tragic poetry its historico-philosophical signature [*ihr geschichtsphilosophische Signatur*]. The tragic relates to the daimonic as does paradox to ambiguity. In all the paradoxes of tragedy . . . ambiguity, the hall-mark of the daimons, is dying away [*ist . . . im Absterben*].
>
> (I 1: 288; *Or.*, 109)

Tragedy is seen here as the site of a particular strifely configuration of Greek existence. Written by a decisive confrontation with that order in which 'the essence is daimon' (I 1: 157; *SW*, 322), namely myth, tragedy happens as a statement of historical intent. It happens as the decisive response of the Greek world to the mythic order of the daimons, as a violent and transformative turning against myth. Tragedy is the site upon which Greek historical man confronts the prevailing mythic realm of the daimons, submitting its overwhelming ambiguities to the discontinuity of tragic paradox. But if tragedy remains for Benjamin a kind of *presentation* in the strictest sense of the term – it is the saying of something, it exposes something or gives something to be seen – he is nevertheless still careful to insist that what is decisive is to be found less in what it is tragedy presents (*das Dargestellte*), than in the presentation itself (*der Darstellung selbst*). The point here concerns how the Greek confrontation with myth is said, how tragedy exposes it or gives it to be seen. For in saying this confrontation, what tragedy exposes or gives to be seen is not so much the 'essence' of it in the sense of what it is, than the confrontation itself in its historical happening. Tragedy is less the dramatic presentation of a confrontation which has already taken place than the 'historico-philosophical' enactment and actualisation of the confrontation itself.

What new insight does the consideration of the 'philosophy of history' provide with respect to the general problematic of tragedy? A preparatory study of early 1916 characterises it in terms of a construction of boundary lines or limits: 'The very least that is to be suspected', remarks Benjamin, 'is that the tragic indicates a *boundary* [*ein Grenze*] no less in the realm of art than in the field of history' (II 1: 133). Translating these remarks back into the concerns of the *Origin of the German Mourning Play* noted above, the historical significance of tragedy lies in the fact that it indicates the point at which one era – that of myth – passes over into another. The *Origin of the German Mourning Play* itself, on the other hand, is even more direct. There, it is a matter of tragedy's assumption of the status of an epochal principle. To say that tragedy is an epochal principle means that it shows the point at which one specific constellation of existence (amongst those constellations called, according to the finite thread of Benjamin's epochal history, myth, tragedy, mourning play, modernity . . . etc.) dies away into another. As the principle of the prior constellation dies away, tragedy comes to the fore as the most essential expression of the new constellation. In the confrontation with myth a new epoch (*Epoche*) is posited (*gesetzt*), and in this positing generates Attic tragedy. And if this epochal positing of tragedy can be identified with that closure located by the essay on the *Elective Affinities*, then it is because it has the historical meaning (*der historische Sinn*) of the end of myth (*Ende des Mythos*) (I 1: 314; *Or.*, 135).

So completely is Benjamin's interpretation of tragedy linked to its status as an epochal principle, so total his assimilation of tragedy, that he does not refer, except very occasionally, and then only in a quite marginal or incidental way, to the tragedies of Aeschylus or Sophocles as examples or figurative translations of that principle, but only to tragedy 'itself' as the essential expression of that principle. Why? Why is it to tragedy that Benjamin grants such a decisive importance in the genealogical unfolding of epochs? What is tragedy if it is such as to trace out the boundaries of an epoch? If tragedy marks the epochal turning from myth to truth as the ground of authentic art and philosophy, does this not also mean that it marks the origin of truth itself? What is tragedy if it marks the origin of truth? These questions lie at the heart of Benjamin's account, and it is only by doing justice to them that he comes, ultimately, to broach the following, overriding question: how can tragedy posit an epoch?

This question begins to find an answer in the context of the meditation on the relation of tragedy to myth which opens the properly tragic phase of the *Origin of the German Mourning Play*. Tragedy is described there not in terms of fabrication or invention – concepts said to be 'incompatible' with tragic art – but in terms of a tendentious transformation (*Umformung*) of legend.[2] With this transformation, says Benjamin, the tragic poet turns the legend in a new direction (*neuen Wendung*). Not, he quickly adds, in the anticipation of or search for tragic constellations. The properly tragic constellation of existence emerges not *in* but *through* this transformation. Even if, in the course of Benjamin's examination of Greek tragedy, this transformative ground appears to slip from view, it none the less remains the case that the whole of that examination is ordered by an inquiry into the epochal significance of this turning. Just why this is so is suggested by the following remarks of 1923, which clearly belong to the gestation of *Origin of the German Mourning Play*. Referring to Aristotle's account of tragedy as the *mimesis* of a particular event,[3] Benjamin states unequivocally that it is legend which provides the substance of Greek tragedy:

> This is why, in the *mimesis* of the fundamental and – if one can say this – ceremonial event that is presented by the legend . . ., with every individual poetic configuration [*Ausgestaltung*] or variant on the fable, a moment of the most essential position-taking of that new poetry [*ein Moment höchst wesentlicher Stellungnahme jener neuen Dichtung*] marks the material of the legend.
>
> (II 1: 248–9)

The primordial history (*Urgeschichte*) of a people, legend, is the most original saying of myth. It is the saying in which the mythic and pre-historical epoch of the existence of a people (*die vorgeschichtliche Epoche ihres Daseins*) finds its expression. But if Benjamin underlines that it is legend which provides the raw material of tragedy, he does not do so in order that tragedy be seen as a dramatisation of that material: as *Umformung* or as *Ausgestaltung*, transformation or configuration, tragedy is only mistakenly understood as legend in dramatic form. Legend provides the 'new poetry' of tragedy with its raw materials only to the extent that the latter is an essential taking of position with respect to that saying. By taking an essential position, tragedy turns legend in a new direction, repositions it in respect of its saying of the existence of a people. Such a position, Benjamin stresses, is not taken aimlessly. It is tendentious. It has a tendency. Not, however, a tendency in the sense of a tending toward something; the tendency harboured by the tragic turning of legend could only be described as a tending *away*. But away from what? Away from the saying of myth in legend. 'Through every minor and yet unpredictably profound interpretation of the material of legend,' writes Benjamin, 'tragedy brings about the destruction [*Abbruch*] of the mythic world-order, and prophetically shakes it with inconspicuous words [*unscheinbaren Worten*]' (II 1: 249).

It would clearly be a mistake, therefore, to try to position tragedy as 'authentic' art, in the sense Benjamin gave to this term in the essay on the *Elective Affinities*. It does not belong to that stage of art which rests on truth. Equally mistaken, however, is the assumption that it belongs to what that essay

197

described as the 'inauthentic', 'theurgic' stage of art. Grounded on myth (*dem Mythos gründenden*) only to the extent that it is destructive of it, tragedy has to be seen, rather, as an opening onto the epochal possibility of authenticity itself, and that means: as an opening onto the possibility of an indifference to myth and the saying of truth – this is, in Benjamin's eyes, the magnificent conception upon which Greek tragedy rests at its height.

*　　*　　*

Yet is it so certain that this conception is one of tragedy alone? Can we be sure that the epochal confrontation with myth is confined solely to tragic art? Is tragedy the only site of this confrontation? Does it describe unequivocally the epochal principle with respect to the closure with myth? Do other voices need to be heard? Why not that of philosophy, for example? Could not philosophy too be said to posit an epoch from out of myth? A note of 1916 would seem to suggest that this is in fact the case: 'Socrates: that is the figure through which the old myths are annihilated and received. . . . In the midst of the terrible struggle, the young philosophy seeks in Plato to assert itself' (II 1: 130). In these remarks at least, it would seem that 'philosophy', just as much as 'tragedy', can assume the epochal status of the end of myth. And yet, without ever actually mentioning tragedy, these remarks also contrive to reinscribe tragedy, to reimpose the framework of tragedy upon this other scene, appearing also to suggest that this struggle of philosophy has itself to be understood as a tragic one: 'Socrates: that is the sacrifice of philosophy to the gods of myth, who demand human sacrifice' (ibid.).

What, then, of this reinscription of tragedy? Is there a tragic aspect to philosophy? An aspect from which philosophy would itself come to be determined as tragedy? Is there a tragedy of philosophy? A tragedy, perhaps, in which philosophy would also be written by the confrontation with myth? Can tragedy be thought as the articulation of philosophy itself?

In the light of such questions, recall the charge levelled by Nietzsche in *Birth of Tragedy* against Euripides and the New Attic Comedies of Menander and Philemon. Nietzsche says: it was at the hands of Euripides that tragedy died its tragic death. Nietzsche says: it was Euripides who drove Dionysus from the tragedy, leaving it free to enjoy its posthumous and senile old age. The corpse of tragedy, Nietzsche says, is now preserved in the New Attic Comedy, where it decays into ever more degenerate imitations.

But Nietzsche *also* says that it was *not* Euripides who fought against tragedy. He says that tragedy did not die tragically at the hands of Euripides, but at the hands of a daimonic power, one neither Apollinian nor Dionysian, which spoke through him: the new-born daimon called Socrates. For Nietzsche, Socrates is the new Orpheus who rises to join Euripides in his struggle against Dionysus.

Did he not, so the old Athenian rumour went, help Euripides to write his plays? 'This is the new opposition: the Dionysian and the Socratic, and the art-work of Greek tragedy was run aground on this.'[4]

Like Nietzsche, Benjamin's concern in his interpretation of tragedy is as much with its death as with its life. 'Here', he writes in the *Origin of the German Mourning Play*, 'it is a matter of its past [*Vergangenheit*]' (I 1: 292; *Or.*, 113). I have already called attention to the link between tragedy and history operative in Benjamin's discussion of tragedy as a founding epochal principle. Here, however, the accent is altogether difference. Now it is less on tragedy as a founding principle than on the way in which that principle itself draws to a close.

If, according to Benjamin, it is a matter of speaking about tragedy in the past tense, then this is because of the privileged relation of tragedy to a particular turning point (*Wendepunkt*) in the history of Greek spirit itself (*der Geschichte des griechischen Geistes selbst*): namely the death of Socrates (I 1: 292; *Or.*, 113).[5] It is in the *Phaedo* that Plato tells of Socrates' death. But this dialogue also tells of Socrates' turn away from the errancy of his youthful inquiry into sensible nature and into beings – away, that is, from the *peri phuseos historia* of the science and philosophy of those who came before him – to *logoi* and to an examination of the truth of beings as a whole.[6] The dialogue which tells of his death also tells, therefore, of Socrates' own turning within Greek spirit, of his turning against the prevailing Greek spirit of his age.

And yet, it is not to this that Benjamin directs us. It is not Socrates' turning within Greek spirit which is, for Benjamin, decisive. Instead, the decisive turning point is to be found at the end of Plato's account of Socrates' counter-turning *historia*. It is to be found in the philosopher's death.

Why? Why is it on his death that Greek spirit turns? Benjamin is unequivocal: it does so because Socrates' death *also* marks the death of tragedy.

Like Nietzsche before him, Benjamin sets Socrates in opposition to tragedy, finding in him the very basis for its destruction. In Plato, Benjamin says, Socrates' *Gespräche* have become the epilogue of tragedy itself. They have become so because, at every point, Socrates – this 'figure' of Plato, according to a note of 1916 (II.1: 130), who marks the turning from the paradoxes of tragedy to the transparency of science – stands opposed to each of the elements of tragedy. This opposition ends with Socratism standing triumphant over the bleeding corpse of tragedy; it is Socrates alone who holds the satyric stage.

At the very heart of this turning in Greek spirit, then, directing it and constituting it from within, the death of tragedy is bound together with that of Socrates. This is a strange, almost monstrous coupling: the death of tragedy is tied in spirit to that of its assassin, the two locked together in a fatal embrace from which neither can emerge alive. And this is why, ultimately, Socrates' death cannot be a tragic one. Certainly, Benjamin concedes, it does in many respects *appear* to be tragic. But however strong such a resemblance may be, in his final conversation, which itself turns on the question of death, Socrates sets Greek spirit turning, sets in place the conditions by virtue of which his death cannot be a tragic one:

> How remote [the 'ideal' of Socrates' death] is from that of the tragic hero Plato could not have indicated more significantly than he did by letting immortality be the subject of his master's last conversation. If, in the *Apology*, the death of Socrates could still have appeared to be tragic . . . , then the Pythagorean mood of the *Phaedo* shows his death to be free of all tragic ties.
>
> (I 1: 293; *Or.*, 114)

And yet, in a crucial departure from Nietzsche, whose text he carefully follows and cites throughout, Benjamin refuses to see the death of tragedy as a tragic one. Which is not to say that it is any finer for Benjamin than it is for Nietzsche. Quite the contrary, in fact. To Benjamin's mind, the death of tragedy is a far meaner affair than Nietzsche could possibly have imagined. Tragedy dies with Socrates because his death is a cruel parody of the tragedy itself: 'And here, as so often, the parody of a form shows its end' (I 1: 292; *Or.*, 113).

Benjamin extends his discourse on Socrates in two central passages, weaving it back and forth between the position of the philosopher and that of the hero, as a description of another epochal turning point: the birth of Socratism from out of the death of tragedy. Here, the tragic law is overturned, the grip of its principle loosened and placed in crisis by the emergence of a new epochal field, namely that of metaphysics. Whereas for Socrates philosophy was to have begun in the pathos of wonderment, for Benjamin it begins in parody. Born from a nihilating parody of the forms of the old myth, philosophy takes over the place of tragedy on the stage of history.

Yet what has consequently to be taken into account is not simply the opposition between Socratic science and tragic art, however destructively parodic such an opposition may be. What has also to be acknowledged is the impossibility of simply submitting tragedy to the privilege of the philosophical question: *ti esti* . . .? In a manner which, in this regard, recalls the epochal indifference of myth to truth, a philosophical account of tragedy – one that would contribute to the 'science' of 'pure aesthetics'[7] – will everywhere find itself checked by tragedy, everywhere run up against points beyond which the phenomenon itself necessarily resists the essential demands made by that question. 'The legends of Socrates', writes Benjamin, 'are an exhaustive secularisation of heroic legend by the betrayal of its daimonic paradoxes to

understanding' (I 1: 292; *Or.*, 113). Whereas tragedy was determined in terms
of a transformative repositioning of legend, Socratism, on the other hand, is
determined as an exhaustion and secularisation of the tragic redirection already
underway, an exhaustion which rests upon a betrayal of what Benjamin takes
to be the outstanding epochal mark of tragedy, namely paradox. In the eyes of
Socrates – his *eye*, Nietzsche will have said[8] – tragedy cannot but appear irra-
tional, a monstrous affront to the clear insight of the philosopher, marred
throughout by paradox. And it is these he will everywhere have betrayed.

With his death, for example. With his own death which, in the *Phaedo*, he
will ultimately rid of its terrors, submitting it to the language of philosophy –
to that 'dazzling unfolding of discourse and consciousness' which characterises
the Socratic *logos* (I 1: 292; *Or.*, 113). But this is, it must be said, more than
just an example. For according to Benjamin, it is only here, in the *Phaedo*, that
the impossibility of a tragic Socrates is fully revealed ('in the *Apology*, the death
of Socrates could *still* have appeared to be tragic'). According to Benjamin, it
is only here, with the parodic death of Socrates, that tragedy actually dies. It
only here that Greek spirit turns. Why? Why here and nowhere else? Why
not in the war raged on tragic art by Socratic science (I.1: 297; *Or.*, 118)?
Why is the turning in Greek spirit only disclosed with the philosopher's death?
Any answer to this question is conspicuously lacking from either of the passages where Benjamin addresses himself to Socrates, and, in several places, he
appears to have in fact forgotten his initial precision with regard to the philosopher's death, finding the ancient turn from tragedy to science already engaged
by Socratism itself. In lieu of any answer from Benjamin, then, let me suggest
the following. It is with Socrates' death that the ancient turn from tragedy is
fully disclosed because it is only here that the philosopher is able to turn on
the extreme limit of tragedy itself. This is, of course, to say more about
tragedy than about its death: it is to say that tragedy turns on death, that it is
in tragic death alone that the properly tragic dimension of tragedy is disclosed.
And what, then, of tragic death? What of tragic death as the very ground of
the tragedy?

In order to answer these questions, let me follow the ancient Athenian off
to the temple, and return to tragedy.

*   *   *

'What tendency is hidden in the tragic? For what does the tragic hero die?'
Recalling his remarks on the *tendenziöse Umformung* of tragic poetry, these are
the questions with which Benjamin begins his reading of the signature of
tragedy.

Answer: tragic poetry rests upon the idea of sacrifice (I 1: 285; *Or.*, 106).[9]
It is in the sacrificial death of the tragic hero alone that the properly tragic

dimension of this poetry is made clear. In sacrifice, tragedy comes to be gathered into its most extreme possibility. Here, the gathering is *not* a gathering of all possibilities into some actuality in the sense of a gathering into a *telos* – this tendency of tragedy to sacrifice, Benjamin says, shelters 'no guaranteed finality' (I 1: 286; *Or.*, 107) – but a gathering into a possibility which cannot be surpassed, a possibility which represents the exhaustion of all possibilities. Consequently, such a gathering cannot be said to intervene suddenly at the end, bringing to a close actions which have taken place quite independently of it. Quite the contrary, in fact, this gathering through sacrifice can be discerned, although only retrospectively, throughout the tragedy as a whole. It is inscribed within it and directs it, not only at those moments when the sacrificial altar holds centre stage, but throughout. One could outline this schema in the following way: sacrifice constitutes the end of tragedy only insofar as, from the outset, tragedy takes its lead from this end which shows itself as such, comes fully into force, only at the very close of the drama. The point is, then, that sacrifice be regarded less as the end of the tragedy than as the form in which it unfolds. Here is how Benjamin begins to formulate this point:

> In terms of its object – the hero – tragic sacrifice is distinct from every other, being at once a first and a final sacrifice. A final sacrifice in the sense of the expiatory sacrifice made to the gods who preside over an ancient right; a first sacrifice in the sense of the representative deed in which new contents [*neue Inhalte*] of the life of a people announce themselves. . . . Tragic death has this double meaning.
>
> (I 1: 285; *Or.*, 106–7)

The double meaning of sacrifice is far from straightforward. The first meaning refers to the sacrifice as an act of atonement of the gods who preside over an ancient right, an expiatory gesture which meets the demands made by that right. The second meaning refers to sacrifice as the act of standing-in-for – *der stellvertretenden Handlung*: the deputising or representative deed – in which a new, as-yet unborn community is gathered together and begins to take shape through the sacrificial object of the hero.

Unproblematic, certainly, inasmuch as sacrifice is, in this regard, the site upon which some object, the hero, is offered to the gods as a stand-in or scapegoat for the community in order to secure its rights, the site of a response to the crushing antinomy which binds together man and the gods; problematic, however, in that Benjamin will not be content merely to allow these two meanings to sit alongside one another, but will want also to turn the second meaning back *against* the first. Thus, the sacrifice of the hero is oriented *not only (nicht nur)* toward the first meaning of sacrifice, but *above all (vorab)* toward

undermining it. If the sacrifice of the hero gathers the tragedy into the exhaustion of its essential possibilities, then it also points beyond such possibilities –
not in the sense of pointing to other possibilities hitherto unremarked, but in
the sense of a profound disruption which, by exhaustively gathering together
such possibilities, also opens onto another space beyond them. Thus, in obey-
ing ancient statutes, tragic sacrifice points *also* to the establishment of new ones
(*alter Satzung willfahrend, neue stiftet*). An expiatory sacrifice according to the
letter (*nach dem Buchstaben*) of the ancient law, tragic death also tears the pages
from that book in the spirit (*im Geist*) of the laws of the new community, con-
signing them – along with the hero – to ashes in the rites of the funeral pyre.

The point here, then, is that tragic sacrifice is the site of a transformation
(*Verwandlung*) from the order of the gods to that of the life of the community.
But how is this transformation to be understood? In the context of a long and
carefully composed semantic chain, the *neue Inhalte* of the community which
are announced by the sacrifice indicate, no doubt, that it has to be understood
as a transformation of support (*Halt*).[10] It is a transformation from an existence
supported (*halten*) by the deadly obligations to the gods into one supported by
the laws of the new community.

But what of the hero? What is his position in all this? If it is his death which
provides the site of this transformation, what supports his existence? Nothing.
Belonging neither to the decaying order of the ancient Olympians nor to that
of the community *in statu nascendi*, the hero marks, rather, the fissure between
the two, the point of the violent passing over from one to the other. Suspended
between the two, his position as a sacrifice cannot be a response to the demand
of an external law. His death, demanded neither by the cruelty of the gods,
nor by the community to which it gives shape, is not imposed from without
but, says Benjamin, takes place as something 'which is intimate, personal and
inherent in him'. A self-sacrifice, then, in which the hero incalculably squan-
ders himself, gives himself up to a self-imposed law – would this not be a sacrifice in the most proper sense of the term? An absolute sacrifice? A sacrifice
with no conceivable hope of return? In fact, the hero is here seen to be placed
in a precarious position, the position of what one could venture to call a tragic
autonomy.[11] In this imposition of autonomy the hero resolutely takes up the
tragedy of an existence (*tragische Dasein*) in which 'his life unfolds [*rollt . . . ab*],
indeed, from [*aus*] death, which is not its end [*sein Ende*] but its form [*seine
Form*]' (I 1: 293; *Or.*, 114).

The schema being advanced here is, quite evidently, identical to the one
which was shown to structure the drama itself. Little wonder, then, that
Benjamin insists that, 'in his spiritual-physical existence, the hero is the framework of the tragic system' (I 1: 294; *Or.*, 115). Little wonder, also, that it is
to this determination, above all – of death not as the termination of a life but,

intrinsic to and operative throughout an existence now revealed as tragic, as the sole form in which the existence of the hero can unfold, but a form which comes fully into force only in and as his being positioned as sacrifice – that Benjamin's remarks here are addressed.

The *Origin of the German Mourning Play* sketches this unfolding of tragic existence in terms of what Benjamin calls the pre-given framework *(vorgegebenen Rahmen)* of the hero's life. With this gift – which, given in advance, guides the unfolding of the hero's existence – the question of fate is raised. Nowhere is Benjamin's interpretation of tragedy more accurately defined than by this outstanding question. For even if fate is not tragic *a priori*, as Benjamin unequivocally stresses at several points, there is no tragic existence which does not unfold under its sign. And yet, the peculiar fate of this gift has so little to do with causality, however, that it could only be understood in relation to freedom. It is, to be sure, the very opposite of freedom; but this opposition only takes place on the common ground of a joint dissociation from anything like a subjection of fate and freedom to causality. By articulating the site of tragedy by way of the link between fate and freedom, Benjamin does not say that tragic art is the presentation of freedom at its most extreme limit, its retrospective recognition and unconditional affirmation in the acceptance of tragic fate. He says, rather, that it is tragedy alone that allows us to think the most peculiar fate of all – the *fatum* of *libertas*.

Tragic fate unfolds toward *(rollt . . . zu)* death. This unfolding toward death, in which the properly tragic *fatum* is thus seen to turn on a reference to finitude, does not fall on the tragic hero from somewhere else but stems, rather, from his own precarious position, namely that of autonomy. Such is, then, the paradox of tragic fate: it is *also* tragic freedom. But what freedom is this? It is the freedom for the hero to give himself that which is most properly his own. He gives himself that which, from the beginning, is his own. And yet in thus giving himself to himself – the ordeal of autonomy – what the hero in fact gives is nothing less than fate, that which is given in advance of him. This is the central paradox of tragic existence. It is the very structure of fate in an existence now disclosed as tragic which means that Benjamin is able to write of the hero not simply that his 'fate unfolds toward death', but also that 'his life unfolds, indeed, from death, which is not its end but its form'.

Up until this point at least, Benjamin's account of fate appears in many ways to align itself along a very traditional axis, translating the principle of autonomy as presented by the critical philosophy – the 'circularity' of freedom and the law described by Kant[12] – into a language of *Schicksal* taken from the conjugation and reconciliation of freedom and necessity projected by German Idealism. In this regard, let me recall that the fate of the hero was broadly stated as follows: 'his life unfolds, indeed, from death, which is not its end but

its form'. With the immediately following sentence, however, a quite different inflection is given to this account: 'tragic existence finds its task only
because it is governed from within [*in ihm selbst gestetzt sind*] by the limits of
linguistic and bodily life given to it from the beginning' (I 1: 293; *Or.*, 114).
If the autonomy which accompanies the hero's resolute embracing of the finitude exposed by his fate is already familiar, what is less so is the limit of language said to be given along with it. It is difficult, moreover, to see exactly
what link there could possibly be between fate and language. All the more so,
indeed, when one sees that Benjamin will want even to understand fate precisely by way of just such a link with language. How? The answer, like fate
itself, turns on the question of necessity (*Notwendigkeit*). The necessity built into
the framework of the hero's existence is, says Benjamin, neither a magical nor
a causal one. It is, rather, the speechless (*sprachlose*) necessity of defiance:

> It would melt away like the snow before the south wind under the
> breath of the word. But the only word which can breathe is unknown
> [*Aber eines ungekannte allein*]. Heroic defiance contains this unknown
> word, locked within itself.
>
> (I 1: 294; *Or.*, 115)

Benjamin calls this silence *hubris*, the hero's refusal to justify himself in the face
of the gods. In this regard, it marks the outstanding site of that decisive
Auseinandersetzung which, I noted at the outset, was said to structure the space
of tragedy. Outstanding because not only does this silence elevate the hero of
the tragedy above the central figures of all other dramatic forms, it also constitutes the proper articulation of what is genuinely tragic (*echter Tragik*) in the
drama. Still, it would be a mistake to think that tragic silence can be reduced
to a failure or default of language. Tragic silence, Benjamin insists, is not the
negation of language. It is neither impossibility, namely the impossibility of
speaking, nor possibility, namely the negative possibility of not speaking.
Rather, it belongs essentially to language as a positive possibility of it. It is,
even, language in its most originary and proper sense.[13] For in order to keep
silent, the hero must have something to say, something to communicate.
'Heroic defiance contains this unknown word, locked within itself.' The
question that needs to be asked, then, is one of how the 'wordless sphere'
(I 3: 839) of the hero is able to bear in this way the entire burden of the
exposition.

And yet, it is not as if the conjunction of language and fate here cannot be
a simple one, and a certain turning commences as soon as the question of language comes into play: a turning into excess. In contrast to the austerity and
irony of Socrates' wilful silence in the face of death, a silence which only

reflects back onto that 'dazzling unfolding of discourse and consciousness' which characterises the Socratic *logos* – the philosopher, says Benjamin, is struck dumb only by falling silence (*verstummt er wo er schweigt*) – in contrast to this, then, the properly tragic hero pays for the right to be silent with his life. In the silence which accompanies and which alone expresses his sacrificial death, however, the very meaning of the tragic conflict is inverted (*denn seine Bedeutung schlagt um*). What had initially appeared as the judgement of the gods upon the hero is now, through the hero's silence, changed into a trial of the gods themselves, a trial in which the hero himself appears as chief witness and, 'against the will of the Gods, displays "the demi-God's honour"' (I 1: 288; *Or.*, 109). Taking care not to cut short this analogy between the formal structure of the Athenian law courts and that of tragedy itself,[14] Benjamin notes that it is the word which takes centre stage in both. Athenian law and tragic drama both turn around the *logos*. What is of principle interest here, however, is not the predominantly linguistic character of their set exchanges, but the point at which the word finds itself able to break free of such constraints, an excess in a way which is in each case unanswerable:

> The important and characteristic feature of Athenian law [*Recht*] is the Dionysian outburst, namely that the drunken, ecstatic word is able to break [*durchbrechen*] through the regular encircling of the *agon*, that a higher justice can emerge more out of the persuasiveness of living discourse [*lebendigen Rede*] than from the trial of conflicting groups struggling either by armed combat or by bounded forms of language [*gebundenen Wortformen*]. The ordeal becomes broken by the *logos* in freedom [*Das Ordal wird durch den* logos *in Freiheit durchbrochen*]. . . . Tragedy is grasped in this picture of the trial proceedings.
>
> (I 1: 295; *Or.*, 116)

Logos, then, refers here not primarily to the various *logoi* or languages – legal or dramatic, for example – of Attic Greece, but to this specific moment of excess in which the word leaps over the boundaries by which such *logoi* are defined. It is a matter of a word which is excessive, of a word which, by exceeding the limits that would otherwise circumscribe it, releases itself into freedom. This word is called ecstatic. But Dionysian? Presumably this, from *The Birth of Tragedy*: 'And now let us think of how into this world built on shining and moderation and artificially dammed up, there sounded, in ever more alluring and magical ways, the ecstatic tone of the Dionysian festival.'[15] And yet, it is not as if Nietzsche had not also written that 'under the magic of the Dionysian . . . singing and dancing, man expresses himself as a member of a higher community: he has forgotten how to walk and speak [*das Sprechen verlernt]*'.[16] It is not as if the ecstatic truth of the Dionysian word is not *also* a forgetting or an un-learning of language, as if the boundless tone of Dionysian ecstasy does not also fly the ground of language. The point is worth insisting upon because if Benjamin does call this word proper to tragedy Dionysian, then he will *also* say that it is the gift of language itself, the word from whose echo coming generations *learn* their language (*erlernen . . . ihre Sprache*) (I 1: 293; *Or.*, 114).

At this point, then, everything gives us to think that tragedy is, in some way, bound up with a certain origin of language.[17] Certainly, it is entirely possible that this thesis will come as no surprise. For if it is in tragedy that the destruction of myth as the ground of existence takes place, this destruction is also an opening onto another ground, one which is perhaps already captured by language, namely by *logos*. As I have already suggested, however, it is by no means certain that Benjamin's remarks – whether those from the essay on Goethe's *Elective Affinities* or these from the *Origin of the German Mourning Play* – can so easily be aligned along such an axis. Equally, it is not as if tragedy can be simply assimilated to that 'authentic' stage of art, in the sense of an art grounded on truth, which Benjamin gave to this term in the essay on the *Elective Affinities*. If one is to follow the thesis according to which tragedy discloses itself as the origin of language, then it will have to be in a way which does not immediately force a direct path from *muthos* to *logos*.

How is it, then, that language finds its origin in tragedy? Here is how Benjamin sketches this gift of language, describing the excess of the tragic word:

> The further behind the tragic word leaves the situation – which can no longer be called tragic when it catches back up – the more surely has the hero escaped the ancient statutes to which, when at the end they overtake him, he flings only the mute shadow [*den stummen Schatten*] of his essence, flings his own self as a sacrifice, whilst his soul is sheltered [*hinübergerettet*] in the word of a distant community. . . . In the countenance of the suffering hero the community learns reverent gratitude [*lernt . . . den ehrfürchtigen Dank*] for the word with which his death endowed it [*sie begabte*] – a word which, with every new direction in which the poet turned legend, lit up another place as a new gift [*an anderer Stelle als erneuertes Geschenk aufleuchtete*]. Far more than tragic pathos, tragic silence becomes the treasure [or shelter: *Hort*] of an experience of the sublime of linguistic expression.
>
> (I 1: 288; *Or.*, 109)

Language, then, begins in the response of the community – its learning thanks or gratitude – to what is given to it by the death of the hero, a death which is now to be thought ecstatically and not metaphysically. From out of this sacrifice, language happens.[18] But what is it that is given by the hero's death? Assuredly not a life. What is given, rather, is the excessive power of the word itself, of the ecstatic word which sounds out beyond itself. Through this excessive power of the word – one which no longer belongs with the faultless imposition of the divine word which it brings to a close, and does not yet belong with those easily spoken *Sitten* (morals, customs, etc.), which constitute the communicable contents of the community onto which this death opens – the gift of another place or another position (*an anderer Stelle*) is revealed. What place? What position? I recall again the inital context of Benjamin's meditation, that context in which tragedy was called an essential position-taking (*wesentlicher Stellungnahme*) with respect to the saying of the existence of a people in legend. The place or the position which, according to the passage being considered here, is given by the gift of language is that of a place or position other than one grounded on or supported by myth.

It is in the silence of the hero, then, that everything is gathered. It is in tragic silence that the ecstatic movement from out of myth finds its outstanding expression. This schema, prepared for from the very beginning of Benjamin's remarks on tragedy in the *Origin of the German Mourning Play*, defines tragedy in terms of language. It is the very structure of the origin of language in an existence now disclosed as tragic. Out of the 'monstrous emptiness [*ungeheurer Leere*]' of the tragic hero, writes Benjamin, 'the distant, new commands of the gods sound out [*tönt . . . wider*], and from this echo [*Echo*], coming generations learn their language' (I 1: 293; *Or.*, 114).

*   *   *

Following these remarks, Benjamin launches upon a remarkable little discourse – he cites, entirely unchanged, a passage from his own essay of 1921, 'Fate and Character'. Already circling around the question of fate, this passage also draws together the entire account of tragedy in the course of a long description of precisely that confrontation with the daimonic remarked at the very outset.

Let me try, then, as briefly as possible, to outline the principal context in which that *Auseinandersetzung* is described.

Although treating of identical concerns, the tone of this earlier examination of fate is markedly different. Here, it is a matter less of an examination of tragic fate as such, than of how fate can be disclosed in the first place. Whereas, according to a famous remark by Leibniz, *fatum* is itself originally *dictum*,[19] for Benjamin it is only in the reading of *dicta* that fate can be disclosed. As much as the art of the clairvoyant or the gypsy woman, therefore, fate is a matter of reading.[20] But whereas the folds of Leibniz's tropology require there to be a specific *dictum* which can give itself as fated and so impose itself as fate – namely the *decretum Dei* – for Benjamin, as one might already suspect from the foregoing remarks on language, the relation of fate to its *dicta* cannot be understood causally. If fate can never be grasped in itself but only through certain traces or signs of its passing, these are not actually fated to appear as such. Indeed, nowhere is the difficulty of reading the *dicta* of fate made more acute than with the divine word. Not only does this word bind fate to a law of causality; it also points toward the error by which fate finds itself locked into a religious context: 'to mention a typical case [*Fall*], fate-imposed misfortune is looked upon as the response [*die Antwort*] of God or the gods to a religious offence' (II 1: 173; *SW*, 203). The error here lies not in the connection of fate to the divine word, but in understanding this case as a fall. For whilst guilt and misfortune do indeed provide the outstanding *dicta* of fate, they are also its only ones. One cannot be fated to innocence or to fortune, for example. Indeed, so little can fortune be thought as a *dictum* of fate that Benjamin instead presents it as the hall-mark of divinity and so of a thorough-going removal from fate itself: 'Fortune is . . . what releases the fortunate man from the chains of the Fates and from the net of his own fate. Not for nothing does Hölderlin call the blissful gods "fateless"' (ibid.).

Once the sole *dicta* of fate are seen to be those of guilt and misfortune, 'for insofar as something is fate, it is misfortune and guilt', then fate can no longer be thought in terms of the context of religion, 'no matter how much the misunderstood concept of guilt appears to refer to it' (II 1: 174; *SW*, 203). The only balance capable of taking the measure of this fate, Benjamin calls right (*Recht*). Only on this balance can misfortune and guilt become measures of the person (*Maßen der Person*). It is in right alone that a fateful kind of existence (*schicksalhafte Art des Daseins*), one unreservedly described by such *dicta*, can come to be measured (I 1: 138; *SW*, 307). The question is, then: what is right? Benjamin calls it 'a remnant of the daimonic level of human existence in which rules of law determined not only the relationships of men, but also their relationships with the gods' (II 1: 174; *SW*, 203).[21] It is due only to a historical confusion of right with justice that such statutes still continue to hold sway long after 'victory over the daimons'.

What of this victory? Where is it won? Where is it that the mythic *Rechtssatzungen* of the daimons are first broken? Benjamin's answer is unequivocal, and it is, of course, tragedy.

Here, now, is the central passage of this essay, the one cited in the *Origin of the German Mourning Play*:

It was not in right but in tragedy that the head of the genius raises itself for the first time from out of the fog of guilt, for in tragedy daimonic fate comes to be broken [durchbrochen]. But not by the supercession of the pagan incalculable interconnection [Verkettung] of guilt and atonement by the purity of the man who has expiated his sins, who is reconciled with the pure God. Rather, in tragedy pagan man recognises himself [besinnt sich] to be better than his God, but this knowledge leaves him without speech, it remains dumb. Without confessing itself, it secretly gathers its forces. . . . There is no question of the 'moral world-order' being restored, but the moral man, still mute, still immature [noch stumm, noch unmündig] – as such is he called the hero – elevates himself in the shaking of that agonised world. The paradox of the birth of the genius in moral speechlessness, moral infantility, is the sublime of tragedy.

(II 1: 174–5; SW, 203 [I 1: 288–9; Or., 109–10])

In connection with this passage several points need briefly to be considered.

The first point concerns the character of that realm from out of which the hero raises himself. Benjamin describes it here as daimonic (dämonisch).[22] The passage indicates that such daimonism is not a matter of a theological 'demonism', but one of fate and its entanglements, of the mythic order of right which is breached in tragedy. The remark from the Origin of the German Mourning Play cited right at the outset is even more expressive of this breach: 'The tragic relates to the daimonic as paradox to ambiguity. In all the paradoxes of tragedy . . . ambiguity, the hallmark of the daimons, is dying away.' In terms of the essence of truth remarked at the very outset, paradox, like ambiguity, remains altogether inconceivable. And yet, unlike the ambiguity of the daimonic, which points nowhere – and this 'nowhere' to which it points is indeed itself and its mythic entanglements – the paradox of tragedy points beyond itself, to its possible resolution at the very least. One could say, orienting the result to the opening onto the epochal possibility of authenticity broached by tragedy: in tragedy, authenticity is already in play and, already, from the outset, in play with the properly tragic itself.

The passage refers, second, to 'the moral man, still mute, still immature – as such is he called a hero'. What man? The man characterised several sentences earlier as 'pagan man', the man who, in tragedy, becomes aware that he exceeds the measures laid down by the gods; but the man also who, in the immediately following sentence, is called 'genius'. What sets the epochal possibility of tragedy in motion is just this awareness on the part of the genius, an awareness which, Benjamin says, is articulated in his speechlessness. Other passages are still more direct – for example, one from the same context, in which Benjamin states that 'the struggle against the daimonism of right is bound to the word of the genius' (I 1: 298; *Or.*, 118). In the light of the foregoing remarks, it is hard not to see in this figure of the genius that of the tragic hero. But there is another point which is essential for grasping the force of this schema. The tragic, Benjamin says here, *sich . . . erhob*, raises himself. The point is that he uses this same term, much earlier, in a fragment of 1916, in developing his account of the relation of language to tragedy: 'in tragedy the eternal rigidity of the spoken word *sich erhebt . . .*' (II 1: 140). In the hero's raising himself, Benjamin continues in the passage being primarily considered, 'daimonic fate comes to be broken [*durchbrochen*]'. Again, an identical remark can be made: it is precisely this formulation which is used in the *Origin of the German Mourning Play* to express the movement of the ecstatic word which 'is able to break through [*durchbrechen*] the *agon*. . . . The ordeal is broken [*durchbrochen*] by the *logos* in freedom' (I 1: 295; *Or.*, 116). The point I want to insist upon here is that of an absolute convergence, one which everywhere borders on identity: the convergence of the hero with language with respect to the opening onto freedom.

Third point: 'The paradox of the birth of the genius in moral speechlessness, moral infantility, is the sublime of tragedy.' The genius of tragedy is still mute (*noch stumm*), still immature (*noch unmündig*); literally, he is still mouthless, *in-fans*, he does not speak. This silence is not something that befalls him; he is mute *in statu nascendi*. And yet the point here is not simply that this figure is silent. Rather, to take as typical the Kantian formulation, whose principal moments Benjamin retains, it is that the genius, trading in *inventio*, can serve as a tutelary figure, one, that is, whose achievements 'serve as a model not for imitation [*Nachmachung*], but for following [*Nachahmung*]'.[23] The point would be that the tragic hero inaugurates a new model, one which, not bound by the rules of mythic fate, exceeds them in the direction of authenticity and truth.

Final point: the passage begins and ends with reference to fate. Indeed, each of the foregoing points has been oriented toward the way in which fate comes to be broken in the fated unfolding of the existence of the hero. Here, Benjamin is once again not so very far from a position of Nietzsche's – a position most concisely expressed in a note of 1870–1 according to which 'the most universal form of *tragic* fate is the victorious defeat'.[24] A fragment of 1923 speaks in this regard of the *seighaften Tode*, the victorious death of the tragic hero (II 1: 267). 'In ancient tragedy', writes Benjamin quite late on in the *Origin of the German Mourning Play*, 'every order of fate denies *itself* [*sich versagenden*]' (I 1: 312; *Or.*, 133). It is as if the unspoken word which accompanies the hero to his fatal end has, in some way, forced fate to testify against itself, speaking out against itself in a way that cannot but call it into question from within.

*   *   *

Benjamin's thinking is not a tragic one – that much, at least on its own terms, is clear. Under the hypothesis of an epochal closure, 'tragedy' has had its day, namely the era in which Greek man rises up against mythic fate and, breaking its daimonic rules, inaugurates a new *fatum*: the *fatum* of *libertas*. Under this hypothesis, tragedy emerges and dies away with and as the epochal close of myth, its grip loosened, its law irretrievably dissolved, dying, finally, at the hands of philosophy. And yet, I begin to wonder whether one can, in fact, sustain the distinction Benjamin demands; whether one can, in other words, exclude tragedy from philosophy only by passing all too quickly over the trace of the tragic which would lie at its origin. The question would be, then, one of a certain excess, a certain echo of the tragic held in reserve from the very beginning, and so also of a certain echoing of this reserve which philosophy will not have been able to silence. In the course of exposing the ancient turn from tragic art to Socratic science, Benjamin also turns, from a language of tension and of excess to one of opposition and conflict, if not out and out war: 'the war [*den Kampf*] which this rationalism had declared on tragic art is decided against tragedy . . .'. If, in the wake of tragedy's destruction of myth, it is this decision which realises the epochal possibility of authenticity broached by tragedy, what is one to make of the manner in which Benjamin's remark continues: '. . . against tragedy with a superiority which in the end hurt the challenger more than the challenged' (I 1: 297; *Or.*, 118). What of this wound? Has it healed? If, according to Benjamin, it is philosophy alone which is left to hold the stage once the tragedy is over, might not some tragic word still echo across the satyric stage? If it is from the echoes which sound from out of 'monstrous emptiness' of the tragic hero that 'coming generations learn their language', might this word not be language itself? And might it not then be that, as Peter Szondi once remarked, 'the history of the philosophy of tragedy is not itself free from the tragic'?[25]

Notes

1 Benjamin's response to Asja Lacis' question concerning his failed *Habilitationsschrift*, *Ursprung des deutschen Trauerspiels*: 'Why do you bother with dead literature?', cited in Walter Benjamin, *Gesammelte Schriften*, edited by Rolf Tiedemann and Herman Schweppenhäuser (Frankfurt am Main; Suhrkamp, 1980) I 3: 879. All references to Benjamin's works are to this edition, henceforth cited by volume and page number without further designation. All translations are my own. References are also given to the following – relentlessly unreliable – English-language editions: Walter Benjamin, *The Origin of German Tragic Drama*, translated by John Osbourne (London: New Left Books, 1977), henceforth *Or.*, Walter Benjamin, *Selected Writings, Volume I: 1913–26*, edited by Marcus Bullock and Michael W. Jennings (Cambridge, MA:

Harvard University Press, 1996), henceforth *SW*. Since translations of works cited here usually include the original pagination in the margins, I have provided such references only where this is not the case.

2 It is important to stress that, with regard to the *Tendenz* of this turning, Benjamin speaks not of *muthos* but of *die Sage*. In part, his use of the term in a preparatory study of 1923, cited below, seems to belong to the citation from Adolf Graf von Schack with which he opens that study (II 1: 246–7), just as its later use in the *Ursprung des deutschen Trauerspiels* reflects the citation from Ulrich von Wilamowitz-Möllendorf (I 1: 284–5; *Or.*, 106) (the author, notably, of *Zukunftphilologie!*, a vitriolic pamphlet of 1872, unsurprisingly not the work cited by Benjamin, directed against the 'ignorance and lack of a love of truth' in Nietzsche's *Birth of Tragedy*; see *Der Streit um Nietzsches 'Geburt der Tragödie'*, edited by K. Grunder [Hildesheim: Olms, 1969], 54). Notwithstanding, one ought to ask: does Benjamin's 'definition' of *die Sage* as the primordial history (*Urgeschichte*) of a people also serve to define his use of the term *Mythos*? Not at all. Admittedly, the following remark on the German Idealist interpretation of tragedy might, on the surface, appear to elide any distinction between these terms: 'The freedom of its interpretation [of tragedy in respect of history] always gives way to the tendentious exactitude of the tragic renewal of myth [*tragischer Mythenerneuerung*]' (I 1: 299; *Or.*, 120). This aside, although even here matters are not so cut and dried, I want simply to draw attention to the fact that, for Benjamin, tragedy is quite obviously a matter of the transformation *not* of *muthos* – as near enough every single one of Benjamin's commentators has stated – but of *die Sage* as the primordial saying of mythic existence.

3 Presumably *Poetics* 1449b 24–5: 'Tragedy is, then, the *mimesis* of elevated action.' Benjamin paraphrases: '. . . *die Tragödie als die besonders geartete* mimesis *eines Geschehens erklärt*' (II 1: 248).

4 Nietzsche, *Die Geburt der Tragödie* in *Werke: Kritische Gesamtausgabe*, edited by Giorgio Colli and Mazzino Montinari (Munich: Walter de Gruyter, Deutscher Taschenbuch, 1988) I: 83; translated by Walter Kaufmann as *The Birth of Tragedy* (New York: Random House, 1967), 82. See also the lecture of 1 February 1870, 'Socrates und die Tragödie' (*Werke* I: 533–49, esp. 540–6), an early draft of §§ 11–15 of *The Birth of Tragedy*. It is worth recalling that, without in any way calling into question the emphasis on Euripides, the lecture of 1870 suggests quite explicitly that the movement which leads from Aeschylean tragedy to the death of tragic art is already underway in Sophocles: 'the gradual decline begins with Sophocles', Nietzsche writes, 'until finally Euripides, in his conscious reaction against Aeschylean tragedy, brings about the end with precipitate haste' (*Werke* I: 549). Benjamin, who could not have known of this lecture at the time of his *Habilitation* (Nietzsche's text was not released by the Archives for publication until 1927, two years after Benjamin completed his *Habilitationsschrift*), makes precisely the same point, remarking that *Antigone*'s illumination by an 'all-too rational concept of duty' means that the death of Sophocles' heroine can now only appear (*erscheinen*) tragic (I 1: 293; *Or.*, 114).

5 Consciously or not, Benjamin draws here on the *Wendepunkt* remarked by Nietzsche in *Birth of Tragedy*: 'Socrates, the one turning point and vortex of so-called world-history [*einen Wendepunkt und Wirbel der sogenannten Weltgeschichte*], (*Werke* I: 100; *Birth of Tragedy*, 96), a turning already announced at the very outset of Nietzsche's text, in the 'Foreword to Richard Wagner' (*Werke* I: 24; *Birth of Tragedy*, 31). This does not mark an end to Benjamin's borrowings from Nietzsche – whose work, Benjamin

Simon Sparks

notes at the outset of his remarks on tragedy, founds his own theses – and one could doubltess read each of the sections of the *Origin of the German Mourning Play* concerned with tragedy as a dialogue with Nietzsche. The Nietzsche presented in John Sallis' fine meditation on tragedy, *Crossing: Nietzsche and the Space of Tragedy* (Chicago: Chicago University Press, 1991), is, to my mind, particularly proximate to the Benjamin presented here.

6 *Phaedo* 99d–e.

7 The term is from Benjamin's essay on Hölderlin of 1914 (II 1: 105) where it refers explicitly to the traditional account of tragedy.

8 The final reference to Nietzsche – this, again from *Birth of Tragedy*: 'Let us think of the Cyclops eye of Socrates fixed on tragedy . . . let us think of this eye to which was denied the pleasure of peering into the Dionysian abysses' (*Werke* 1: 92; *Birth of Tragedy*, 89). Reiner Schürmann, one of the finest recent commentators on tragedy, has convincingly drawn attention to the possibility of translating this Socratic cyclopticism onto the structure of tragedy itself. For Schürmann,

> tragedy always traces a path of sight [*un parcours des yeux*]. The hero *sees* laws in conflict. Then – the moment of tragic denial – he *blinds* himself to one of them, keeping his *gaze fixed* on the other. . . . There follows then a catastrophe which *opens his eyes*: the moment of tragic truth . . . From denial to recognition, blindness is transmuted. Hubristic sightlessness changes into visionary blindness.

See *Des Hégémonies brisées* (Mauvezin: T. E. R., 1996), 40; Schürmann's emphasis. Although Schürmann does not mention Nietzsche's remarks, his suggestion that the philosopher, like Agamemnon, also serves to lay down the law by refusing a counter law, shows his concern to ascribe a tragic origin to philosophy.

9 There is, of course, nothing particularly new about a turn to sacrifice with respect to tragedy. And, in fact, the idea of sacrifice presented by Benjamin does indeed call to mind the tradition of questioning which has sought always to place the *thumele* at the very centre of the tragic stage (a tradition, moreover, already evoked by the word itself: what is tragedy if not the song of the goat, *no tragos*, the animal of immemorial sacrifice?). In this regard, one thinks most immediately of Hegel's article on natural law in which ethical life finds itself presented as the point at which the tragic comes to be articulated in absolute terms, but just as much of the invitation, spoken by an ancient Athenian, with which Nietzsche brings *The Birth of Tragedy* to a close: 'But now follow me to the tragedy and sacrifice with me in the temple of both gods' (*Werke* I: 156; *Birth of Tragedy*, 144). Equally, one would have also to refer here to Hölderlin, who will not cease to insist upon Empedocles' position as 'a sacrifice of his time'; see Friedrich Hölderlin, 'Grund zum Empedokles' in *Werke und Briefe*, edited by Friedrich Beißner and Jochen Schmidt (Frankfurt am Main: Insel, 1982), 578.

10 Thus, in addition to the new contents (*neue Inhalte*) announced by the sacrifice (I 1: 285; *Or.*, 107): the unarticulated content of the hero's achievements (*der Gehalt der Heroenwerke*) (I 1: 287; *Or.*, 108), the coming word contained (*erhält*) by his defiance (I 1: 294; *Or.*, 115), the composure (*Haltung*) of Greek man in the face of fate (I 3: 879) – at each of the disjunctive moments which structure Benjamin's reading of tragedy, it is a matter of such support.

11 The reference here is to Kant and the *Groundwork* of 1785, in which he describes philosophy, now placed in a precarious position (*einen mißlichen Standpunkt*), as the guardian or self-supporter of its own laws (*als Selbsthalterin ihrer Gesetze*); see the *Grundlegung zur Metaphysik der Sitten* in *Kants Gesammelte Schriften*, edited by the Preussische Akademie der Wissenschaft (Berlin: Walter de Gruyter 1902–) IV: 425, henceforth Ak., volume and page number. Doubtless Benjamin is *not* thinking of Kant at this point, yet it is to my mind uncertain that he can here sustain his insistence upon 'the independence of the tragic from *ethos*' (I 1: 280; *Or.*, 102). The transformation marked by the hero, which might be expressed in the – Hegelian – terms employed in a later section of the *Ürsprung des deutschen Trauerspiels*, from religious society (*religiöser Gemeinschaft*) to ethical community (*sittlicher Gesellschaft*) (I 1: 300; *Or.*, 121), seems to me to allow one to read tragedy not simply as the originary saying of truth, but as the originary saying of ethics as well. It is in this light that one would have to read the following remark from a preparatory essay of 1923 in which Benjamin will speak of tragedy as 'the ethical unfolding of mythical occurrences [*die sittliche Enfaltung eines mythischen Vorgangs*]' (II 1: 265). That Benjamin's central objection to the ethical interpretation of tragedy is to the imposition onto properly tragic action of a certain moral framework does not, I think, preclude the possibility of such a reading.

12 See, for example, the *Groundwork for the Metaphysics of Morals*, Ak. IV: 450f.
13 Thus a note of 1916:

> Not only does the tragic exist exclusively in the realm of dramatic human discourse [*Rede*]; it is even the only form originarily suitable [*ursprünglich eignet*] to human discursive exchange [*Wechselrede*]. Which is to say that there is nothing tragic outside of discursive exchange between men and that there is no other form of discursive exchange than the tragic.
>
> (II 1: 137)

Tragedy, Benjamin suggests in this note, is that form of language, namely discourse, in which language itself comes originally to be disclosed as such – disclosed, that is, *not* as the site of some supposed original meaning of language which might come to be lost, but as 'the word as the pure carrier [*reiner Träger*] of its meaning . . . the pure word'. Benjamin calls tragic this pure appearance (*reinen Erscheinungen*) of language, adding: 'In tragedy, the word and the tragic arise simultaneously' (II 1: 138). See also note 16, below.

14 In point of fact, this analogy belongs not to Benjamin, but to his friend Florens Christian Rang, with whom he conducted a lengthy correspondence during the gestation of his *Habilitationsschrift*. Throughout, Benjamin relied heavily on Rang's knowledge of the historical origins of tragedy, noting at one point that 'on the question of Greek theatre I am and remain wholly dependent upon you' (I 3: 892). In response to Benjamin's inquiry of early January 1924 as to whether there is any 'historical or merely factual [*sachlicher*]' 'connection . . . between the dianoetic forms of Sophocles and Euripides and Attic legal proceedings' (ibid.), Rang replied at length, drawing his friend's attention to the properly dialogic structure of the antique trial, and noting that what is characteristic of Attic law is that 'the drunken, ecstatic word is allowed to break through the regular encircling of the *agon*' (I 3: 894), a reply which Benjamin copied unchanged and at length into the body of his

work (see I 1: 295; *Or.*, 116). All the material is collected by the editors of Benjamin's *Gesammelte Schriften* (I 3: 887–95). The relation of the verbal formality or systematicity of the dramatic conflict – most evidently in the staged conflict of the Euripidean drama, but also, and to slightly different effect, in Sophocles (in *Electra*, for example, the central exchange between Clytaemnestra and Electra herself [516–22]) – to the set-speeches of the Athenian courts is summed up by Benjamin in the *Ursprung des deutschen Trauerspiels* as follows: 'Athletic contests, law and tragedy constitute the great agonal trinity of Greek life . . . and they are bound together under the sign of the contract' between the hero and the gods (I 1: 294–5; *Or.*, 115).

15 *Werke* I: 40–1; *Birth of Tragedy*, 46.
16 *Werke* I: 29–30; *Birth of Tragedy*, 37.
17 In a fragment 'Über Sprache überhaupt und über die Sprache des Menschens', contemporaneous with this one and also a preliminary study for the *Ursprung des deutschen Trauerspiels*, Benjamin will, in passing, draw attention to the 'tragic relationship which prevails between the languages of speaking men [*die . . . tragischen Verhältnis zwischen den Sprachen der sprechenden Menschen waltet*]' (II. 1: 156; *SW*, 73). In the light of this remark and the following reading of the *Ursprung des deutschen Trauerspiels*, one could inquire as to the relation of the gift of language disclosed by tragic fate, which, as I shall argue, directs Benjamin's reading of tragedy, and the origin of (human) language remarked in this fragment of 1917, an origin which comes about on the basis of the most divine fate of all: '. . . thou shalt surely die' (Genesis 2: 17). It seems to me that one *could* read these two texts together in such a way that would allow for a more expansive reading of the emergence of language from out of properly tragic guilt.
18 In this regard, does one's gaze not inevitably fall on Heidegger? *Not*, I think, on the lectures on Hölderlin of 1934–5, for whom the *sacrifice of death* (indeed, for Heidegger could there be any other?) as the giving of that which is most properly my own, would be the founding gesture of an *ursprüngliche Gemeinschaft*. See *Hölderlins Hymnen 'Germanien' und 'Der Rhein'* Gesamtausgabe 39) (Frankfurt am Main: Klostermann, 1989), 72–3. Not this Heidegger, then, but, I would say, the Heidegger of the Afterword to 'What is Metaphysics?', for whom sacrifice is the concealed thanks (*der verborgene Dank*) of an essential thinking (*das wesentliche Denken*), a thanking which he refers to language itself, saying in a marginal note that this 'speechless answer of thanking in sacrifice' 'is the origin of the human word [*ist der Ur-sprung des menschlichen Wortes*]'. See *Wegmarken* (Frankfurt am Main: Klostermann, 1996), 310 and note.
19 See Gottfried Wilhelm Leibniz, *Die philosophische Schriften*, edited by C.J. Gerhardt (Berlin: Weidmann, 1890) V: 139–40; translated and edited by Leroy E. Loemker as *Philosophical Papers and Letters* (Boston: Reidel, 1976), 122.
20 Benjamin's implicit engagement with Kant throughout 'Schicksal und Charakter' seems, quite remarkably, to have gone unnoticed by commentators. This engagement extends beyond the simple exchange of figures in which Benjamin indulges – here, the gypsy women who appears in 'Der Streit der Fakultäten', Kant's last philosophical work, in order to denote the possibility of soothsaying history (*wahrsagende Geschichtserzählung*), of history *a priori* (Ak. VII: 79) – and embraces the whole analysis of fate. Thus, in his insistence that reading the *dicta* of fate 'is no easy matter', Benjamin clearly aligns himself with the disquiet remarked by Kant

at the outset of the Analytic of Concepts: along with the concept of fortune, the concept of fate is, Kant writes, one of those 'usurped concepts' which 'run around with almost universal indulgence yet which are from time to time challenged by the question: *quid juris?*' Since 'no clear legal ground [*Rechtsgrund*]' can ever be adduced for the employment of such terms, either from reason or from experience, they serve only to embarrass and to confuse. See *Kritik der reinen Vernunft*, edited by Raymund Schmidt (Hamburg: Felix Meiner, 1956) A 84–5; B 117. And yet, however questionable the concept of fate may be, it is not as if it could itself ever be usurped. Indeed, its very questionability provides the starting point not merely for Benjamin's own text, but for the critical enterprise itself, which, as one knows, takes its leave from the 'peculiar fate [*das besondere Schicksal*]' remarked by Kant at the outset of the *Critique of Pure Reason*, the fact that certain questions are fated to arise to reason. Such questions are fated to arise, Kant remarks, because assigned to reason by reason itself (A viii). It is in response to such embarrassment and confusion that Benjamin seeks to provide a 'genuine' concept of fate, one 'which takes in fate in tragedy as well as the foresights [*Absichten*] of the fortune-teller' (II 1: 176; *SW*, 204). Indeed, the assertion of *Recht* as the measure of fate begs the question of whether or not one can say that Benjamin has therefore provided fate with the *Rechtsgrund* it was so desperately lacking in Kant.

21 Equally, in 'Toward a Critique of Violence' of the following year, Benjamin will draw attention to the mythic – if not properly daimonic – foundations of right (cf. II 1: 197–203; *SW*, 248–52).

22 Benjamin's most extensive remarks on the daimonic are to be found in the first part of his essay on Goethe's *Elective Affinities*, particularly I 1: 146–54; *SW*, 314–20. Whilst one must doubtless hear in Benjamin's use of the word an echo of the classical paradigm of the daimons, namely the words of Diotima of Mantinea, spoken to Sophocles in the *Symposium* – to daimonion, she tells him, 'is midway between what is divine and what is mortal' (*Symposium* 202d; in a contemporaneous fragment entitled 'Schemata zum Psychophysichen', Benjamin cites precisely this remark in the following, his own, translation: 'Dämonische ist mitten zwechen Gott und Sterblichem' [VI: 86]) – one must also hear echoed the final words of Goethe's 'Wahrheit und Dichtung', discussed in Benjamin's essay on the *Elective Affinities*. There, the poet grasps the daimonic as something manifest in nature, something *of* nature. Neither divine nor human, malevolent nor angelic, it expresses itself only in contradictions (*Widersprüchen*). It can be expressed neither by a concept nor by a word. Like the 'empire of the *ur*-phenomena', nature, in which it manifests itself and to which it is wedded, it 'can never be entirely illuminated by thought'. It penetrates the boundaries which limit us (*uns begrenzt*), manipulating the conditions of time and space. 'This essence', writes Goethe, 'I called daimonic' (cited I 1: 150; *SW*, 316). Equally, one should not discount the presence here of Kierkegaard's *The Concept of Anxiety* – which Benjamin could have read in an early translation by Theodor Haecker under the title *Kritik der Gegenwart* (Basel: Hess, 1914). I am thinking, most particularly, of the final section of that work, in which the Danish philosopher ponders not only of 'the relation of the immediate genius to fate', but also the *communicatio idiomatum* of the daimonic, a name, Kierkegaard says, only rarely spoken today; see *The Concept of Anxiety*, translated by Reider Thomte and Albert B. Anderson (Princeton: Princeton University Press, 1980), 107 and 118. This seems all the more likely given the massive presence of Kierkegaard

in the *Ursprung des deutschen Trauerspiels*: not only in Benjamin's famous concluding remarks – written in 1917 and so before 'Schicksal und Charakter' – on *Geschwätz* and the fall from linguistic immediacy (I 1: 407–9, *Or.*, 233–5), also drawn from *The Concept of Anxiety*, but, equally, in the meditation on the irony of Socrates' non-tragic death, a meditation which clearly bears the imprint of Kierkegaard's own dissertation; see *The Concept of Irony*, translated by Howard V. Hong and Edna V. Hong (Princeton: Princeton University Press, 1989), 270–1, and Sylviane Agacinski, *Aparté: Conceptions et morts de Sören Kierkegaard* (Paris: Aubier-Flammarion, 1977), 33–5. Here I can only refer to David Farrell Krell's remarkable analyses of the daimonic in *Daimon Life: Heidegger and Life-Philosophy* (Bloomington: Indiana University Press 1992). Although this work is devoted to Heidegger and his readers, much of what is said there could be extended to Benjamin. Indeed, Krell himself pauses momentarily in order to draw our attention to the daimons of the essay on Goethe, in order, he says, to indicate 'the alarming "spread" of the daimons – of daimon life, or of "daimon life", if you will'(7).

23 Kant, *Critique of Judgement*, Ak. V: 309.
24 Nietzsche, *Werke* VIII: 192.
25 Peter Szondi, *Versuch über das Tragische* in *Schriften*, edited by Jean Bollack (Frankfurt am Main: Suhrkamp, 1979) I: 200.

Part VI

Last Words

11

Aphasia: or the last word

Marc Froment-Meurice

Crénom!

      – remark attributed to Charles Baudelaire

'This is what is tragic about us: that we leave the realm of the living silently, packed into some container or other, not that we, consumed by flames, atone for the flame we could not possibly control.' These words appear in a letter Hölderlin wrote on 4 December 1801 to his friend Böhlendorff, thanking him for having sent his play *Fernando*, which Hölderlin saw as 'a *real* modern tragedy'. The compliment is an exaggeration, like everything that comes from a poet close to losing all sense of measure, someone engaged in a bitter confrontation with what he called 'the fire of the heavens'. Jean Beaufret was right when he pointed out that the play would have 'faded into oblivion' were it not for the fact that Hölderlin cited two verses of it.[1] Yet Beaufret missed what, according to Hölderlin, makes this a *real* modern tragedy. Putting it brutally: what is tragic about modernity is that there is no such thing as the modern tragic. It is useless, even fallacious, to look to *Oedipus at Colonus* for

> almost a modern or Hesperian tragedy, the tragedy Hölderlin wanted
> to write, the tragedy he fell short of in each successive version of
> *Empedocles*, and the promise of which he thought he had discerned, at
> last, in his friend Böhlendorff's *Fernando*.[2]

With all due respect to my old master, I cannot agree with him: first, the words 'modern or *Hesperian*' suggest that giving the 'authentic' definition of poetic modernity would be a matter of defining the modern *Hesperian*. In fact, if '*Hesperian*' has any meaning at all, it is as the opposite of 'modern', a sort of detour which is not exempt from return – to the Greeks, even if this return has nothing to do with neo-classicism, and indeed follows no known model. In addition, how can one think of *The Death of Empedocles* – in whichever version

221

it comes down to us – as a modern tragedy if the very name of Empedocles
evokes *fire* – here, the fire of the volcano – and a return, albeit deferred or
diverted, to the principle of *hen kai pan*, the principle of the 'aorgic'? If the
'statutory' principle tries to apply a *brake*, it is nevertheless related to this rage
without which there is no tragedy. For it is clear what Hölderlin saw as modern tragedy: it is the total absence of flame and sacrifice, the sheer lack of
everything divine – and a lack which is not even recognised as such. If his
friend's play struck him, it is not because he saw there, by means of some sort
of projection, an affinity with his own attempts, but because the play was nothing, and had nothing tragic about it; does he not try to convince his friend that
the Greeks are indispensable (*unentbehrlich*) to us? The modern 'fate' he
describes in images as prosaic as packing a box, or canning (*coffin* as *container*)
– as if leaving the world were like leaving a fast food restaurant with a meal
'to-go' – clearly does not need the Greeks. Finally, what right do we have to
think of *The Death of Empedocles* as a failed tragedy? If there is a failure, it is
not a question of simply missing the mark; is it not, rather, the sign of a more
fundamental impasse – a sign that no modern tragedy is even close to attain-
ing *the* tragic, that this 'absence of fate' is *our* fate? It might seem paradoxical
that, in one sense, this failure alone is what coincides with our lot – as athe-
ists – but I will give an example of the heroic virtue of the not [*pas*] (of god,
and therefore of the tragic): I will offer here a reading of Maurice Blanchot's
The Last Word.[3]

*　*　*

'Philosophy and tragedy.' That 'philosophy' comes first might already come as
a surprise, if philosophy was born *after* tragedy, or at least at a time when it
already dominated the scene. The consequences Nietzsche drew from this are
well known, consequences which Hegel had already inscribed with the departure of the philosophical spirit in the form of its emblem, the owl. What
Nietzsche would interpret as the sign of decadence, calling for a return to the
properly tragic, pre-Socratic origin of philosophy, was, for Hegel, the indication of a more comprehensive maturity, a universality which would surpass all,
integrating tragic particularity as it went. For both, however, tragedy remains
a *Greek* (not modern) model. Similarly, Heidegger, following Hölderlin, could
never forget the origin which seemed to condemn all modern tragedy to being
no more than imitation – more or less successful but nevertheless failed because
it is an imitation – of the Greek model. It is as though no philosophy can overcome its fondness for that initial catastrophe, its posthumous birth, posthumous
in a double sense: it is born of a dying father (or mother), and is stillborn, in
the pale light of dawn, too late, as though it were its own survivor – after the
drama, desiring it all the while, from its first step it walks backward. Walking

222

backward, it inscribes the return of the birth to self as its avowed or hidden plan, inscribing it in all its forms, and with the ambivalence of what Freud, using the name (at least) of the tragic hero *par excellence*, would determine as the Oedipus Complex: kill the father, sleep with the mother – kill tragedy in order to be more tragic than it.

Are we obliged, then, to see Socrates – as Nietzsche did – as the grave-digger of Greek tragedy? Socrates is not generally seen as a tragic figure, and, if he is seen as a hero, it is in a sense too human to be tragic. Human, too human: a champion of 'measure in all things', with the difference that he pushed this ideal so far that it too appeared excessive. Thus Pierre Boutang could say that, if he is never drunk, it is that he is always drunk, even when he is sober, 'drunk with that small difference that mocks the *medan agan*, the nothing to excess [*rien de trop*], the secret joke that the Greeks translated into action as *a bit much* [*un rien trop*]'.[4] A bit too human, an example of a rule which – if the Greeks did indeed desire it – was quite an exception for a fundamentally unreasonable people, extravagant in their myths and in insanities of all sorts. Nietzsche had the virtue of rediscovering this brilliant infancy of a world which nevertheless gave birth to 'reason'. Hölderlin prepared the way, naming what is properly Greek 'the fire of the heavens', in contrast to which sobriety is our fate by birth. If *hubris* is the ultimate danger, as tragedy demonstrates with Oedipus as well as with Antigone, it is because it is so common, so thoroughly shared that it must be exorcised by tragic purification, and each tragic destiny will be an example not to be followed: it is our opposite, and rather than admiration there is a 'salutariness' – fear in the face of these sacred monsters, fear so great that everyone knows (according to the famous definition from the stasimon in *Antigone*) that there is nothing more monstrous, more terrifying (*Ungeheuer*, in Hölderlin's translation[5]) on earth than this apparently so innocuous animal: man.

Excess dominates, which is why there *must* be tragedy: limits by *default*. This is not the case with Socrates, who internalised these limits to the point where Nietzsche thought of him as a monster, but, contrary to all monstrosity, a monster of consciousness, critique, mastery.[6] Nor, in another sense, is it the case with the Moderns, who simply no longer had access to the transports which carried the Greeks beyond themselves: we are barbarians to the point of seeing Dionysian excess as mere barbarianism.

Thus, when Socrates said, in the *Symposium*, that his wisdom was 'surely as worthless and ambiguous as a dream', Agathon replied: 'You're being outrageous' (175e). But if Socrates commits an outrage,[7] if he is guilty of *hubris*, it is by a sort of monstrous inversion of the relation to limit. It then seems that he can never be drunk, or beside himself, because he has so carefully followed the Delphic oracle that he never forgets himself. He has found his limits so

223

well that he has surpassed them all, including death, not only by inventing immortality, but by making himself immortal by means of *logos* – always immortal. But only the gods are immortal, and this, from a Greek perspective, justified sentencing Socrates to death.

Is this a tragic event? Perhaps, but in a paradoxical sense, since it would be the tragedy of the end of tragedy, or the birth of philosophy: death without pathos, *absolutely flat*, death 'with no fuss' ['*sans phrases*'], as Blanchot put it. What is most astonishing is that – thanks to Plato's grandiose dramatisation – this rather miserable end (compared to Achilles' or Hector's) became a model of heroism. It took the staggering generosity of an Alcibiades to get us to swallow Socrates' bravery in the wars. (He didn't run away! But we have no idea if he fought or killed anyone.) Who could credit the courage of a man who is not afraid of death for the simple reason that he believes he is immortal? Achilles knows he is going to die, but he prefers glory to that 'cobbler's life' which one must lead as a survivor and which Hölderlin saw – to his horror – as the modern fate. In the end, Socrates settled for swallowing the hemlock in order to have done with his wretched fellow citizens. He goes so far as to remember his little debts – the cock to Asclepius – as if death were no more than a detail of everyday life. Ha! (A Homeric laugh.) That would be funny – and perhaps *truly heroic* – if he had himself laughed, and if this laughable reflection had not sprung from a 'disinterest' that was more than interested, if it had not been the result of a calculation which indeed heralded the stroke of genius of Christianity (as Nietzsche put it) – the pretence that killed two birds with one stone: granting oneself the luxury of being heroic while, as Baudelaire says, both performing 'an act of charity and getting a good deal'. Socrates *would have had to* laugh (up Plato's sleeve) at having so successfully fooled us into taking so seriously a death in which he never believed.

At the end of the *Symposium* we read: 'Socrates was forcing them to accept that the same man could not know how to compose both a comedy and a tragedy' (223d). Dawn is breaking on this equivalence of tragedy and comedy. It is the advent of philosophy, the anticipation of tragedy's becoming comedy in the *Phenomenology*. All tragedy ends in farce, but this *is* what is most tragic, in a sense shown only by Bataille's laughter or Beckett's absurdity. 'But what about Socratic irony?' Well, maybe that too is only a trick, a triviality trying to make us believe that there is a hidden treasure after all. A Greek would not let himself be taken in by such games: everything is exposed, that is the *only* secret – the Greeks' 'athletic' bodies testify to as much.

Hegel writes: 'The hero who appears before the onlookers splits up into his mask and the actor, into the person in the play and the actual self.'[8] This division gives the actor his rule: he must forget his 'effective Self' in order to identify with his character, but he must not forget himself *as* actor for fear of becoming the mask, a death mask insofar as it can no longer be detached from the 'effective Self'. For Hegel, this is no more than a stage in the process of reaching the absolute Self through the negation of every character – *typos* which is no more than an abstract universal, a 'type'. By letting the mask fall, by showing *that* he is a player (albeit of a tragic destiny), the actor reveals the truth – *that* it is tragedy but that it, at the same time, delivers the *coup de grâce* to tragedy.

> The self . . . plays with the mask which it once put on in order to act its part [the *histrion*]; but it as quickly breaks out again from this illusory character and stands forth in its own nakedness and ordinariness, which it shows to be not distinct from the genuine self, the actor, or from the spectator.[9]

It is as if the mask were only a suit of clothes one could take off without damaging the body itself: naked, ordinary, common, shared by all; what is more, the Hegelian reduction of all transcendence – of every trance and dance – ends up quite simply suppressing the tragic (which explains why Hegel interprets Antigone as representing the sedition of the particular, or the feminine, against the State). The difference which marks the tragic hero is not confined to a particular sign (a costume, a sceptre, any apparent mark of recognition, the name, for instance: is an anonymous tragedy even thinkable?). Hegel misses tragic singularity because he forgets what, according to Aristotle, is the second element of the tragic effect. Beyond terrifying, tragedy must evoke sym-pathy[10] (I prefer this word to 'compassion' or 'pity', which are too moral by far), that is, the spectators' ability to identify with the actor, or rather with the *persona* he embodies: Oedipus is, after all, *also* the first on the scene, and his lot could have fallen to each of us. If the ordinary were not the extraordinary, there would be no way of sharing – through mediation, or at a distance: by the distance maintained from the mask, from the game – which will, from then on, be a matter of indifference to us. Difference is what is most thoroughly shared, precisely because nakedness is not at all ordinary, or because it characterises the human being in its proper monstrosity, a being with no shelter, exposed, too natural to be natural. The mask, then, plays this veiling role, acting as a protector because it introduces a thin surface which is enough to set at a distance this unnameable, chaotic, terrifying depth which is the Face.[11]

According to Nietzsche, man is an animal whose nature has not yet been fixed.[12] This is why 'man' is a transitory term, a passage towards the beyond of man, the super-human; but that in turn cannot be taken as a term, that is, an end, since it is essentially determined by limitlessness. 'I carry on my shoulders the fate of humanity', Nietzsche writes in *Ecce Homo*. This appears to common sense as the epitome of presumption and impertinence. But it is impossible to think tragically, 'Dionysically', without im-pertinence, without surpassing the limits, not only those of what is permitted, or reasonable, but *all* limits.

Nietzsche was ingenious enough not to propose *a* philosophy as if it were a recipe, or a system. He proposed nothing more than tragic philosophy, but in such a way that the *proposal* had to be indecent, impossible. For him, tragic existence, as opposed to Kant's metronomic regularity, is 'life lived in ice and in the high mountains', solitudes – trade-mark – without even the (de)railing of Being. Such a position can be compared to nothing; it is, rather, a de/position, a *tabula rasa*, and not only of the past. Violence – *Gewalt*, which Heidegger takes up in his *Introduction to Metaphysics*, the most Nietzschean and therefore most tragic of his books – is, from the *beginning* of philosophy, its source and its power, and with Nietzsche it bursts into a final firework display, the last sparks of which we live today. This is the Apocalypse, the end of humanity – and of philosophy; and here, *Ecce Homo*. Man presents himself precisely as what grinds every presentation to pieces, every human 'essence', as what has surpassed the limits and even the name of man: 'I am not a human being, I am made of dynamite.' Such extra-vagance would have to be measured before we condemn or exalt it. But how and against what to measure it? Recognise this much: something happened – to which nothing will hark back. The irreversible, an absolute limit. But there is no limit that is not destined to be surpassed. To say 'limit', to set a limit, is to already imply its possible – and therefore actual – transgression. Nevertheless, showing the limit as limit constitutes the end of the limit, its limit – the last word. The limit is unlimited, exposed down to its most intimate interiority, exploded: like a revulsion of the interior, emptied of its entrails, or turned into surface – and nothing else, or the nothing *itself*.

Nothing: experience. And once again, not a philosophy; nothing but experience, and again, not *an* experience – at least not personal experience: 'but let's leave Mr. Nietzsche there', to use an expression from the *Gay Science* which was one of the epigraphs for Bataille's *On Nietzsche*. Experience opens onto a community, it is the experience of sharing, and the sharing of experience itself; of sharing of the Same, a Same identical to nothing. Experience, however interior, demands to be communicated, but it always remains a demand, never a fact, contrary to the common (common sense). What it communicates is not in fact communicable or, rather, it is communicated only in its impossibility – as Trakl said: 'One can absolutely not communicate.' Because to communicate, at its limit, is to destroy oneself as in sexual or orgiastic union. At the moment of union, as at the moment of death, there is also limitless separation. In Hölderlin's words:

The presentation of the tragic rests mainly upon this: that the monstrous – how god and human mate, and [how] the power of nature and what is innermost in man boundlessly become one, in fury – can be understood by the fact that the boundless becoming-one purifies itself though a boundless separation.[13]

In purification one hears an echo of the *katharsis* which Aristotle read into tragic *pathos*; but it is not a simple purgative. Becoming-one, the divine and the human, their boundless belonging [*appartenance*] is achieved by a departure [*départ*], or, better yet, a disowning [*départenance*], which is also without bounds. No mediation, not even the not as mediation; the place of the transport, of the *caesura,* must remain empty. This is why the act of copulation, the little linking word 'is', remains meaningless. 'Is' is not, is nothing, has no meaning. No one can be, in the full sense, limitless being-with, without bonds, without being *immediately being-without*, without bounds.

If experience immediately transcends the subject, it also brings about the fall of transcendence. It presents nothing presentable, even under the name 'God'. God is dead, but the word signifies nothing, or signifies everything but a fact: there is no death certificate to show, no announcement to send out. It would be something only someone demented could read. Only the insane can say 'I am dead'. And maybe that is what happens; but the demented one who announces the death of God is dead and buried, buried by his own words. I is another, but there is no other of the other; I is alienated by the simple fact that it has passed to the third person – become Nobody [*Personne*] – passed into the desert of copulation without object.

Experience oscillates between the summit (the extreme of the possible, which turns towards the impossible) and descent, a word in which one hears what is positive in the ends proposed. Zarathustra began his story with a descent. Summit and descent are not opposed, like good and evil: 'Just as the summit is, in the end, only the inaccessible, the descent is, from the beginning, inevitable.'[14] History always begins with a descent or decline, the catastrophe of beginning at the very moment it appears: *incipit tragoedia*. The limit recoils into the limitless. Love ends as soon as the limits of the loved one are reached, because love is the will to lose one's limits, to give [*dé/penser*] without limits. But unlimited transgression is impossible; to transgress Creon's order, for example, is not just to lift the interdiction, but to reaffirm the legitimacy of the edict by the very means by which it is *said* [*dit*]. Unlimited transgression, as it is thought – no, as Bataille in fact experienced it – is, precisely as impossible, the place of experience. It can be located on no map, but is never the less *there*.

Is Sade, then, a tragic author? He at least shows the straight, strict, almost dialectical (were it not so dazzling) relationship between pleasure and transgression. *To say everything* can only reach the very limit of saying: the silence of the body in the hidden room, where, unlike in the boudoir, one can no longer talk philosophy, but can just let out cries and sighs. Not even a universe as frightful as that of *One Hundred and Twenty Days of Sodom* can produce unlimited violence, because the violence is expressed in a language that is itself measured (like discourse, with regular syntax). In torture, just like in extreme pleasure, an objective limit is marked, the limit of language: the only absolute transgression would be that of saying [*le dire*] itself rather than of this or that interdiction. Hölderlin evoked a word which would kill *immediately*, not only by its consequences and translations. Is a word which kills speech only imaginable? Language keeps to that side of its limits which can be reached; on the other side there are no longer even sides. The paradox of Sadian discourse – letting beings who are without faith or law speak but so as to make them reason to excess, and to the point of nausea – recalls (but inverts) the discourse of experience, devoted to the unsayable even as it tends to infinite community. It can communicate nothing sane, and plunges each one into extreme destitution and solitude, just as the work of Sade can only end up as a reasoned (almost Socratic) catalogue of all the most delirious perversions.

Experience, going to the limit and the very limit of limit, can never be 'made' ['*faite*'] without being undone [*défaite*], deposed. In the end, in experience 'one is left, like a child [abandoned] one night, naked, in the depths of the woods,'[15] and its community can only remain deserted. Desert, the very place of experience, the uninhabitable trance: open, but to no-one, to a place determined only by the unlimited limit. Whatever gives itself over to excess is an annunciation, but one that carries no content and takes no prisoners. Everything – on condition of being nothing at all, no object. Or the ocean: 'But where does all that is grand and sublime in man finally flow? Is there no ocean for these torrents? – Be that ocean: there will be one.'[16] Bataille concluded: 'Better than the image of Dionysus Philosophos, the loss of this ocean and this bare demand: "Be this ocean", designates experience and the extreme to which it tends.' The ocean and the desert are the extreme metaphors for what is beyond metaphor, the figures of meaning when meaning changes its figure.

Perhaps 'literature' returns at this point, not to save us from the tragic or from the abyss (which is too grand a word, anyway, and too filosofik), nor to plunge us into it as though into holy water, but perhaps just to testify to a possibility – *the impossible*. I have come to *The Last Word* I mentioned earlier. And I will go immediately to its end, its last word: 'But his tranquillity reassured her, and, when the fall of the tower flung them outside, all three fell without saying a word.' The last word, then, is 'without saying a word'. The last word is the word 'word'. Just as the end is the end – of Blanchot's *Après coup*: 'And there is nonetheless still meditation to be done, even on death with no eulogies [*sans phrases*], perhaps without end, to the *end*.' Death can never be said without eulogies [*sans phrases*], since there will always be florid words to be said; the last word can never be said, at least *not without* saying a word (since silence is another one).

As Blanchot himself said, this account of the end of everything can only be a fiction –

> . . . telling the story of total destruction – in which the account itself would also have had to have perished – as if it had happened is as impossible as it is absurd, at least to the extent that it does not feign prophecy, announcing to the past a future that is already there.
>
> (*AC*, 93–4)

The prophetic nature of the said is even more obvious in the earlier piece, 'The Idyll', a premonition of the 'end' of history – the death camps. At least this is what certain philosophers[17] have said of this 'event' improperly called by the place-name, Auschwitz: that it is the last word of the West. It can be said, but in saying it all reality vanishes into the night and fog of an event which will never come to be an event, at least not as an event of or in history. The last word must be the end, of everything, including or beginning with the end of the word (and therefore of history, as its telling). It would be nearly better to say that Auschwitz – a generic name, since there is no proper one[18] – never happened, not in denial, but because no place can 'accommodate' what has never said its word, and therefore whose place it never was to say it. If these places exist, if Auschwitz can be visited, and if there are even guided tours, and supermarkets, and convents there, then these places can recall nothing, to no one: there is no memory when there is no possibility of forgetting.

'The last word' stands in much the same place. Like all history, like all stories, it happened one day, once upon a time: 'The words I heard that day sounded bad to my ears, in the most beautiful street in the town.' It becomes clear quickly enough, indeed, from the first question the narrator poses to the first person who happens to pass: 'Well, what's the watchword [*mot d'ordre*]?', but it could also be read after the fact [*après coup*], in *Après coup* (*AC*, 93), that it 'springs from an abrupt summoning of language, of the strange resolution to deprive this one of his support, the watchword'. An explanation comes after the fact, in parentheses: '(no more constraining or affirmative language, i.e., no more language – but no: always a word for saying and not saying it)' – an explanation that the watchword is the last word. In fact, the last word is not only the one that comes last, but also something that loops back and puts the

end, as *telos*, at the head – getting it into its head that it is the head, the com-
mander – the first: principle, *arche*. 'And that's my last word,' the negotiator
says, to put an end to the negotiation, but also to carry the day, to settle the
matter. That's my last word, and the interlocutor has no choice but to shut
up. Prescriptive language, language of the Law promulgated until the advent of
a new order, or indefinitely if another does not come to put an end to it by
contesting its claim to have the last word. In the guise of being the last word,
the watchword forbids all others (words or orders); but it calls them up just
as much as it forbids them.

One could go so far as to claim that every word is of the order of the watchword, prescriptive and non-declarative in the terminology of speech acts (terminology which makes one wonder if it is a last word of language acts). A
statement which seems to be purely declarative must also be prescriptive, in
order to be a statement. As a pro-position, it states, issues an order, albeit
only its own: it demands that it be heard, understood, followed – in the order
it prescribes, the order of discourse: syntax. *Syntaxis* is the order of lines on a
battlefield – a page. Whatever the content of a discourse, there is always a
direction to be followed, and it is never *neutral*. Listen to the first words of
one who has lost the watchword: 'Your language only half pleases me. Are you
sure of your words? – No, I say, shrugging my shoulders; how can I be sure
of them? It's a risk one takes.' It quickly becomes clear that he contravenes
what regulates the use of words even more than syntax: the adequation of language to intention and even the presence of this intention. Someone who does
not know what he says or wants to say is senseless, mad . . . Nevertheless,
madness, the madness of the day, lies in wait for anyone who speaks, since no
language is proper (to him), since its engagement is above all a hostage-taking,
a language-lying [*langage-ment*]. The promise one makes to say what one means
always runs up against language which has no says without wanting-to-say. The
example, from *The Death Sentence*, is the marriage proposal which can only be
formulated in a foreign language, and, though the response is given in yet
another foreign language, it is nevertheless translated, without the slightest
word being understood. Every word betrays, and in a double sense: the sense
of going back on one's word, and of revelation.

The narrator, in search of the lost watchword, goes, naturally enough, to
the library: a place of exemplary order, not only because books, the guaran-
tors of knowledge, are there, but because one can be sure that they will be
arranged in a very particular – probably alphabetical – order. This library has
nothing but empty shelves. Only when he is thrown into a cell does the narrator find a book to his purposes, a book 'which seemed open on the table'.
False purpose: no book is destined for a single recipient, even if it is dedicated
to him. In the cell he finds a rather shadowy old woman who is taking off her

clothes – the book is always an old whore, but, at the same time, there is no nude, or nakedness is, like the black shift which covers the body of the old woman, no more than a shroud. He asks the woman: 'Can you read?' An infantile question that every book asks, implicitly, and one a person should not rush to answer on the basis of the fact that he is not illiterate: if the old woman represents the book as its literality, she can only be ruined in spelling out the very word 'ruin'. No one escapes this ruination. Indeed, every book is the ruination of the letter, which is condemned to erase itself as a letter if it wants to offer something to be read.

The book presents itself as 'an extract from the discourse on the third estate', a mythic discourse that talks about origin and therefore its degradation. Saying that there was a time when language no longer linked words to one another in simple relations, it then surmises that there was another time when, in contrast, everything was related according to a simple, unequivocal, immutable order: I say what I mean, take me at my word. But this discourse runs up against the interdiction, the indirect return of the lost watchword: 'no more language', they say, because it is an instrument that is impossible to manipulate, or because it masters the one who should master it – after all, who can guarantee that words correspond to intentions, and what language could be used to affirm it? Interdiction sustains the desire for transgression. The law generates its own breaking (Hegel says, in the same vein, that the law is criminal). The *simple* fact that there is a language that is the double of the existing one implies that all language is double, capable of saying what is just as easily as what is not, of calling into being what is not and causing what is to disappear. On account of this primordial ambiguity – *Oedipus the King* is, according to Karl Reinhardt, the tragedy of appearance – one arrives at this paradoxical situation: 'reasonable people decided to stop talking'. 'Those to whom nothing was forbidden', because they were the incarnation of the watchword, those who knew what it meant to speak, fell silent, or, worse still, abused the language, 'diverting it from its natural course'. Aware of what words *can* always say and therefore *do* say something they do not mean, reasonable people use language for keeping silent rather than for speaking. They use it more foolishly than the fools who do not even know what they are saying.

'Why was this book so different from the others?'(*AC*, 62). This is the question which will liberate him, throw him out of the cell. Now 'there is no library anymore', no more order to follow, no more intention: 'Now everyone will read as he wishes' (*AC*, 63) – but this apparent liberty is an illusion. 'I would like to kill you,' he says to the old woman who has just told him the news 'with a malicious smile'. All that remains of language are 'the forms of a long sentence crushed by the stamping of the crowd', a word that could be heard through any crowd's roar: *until*. It is the end word, in the sense that by forbidding us to envisage any end, it puts an end to all meaning. 'By means of the *until*, time throws obstacles in its way, and becomes the ruin of itself.' If there is no longer an end, there is also no more failure; but the absence of failure, the throwing of obstacles, far from being a success, is the most tragic thing that could happen: that nothing more should happen, that time should become its own ruin (Hölderlin talks of time become a desert, 'like Niobe').

What is there . . . ? [*Qu'est-ce qu'il y a . . .?*] He runs away, the dogs of justice let him go by ('I was judge. Who could condemn me?'); it is only long after he is gone that they begin to howl again: 'trembling, smothered howling which, at this time of the day, rang out like an echo of the word *"there is"*' (*AC*, 66). '*There is*' would thus be the last word, since it says what all words say or do: that there is. Without '*there is*', there is nothing, not even 'nothing'. The identity of being and *logos*, which rests on the onto-logical difference between *what* there is and the '*there is*' itself, which is no part of what there is so as to be able to allow what there is to take place. The word '*there is*' is also the watchword of justice, in that it determines the order of things, that they be rather than not be, but if it justifies everything in its being there, it cannot justify itself in the same way. The theodicy of the world has no *dike*, the Law without law, the unjustifiable because it justifies everything. The word itself verifies as much, 'there is', which means nothing, which has no determinable subject – the 'there' ['*il/Es*'] which Blanchot will call the Neutral, which Heidegger will try to identify as *Ereignis*, which is no one and no instance, which is not, but which gives being . . . that would be the last word if it were indeed a word. After all, the fact that it is heard only as an echo through the muffled howling of the dogs – the occasional instruments of justice, of ontotheological Dike – means, above all, that it cannot reach the status that it gives to every word. There is no '*there is*' or there is only its distorted echo, a muffled howling, which is heard again when one enters the pavilion where the children are locked away, 'those who agree to talk only by screaming and crying' (*AC*, 66). As tradition has it, children are those who speak only by being incapable of speech. This incapacity, unlike a material impossibility (a stone cannot be reproached for not being able to talk), marks the primitive state of the human being. Speaking, in the sense of *logos*, is a matter not of emitting sounds, but of being able to answer for oneself, being able to be responsible. A word must be able to answer for itself, to say what it means, it must keep its word. We naïvely believe that the crying child expresses himself, and therefore 'speaks'. Heidegger destroys this naïve, positivist conception: a dog also expresses himself when he barks, but it would be eccentric to take his barking for a language. Language appears only when there is a difference between medium and intention: a word like 'pain' is not itself painful, it is not of the same nature as pain, while a cry *of* pain is already painful.

That learning language should also be learning difference, a tearing away from all immediacy (or nature), from all self-identity, is shown in the scene where the adult appears before the children as utterly Other: 'Are you the teacher, or God?', they ask him. They wait for him to identify himself with that Other, but he cannot do it: 'I too am a child in the cradle, and I need to talk in cries and tears.' His privilege is being closer to the origin or to birth than the child, who, because he is a child, cannot be *close*, or can be only too close, in a proximity that is without proximity since it involves no distance, no difference, no relation. It is what Heidegger called the structure of de-distancing (*Ent-fernung*), another name for difference: speech de-distances in that it brings together (things and, perhaps above all, the mother, the primary image of origin), but as it brings together it displaces everything in its space – different, unreal – its spacing which is also its property. Language is the house [*de-meure*] of Being in that Being is not part of what there is, and so the house is empty. Cries and tears, taken to be the origin of speech (as pure ex-pression, an outward display driven by a *Trieb*), arc infinitely separated from that origin from the moment they are expressed. 'Listen, I say to them . . . ', 'be reasonable, I say to him', and, right up to the last moment, he says nothing else, nothing but demands destined not to be understood because the condition for the possibility of all understanding – a common language – is missing. Only difference can establish the common. Far from being the basic given, it is what appears only at the end of a long process of wresting away from the idiom. Just as a language at the origin of language must be presupposed, presupposing an already which can appear as such only after the fact [*après coup*], which is indeed produced by the afterwards [*après coup*], its incision [*coup*] in the cut [*coupure*] which marks the appearance of language, of the *Als-Struktur*, so also community presupposes itself, since it can establish itself only by means of extreme violence: e-ducation, being drawn out of oneself by means of communal discipline. 'The pupil quietly listens to the master. He is given lessons by him, and loves him. He makes progress. But if, one day, he sees that the master is God, he scorns him and knows no more' (*AC*, 72).

The master is recognised as such in the fact that the only place he can take is beside his own statue; he has the status of the master but must never entirely identify with it, for fear of becoming a mere statue. Representation – of the master, of knowledge, of God – can only be a side-show (an example, *Beispiel*), and all examples are dangerous: there is no adequate representation of God. Now, if all models run the risk of being fetishes, idols of stone or plaster, then there is no place for the master, and he – like God – can only present himself *in absentia*. The master is he who is not there, not the master *in person*, but only he who re-presents him, like the word 'master'. He is actor rather than author. The singularity of this re-presentation must be understood right to the point of paradox which draws the derision of the pupils. With his last words ('if, one day, he sees that the master is God . . . '), the master, who took the master's place on the understanding that it could never be taken but must remain empty – just as *Da-sein* takes the place of being as long as it is *nothing* (or not a what) – has himself chased out of the classroom and becomes who he is: no-one is master [*maître à penser*] except in exile.

It becomes clear why the master is scorned by his pupils. Surely it should be the reverse: the pupil one day sees that his beloved master (there is no such thing as a hated master, according to the slavish crowd), his idol, is *not* God, but only a plaster idol, and from that point despises him and refuses to learn. None the less, the reverse of this is true. The day the pupil sees that the master is the same as God, that is, *no-one*, no-one with whom he can identify, he spits on him. He is not looking for knowledge (or if so, it is knowledge that he imagines in the form of a thing, something to own), he is looking for the state he thinks he can reach by imitation alone. God's unpresentability destroys entirely the pupil's ideology, which lets him believe that the difference between himself and the master is difference of position. The master can only ever master this difference in the knowledge that it never appears in any form, never even appears as such, that is, in the knowledge that he cannot master it, which means he remains a child, speaking in cries and tears which are no longer expressions of desire but expressions of his acknowledged *impotence*. This infinite distance can itself arise only when it does not arise as a masterable difference. It is the incommensurability of difference which gauges the identity of the master as not being God, but a 'not' is the only relation to God that is not idolatrous. On the other hand, the pupil who sees that his master (Hitler, Stalin, the list goes on) is not God revolts against the master, against what he, in his ignorance, took for the Law. From that moment, thinking himself his own master, he falls into infinite slavery (as Baudelaire said: 'riddled with democracy and syphilis'). He would prefer to worship the plaster statue because at least a statue does not give orders.

'Since the watchword was suppressed . . . , I am just one voice among others.' That is the common condition: 'God' is certainly not a voice among others, but, insofar as he must go by way of language, that is all he can appear as; he can never appear as the One. The disappearance of authority – and the author, and orders – comes as a relief. None of the books in the text has an author. The first declares the law: 'Fear is your only master.' Still, God expresses himself in fear and trembling. It is fear with no object; a reply to the question 'what are you afraid of?' is impossible, because a reply would *ipso facto* annihilate the fear. The one who fears nothing learns – and understands

– nothing. Absolute knowledge is the same as absolute ignorance: the whole of *The Last Word* can be read as a commentary on Hegel (the absolute lord is death); but that is already inscribed as a philosophical *topos*. The only one who can learn is the one who knows that he does not know, and if God is defined as omniscient, he must be ignorant. He has nothing more to fear, but only in the sense that, like the dead, nothing more can happen to him. Like the plaster statue, he cannot fear, and can learn nothing.

Now, if the master (or God) declares that he is only one voice among others, he risks losing all authority, or no longer being heard as the voice of the master: no fear. Caught in this vice, he can never be what he must be. What is said of the master also holds for the author, who is, but must not be, 'one voice among others'. He must know (or must have known) what he wants to say; but this is the mark of writing, that it knows nothing of what it wants to say. Not that it says anything and everything, but that, if it knew in advance what it wanted to say, it could not happen. It happens only in not happening. It has the advantage, over the spoken word, of not trembling, but, without trembling, it knows nothing; being fixed, it is reassuring: 'and once again I wrote the text on the blackboard to make it familiar to everyone' (*AC*, 69) – but this assurance is once again anything but reassuring, because vacant repetition by heart demonstrates, again, the absence of all authority.

What is the relation between the two extracts (*AC*, 69)? The second is taken 'from the same work' (on the third estate? the excluded third?). It is the 'last lines of the fable of the beseiged': the legend of the survivor. The 'extra' individual from the first is also the last survivor who cannot be included in the 'general list' because there can be no account of him, no story about him: no witness is possible. There is no witness for the witness, Celan said. 'No one can say it', no one can say what happened to him, including (or least of all) himself. But under these conditions – an event which, not being an event, cannot be said – the commentary, which sets out to 'efface all these words and substitute the word "not" ["ne pas"]' (would this 'not' be the last word, including the no words that would follow it?), would utter the last word of all narrative, indeed of all writing insofar as its law begins with the effacing of all trace of writing. Its law is to set itself beyond law, and in this way to give itself law. The last survivor cannot testify to what happened to him, 'he knows nothing, and he can express what happened to him only by saying: nothing happened'. Saying this, he says what happened to him, since this is the only way he can say it. He says the truth of what saying is: the difference which, given that a narrative cannot be identical to an event, makes his narrative possible. If this were equal to that, neither one could be.

To understand this difference, one must first grasp the relation between narrative and event. It is generally assumed that the thing to be narrated, the event

– whether real or fictional – must precede its narration. Which is why all narratives, more or less, are in the past tense. Take the example of the last survivor who fled the beseiged town – a fable, presented as such: no one is expected to believe the reality of the facts – what is inevitable is that, *if* it took place, it must have happened before any narrative *of* what took place. But then, how is one to say what, as soon as it happens, has no word or speech that would allow it to be said? To say that there is no narration of the present is to say that nothing happens, or that saying is the only event, already in the past. 'To happen', 'to take place', can happen or take place only in the space of a saying which marks it as such, as taking place. Here, space does not mean an empty frame, nor a formative matrix; it is the originary leap (*Ur-sprung*) by which place separates itself in advance – *chora* – from what takes place. The *'there is'* reaches itself only by departing [*en départenant*], deferring/differing [*se différant*] itself in what there is, and which it allowed to be recounted instead of, and in the place of, the (always non-existent) *there is* itself. The narrative always comes too late for the very reason that it precedes every event which it allows to happen, that is, dismisses. The event – the place of the tragic – is what never attains to being – above all in narrative – or what reaches it only in not reaching it, like 'death'. This is also why all narrative is, strictly speaking, mortal: it never attains to being, to being the event which it recounts, and, by the same token, becomes the event itself in its unsurpassable facticity: effacing what it recounts, it writes it *for the first time.*

Take this quotation from *The Death Sentence*, for example:[19] 'It's a secondary question, just as knowing whether things really happened like that is insignificant.' It is an affirmation which, in 'reality', would be shocking. Imagine a witness beginning his testimony: 'It doesn't really matter if things (the murder, for instance) really happened like this . . .' He would be immediately dismissed. A false witness would be better, because he would at least be credible. Sure, he does not tell the truth, but by deliberately not telling it he presupposes that there is a truth, and maybe even that he is the only one who knows it. (To tell a lie, one must know the truth.) On the contrary, the witness who declares that the facts are not at all important, that they can be suppressed and, if they are not suppressed, 'others come and take their place, and take on the same meaning and the story is the same', cannot be taken seriously, however, he may be the only *true* witness.

Death is the absolute lord. This is also to say: there is no master, since death is what does not happen (to beings, or to being said) and it does not cease, or ceases only by stopping what never stops happening, dying. Death interrupts dying; it is this sentence [*arrêt*]. At the same time, it does not provide the occasion [*lieu*] for any narrative (nothing about it is observable, verifiable) and there is narrative only in the place it provides – separated from all places. Dying, like speaking, takes place only in its cessation, in the afterwards [*l'après coup*] which precedes it. The figure of the judge is the figure of a 'young mute' (*AC*, 71):

> Here is our judge . . . In whose name would you judge him? Who would make you dismiss him? Poor childen, for such a wound, the cause of language, imposes no restraint on you!

The wound is the 'cause' (or the thing) of language in a double sense: because we speak only in order to have nothing more to say, and because this last word is nowhere to be found. It 'cannot be a word, nor the absence of word, nor something other than a word': not a word, because any word would no longer be a word; not the absence of word, because every word is the last one; not something other than a word, because there is nothing that is not also, and above all, a word. The same could be said of death, which cannot be a word, nor the absence of word, nor something other than a word. This word which is not a word, without being its absence or something else, is what *The Last Word* says, but without being it. Saying without being does not say it, and says it so much better. Saying as *The Last Word* which is not the last word and is not some*thing* else either. Saying in *repeating* it, even given that it has to be impossible to repeat the last word. But this repetition [*redite*] is, as the afterwards [*l'après coup*], the law of this saying which says the law only as it gives it as impossible – and thus as the law. Oedipus never stops gouging out his eyes, Antigone never stops hanging herself in the tomb, and the poet never stops telling it to us, making us the survivors of our own death. No one can call himself the last survivor (including, and above all, the last survivor of language) and, therefore, there is narrative only in this *writing of the disaster*. Because the disaster affects *everything*, it is the very source of the word which is the disaster itself, in that it does not come to say itself, even as the last word.

Translated by Anne O'Byrne

Notes

1 Jean Beaufret, 'Hölderlin et Sophocle', preface to *Remarques sur Oedipe, Remarques sur Antigone*, (Paris: 10/18, 1965), 38.
2 Ibid., 38.
3 See *Après Coup* (Paris: Editions de Minuit, 1983). Henceforth *AC* in the main text.
4 Platon, *Le Banquet*, translated and with a commentary by Pierre Boutang (Paris: Hermann, 1972), 120.
5 Heidegger, of course, preferred *Unheimliche*; indeed, he did not hesitate to criticise

Hölderlin's translation, particularly of Antigone and Ismene's dialogue. Cf. *Hölderlins Hymne 'Der Ister'*, (Gesamtausgabe 53) (Frankfurt-am-Main: Klostermann, 1984), 122.

6 'While in all productive men it is instinct that is the creative-affirmative force, and consciousness acts critically and dissuasively, in Socrates it is instinct that becomes the critic, and consciousness that becomes the creator – truly a monster *per defectum!*' Nietzsche, *The Birth of Tragedy*, translated by Walter Kaufmann (New York: Random, 1967), §13.

7 A word which carries an echo of rage, but comes from outside – beyond. *Outrage à la pudeur*: indecent behaviour.

8 Hegel, *The Phenomenology of Spirit*, translated by A.V.Miller (Oxford: Oxford University Press, 1977), 450.

9 Ibid., 450.

10 In *The Birth of Tragedy*, Nietzsche speaks of a magic mirror in which the Greeks saw themselves transformed into the chorus, and which he saw as the primitive element of tragedy. But I regard talk of 'transformation' as useless, insofar as the *being* of this people is mythical – Homeric, perhaps – from the very beginning; if there is no Greek religion it is because there was never any difference between gods and mortals – except death.

11 A faint echo of this terror is to be heard in the way Levinas appeals to the Face as the immediate exposition of the infinitely other, but he then passes it all through his sterilising 'ethics'.

12 *Beyond Good and Evil*, §3.

13 Hölderlin, 'Remarks on Oedipus' in *Friedrich Hölderlin: Essays and Letters on Theory*, translated and edited by Thomas Pfau (Albany: SUNY, 1988), 107.

14 Georges Bataille, *Oeuvres complètes* (Paris: Gallimard, 1973) IV: 57.

15 Ibid., V: 68.

16 Nietzsche, cited in ibid., V: 40.

17 See particularly Philippe Lacoue-Labarthe, *Heidegger, Art and Politics*, translated by Chris Turner (Oxford: Basil Blackwell, 1990).

18 The most beautiful proper name, the extreme opposite of 'Auschwitz', is the name of the heroine of *The Blue of Noon*: 'Dirty'. 'As beautiful as she was drunk.'

19 Maurice Blanchot, *L'arrêt de mort* (Paris: Galillée, 1948), 126.

Index

absolute, the 17–20; the comic and 49–50; as eternal freedom 66; ethico-political and 21; sensible presentation (*Darstellung*) 119; speculative reality 18; technologicl 180; tragic and 19–20, 27, 33, 73, 119
Achilles 224
adversary, forms of 85
Aeschylus 18, 123, 196; *Orestia* 16–17
aesthetic 145; experience 141; judgement 3; *listener* 155
aesthetics 100–1, 142, 145, 149–50
agon 128–9, 206
Alcibiades 224
Alexander 30–1
'Anmerkungen to Sophocles' *see* 'Remarks on *Antigone*'
antagonistic process, tragic mechanism and 134
Antigone 113, 131, 237; Hegel and 51, 109, 225; Heidegger and 183–4; Hölderlin on 122–3, 125–6, 223; translation by Hölderlin 60, 111–12, 118, 123, 126–7, 133; as victim 110
antique *polis* 13–14
aorgic: principle 222; realm of nature 102, 104, 107, 112
Aphrodite 94, 111
Apollinian 61, 145, 148, 179, 198; *illusion* 154, 157
Apollo 18, 101, 104, 111
appearance (*Schein*) 61, 146–8
arche 230
arche-partition 69, 72
arche-separation (*Urtheilung*), 'I am I' 64
arche-unity 66–7
Archimedean point 180
Areopage, Athenian people and 18
Ares, 'spirit of battle' 111
Aristophanes 41, 50, 53; *Birds, The* and 111
Aristotle 88, 91, 98, 113, 123, 131; being

and appearing 173; circular motion 93-4; Herodotus and 182; higher nexus 112; Hölderlin and 96–7, 104, 124; *katharisis* 126, 227; *mimesis* 129, 197; *muthos* 120, 124; *phronesis* 176; *praxis* 181; problem of *lexis* 61; reconciliation 11–12; *Rhetoric* 183; superior delight 107; *theoreia* 176; tragic effect 225; *Wesen* and 170; lectures on 'ethics' 169, 171-3, 175, 181; *Nicomachean Ethics* 90, 92–3, 175–6, 181; *Organon* 94–5; *Physics* 94–5; *Poetics, The* 1, 78, 89–90, 92, 95–7, 99, 132, 177–9, 181–2
art: aesthetics, science of 145, 149–50; authentic 194, 197; problematics of 3; rebirth of 152; religion and 41–2; science and 92; tragic 80, 90, 159, 198
'Art-religion', tragedy one genre amongst others 25–6
artistic presentation (*Darstellung*) 42
Athena, conflict and 18
Attic tragedy 41, 118, 196
Auschwitz 229
authentic thinkers 193

basic or fundamental tone (*Hauptton*) 61
Bataille, Georges 224, 226-8; *On Nietzsche* 226
Baudelaire, Charles 221, 224, 234
Beaufret, Jean 178, 221
beautiful, the 3, 21, 24, 29
Beckett, Samuel 224
becoming and being 144, 146, 148
being (*Seyn*) 63–4, 144, 226, 233
belonging 183, 227
Benjamin, Walter: gift of language 207; Socrates and 200, 206; 'Fate and Character' 208; 'Myth and Truth' 193–4, 196–7, 199; *Origin of the German Mourning Play* 195–7, 199, 204, 207, 208–11

239